Additional Praise for Rami and *I Will Teach You to Be R...*

"Ramit Sethi is a rising star in the world of personal finance writing . . . one singularly attuned to the sensibilities of his generation. . . . His style is part frat boy and part Silicon Valley geek, with a little bit of San Francisco hipster thrown in."
—SAN FRANCISCO CHRONICLE

". . . one of our favorite personal finance sites." **—LIFEHACKER**

"The easiest way to get rich is to inherit. This is the second best way—knowledge and some discipline. If you're bold enough to do the right thing, Ramit will show you how. Highly recommended."
—SETH GODIN, AUTHOR OF *THIS IS MARKETING*

"The common perception about personal finance books is that the advice is loaded with technical terms and jargon. On this front, *I Will Teach You to Be Rich* comes as a complete surprise. It is written in an extremely breezy style, but it doesn't mean that it contains frivolous advice. On the contrary, it packs useful information for beginners on how they can manage their money."
—ECONOMIC TIMES

". . . particularly appealing to the younger generation with its easy-to-read, no-holds-barred language."
—BUSINESS INSIDER

Real Reader Results

"Ramit's teaching that frugality isn't about 'spending nothing' but rather about spending extravagantly on the things we love changed our outlook on life. My wife and I retired from full-time work at ages 33 and 35, respectively, and adventure around the country in an Airstream RV. We wake up every morning excited and energetic because we control every minute of our day."

—STEVE ADCOCK

"When I was 30, I had no 401k and a student loan of $16,000. Now I'm 35, I have no student-loan debt, a healthy 401k, an IRA, an additional investment account, and one secured credit card which I use to pay my monthly bills. I used IWT to do all of this and now spend most of my money on what I love, which is my kids, food, and ebooks."

—ARIEL STEWART

"Since implementing a fully automated system in 2011, my net worth went from zero to close to $450k. I never have to worry about money—I have enough for bills, any indulgence, and maxing out retirement accounts (Roth and 401k)."

—ROSS FLETCHER

"I read your book in 2010 when I was a 25-year-old executive assistant at a tiny book publisher making $28,000. I'm now leading a full team of writers in San Francisco and making $155,000."

—CLAIRE PEACOCK

"After reading your book, I negotiated a $175 monthly reduction in apartment rent by offering a long-term extended lease and putting the apartment as a preferred vendor. Landlord agreed immediately, and that saved me over $3,500!"

—SAMEER DESAI

"I've got over $100,000 growing for retirement, $8,000 in the personal investment account, and have next year's Roth contribution already set aside in an interest-bearing account."

—DAVID CHAMBERS

"After applying the lessons from the book, I paid off one credit card within 6 months and renegotiated terms with my medical expenses that saved me $5,000 instantly. Within another two years I was totally credit-card and medical-debt free. I'm now 34, still debt free and over a month ahead in expenses."

—HILARY BUUCK

"At first your chapter on debt freaked me out—you can't just get out of debt so fast! Then I realized making more money was not scary or daunting, but very doable. I went from making around $4,000 a month to $8,000 a month from my company. I had 4,500 in debt that is now down to $900 (soon it'll be at $0)."

—REENA BHANSALI

"I've used the IWT principles to pay down $40,000 in debt inside two years by negotiating a raise and taking on my first side-gig projects with the '1K on the Side' project. And with the automation principles, and paying ourselves first, my wife and I built close to $200,000 in savings in the last two years."

—SEAN WILKINS

"I took this book on a Caribbean cruise and couldn't put it down. It led me to getting a $20,000 salary increase in my day job and starting a side business as a career coach, earning thousands each month. It helped me negotiate down bills and fees, increase my credit limit, grow a healthy retirement fund and savings, and fundamentally change my mindset about earning money."

—MARY GRACE GARDNER

"I went from having nothing in my investment accounts to having over $55,000 to date."

—ALEX CRAIG

"I didn't have any credit card debt so I was able to implement the whole book in about three weeks. After that, I kind of forgot about it. Eight years later I was worth close to $200,000 with no debt as a retail employee."

—DANIEL LEE REIFENBERGER

"I changed my student loans from 20-year loans to 10-year loans. I had no idea the difference, and it ended up saving me over $10k. . . . Just by paying an extra $50 a month."

—LYLA NUTT

"When I was 25, I had $8,500 of credit card debt, and $3,000 of other debt. IWT gave me the manageable steps to get out of my hole, better use my credit cards, not live check to check, pay off what I owed, and start saving. At 28, I have $50,000 in savings, am debt-free, have automated my finances, and I am going to buy a house this year."

—ALLISON REYNOLDS

"In four years after I read IWT, I've saved $40,000 using dollar cost averaging to contribute to my $20,000 index tracking fund. I received one promotion and four raises, increasing my earning potential by 70 percent :)"

—BEVAN HIRST

"Without the book, I wouldn't have started my retirement account. It showed me what to open and how to use systems to automatically save my money for future purchases. So far I have $40,000+ in retirement by maxing out my Roth every year."

—JAMES MONROE ŜTEVKO

"I was 25 when I read the book. I had a crappy job, very little savings, and even less of a clue what to do with my money. I implemented IWT systems and I got a new job (with a 20 percent raise) at a company where I've flourished for the past five years. I have $100,000 in my retirement accounts and six months' salary in an emergency account, along with other savings for various goals."

—SHEILA MASTERSON

"Before, I felt guilty because at 37 I should have had my stuff together. Now everything is completely automated. I feel more confident and can spend guilt-free with the money left over. Since reading your book, I maxed out my Roth IRA, made a $7,000 emergency savings account, have a growing investment account, and have multiple accounts for special purchases."

—QUINN ZEDA

Also by Ramit Sethi

I Will Teach You to Be Rich: The Journal

Money for Couples

I WILL TEACH YOU TO BE RICH

No Guilt. No Excuses. No BS.
Just a 6-Week Program That Works

RAMIT SETHI

SECOND EDITION

WORKMAN PUBLISHING
NEW YORK

For free bonuses, including ready-to-use templates to increase your income, visit iwillteachyoutoberich.com/bonus.

Workman
Workman Publishing
Hachette Book Group, Inc.
1290 Avenue of the Americas
New York, NY 10104
workman.com

Workman is an imprint of Workman Publishing, a division of Hachette Book Group, Inc. The Workman name and logo are registered trademarks of Hachette Book Group, Inc.

Design by Janet Parker and Jean-Marc Troadec
Back cover photo by Peter Hurley

The publisher is not responsible for websites (or their content) that are not owned by the publisher.

Workman books may be purchased in bulk for business, educational, or promotional use. For information, please contact your local bookseller or the Hachette Book Group Special Markets Department at special.markets@hbgusa.com.

Library of Congress Cataloging-in-Publication Data is available.

ISBN 978-1-5235-0574-6

Second Edition April 2019

Printed in the United States of America on responsibly sourced paper.

21 20

To my wife,
Cassandra.
You're the best part
of every day.

Contents

AN OPEN LETTER TO NEW READERS

If you listened to all the internet influencers telling you the things you "need" to do every morning, here's what your day would look like:

4:00 a.m. wake up

4:01 a.m. meditate

5:00 a.m. drink 37 gallons of water

5:33 a.m. gratitude journal

10:45 a.m. eat (keto only)

11:00 a.m. track every penny of spending from the last 16 years

11:01 a.m. die

I dunno, guys. I prefer advice that actually works. And when I took a hard look at the advice I gave in this book a decade ago, I realized one thing: I was right.

If you bought this book ten years ago and followed the exact advice in it, here's what you would have accomplished by now.

- If you had invested just $100/month, that $12,000 would have turned into over $20,000 (The S&P 500 averaged around 13 percent annually over the last decade.)

- If you had aggressively invested $1,000/month, that $120,000 you contributed would have grown to more than $200,000.

- You would be spending less than 90 minutes per month on your money.

- You would have been able to take multiple vacations and fly business class—completely free—using credit card points.

■ Money would have gone from a source of anxiety and confusion to one of calm and possibility.

As you'll see in this book, I do things differently than typical money "experts." I won't lecture you about cutting back on lattes (buy as many as you want). I won't try to convince you to keep a budget (I have a better method). And one more thing: I'm a real guy. I post on Instagram and Twitter (@ramit) and I write for millions of people on my blog and newsletter almost every day (iwillteachyoutoberich.com). So let's start off doing something different: I want to hear from you. Really! Send me an email (ramit.sethi@iwillteachyoutoberich.com, subject: new book reader) and tell me two things:

1. What made you decide to take control of your money today?

2. What does your Rich Life look like? (Please be specific!)

I read every email and I try to respond to as many as possible.

What has *I Will Teach You to Be Rich* allowed you to do?

One of my greatest joys is hearing from you about how you've applied my material to change your life. I asked some of my readers to share their results.

I paid off $10,000 in credit card debt that I accumulated while unemployed, bought a condo in San Francisco, and am now debt-free and building my retirement funds.

—JULIANA BRODSKY, 38

I have $200,000 in retirement savings and countless vacations paid for by creating specific savings accounts for them; it's hard to put a specific number on that.

—KYLE SLATTERY, 30

I travel internationally for a month 1 or 2 times a year. Last year it was South Africa; this year, Korea.

—ESLI LIGAYA, 34

The Rich Life is about freedom. In my case it allowed me to take 9 months off work and travel throughout Argentina, Colombia, and the US. And now it's allowing my wife to take a 6-month break from work to figure out what's next.

—SEAN WILKINS, 39

We were able to put three children into private school on one full-time income.

—BRYAN DILBERT, 32

All that said, I'll admit that I wasn't perfect. Ten years ago, I made three mistakes when writing the first edition of this book.

My first mistake was that I didn't cover the emotions around money. I spent time covering the nuts and bolts of personal finance—I gave you the perfect word-for-word scripts to get late fees waived (page 42), the exact asset allocation I use for investing (page 148), and even how to manage money with your partner (page 292)—but if you don't tackle your invisible money scripts, none of it matters.

Invisible scripts are the messages you've absorbed from your parents and society that guide your decisions for decades—and often without even being aware of it. Do any of these sound familiar?

- "You're throwing your money away on rent."

- "We don't talk about money in this house."

- "Credit cards are a scam."

- "Stop spending money on lattes."

- "Money changes people."

- "You don't get that level of wealth without making a few shady deals here and there."

- "The stock market is gambling."

- "Student loans are a scam."

In this edition, I'll show you what the most insidious, powerful invisible money scripts are—and how to beat them.

The second mistake I made was being too overbearing. The truth is, you can choose what your Rich Life is *and* how you get there. In the original book, I did write about the different definitions of a Rich Life, but I didn't acknowledge that we might take *different routes* to get there.

For example, your Rich Life might be to live in Manhattan. It might be to ski forty days a year in Utah, or to save and buy a house with a huge yard for your kids, or to fund an elementary school in Croatia. That's your choice.

But how you get there is *also* your choice. Some people choose the traditional route of saving 10 percent, investing 10 percent, and slowly working their way to a comfortable Rich Life. Others save 50 percent of their income and quickly reach the "crossover point" where their investments pay for their life—forever. (This is called "FIRE," or Financial Independence, Retire Early, which I cover on page 217.)

You choose your Rich Life. And in this edition, I want to show you different ways to get there. To do that, I've included lots of examples of people who took unconventional routes to create their Rich Lives.

Finally, the third mistake. Let me just say that I've messed up quite a few things in my life: I've hired and fired the wrong people. I ruined my chance at a TED talk by walking into the meeting unprepared. I was six feet and 127 pounds into my mid-twenties, looking like a hairy Indian Gumby. But nothing compares to my worst mistake of all:

Writing the actual interest rates of banks in the original edition of this book.

Here's what I wrote back then:

"Online banks pay a higher interest rate for savings accounts—about 2.5 to 5 percent, which would produce $25 to $50 interest per year on that $1,000, compared with $5 per year on the Big Bank savings account."

The information was right . . . at the time. The problem is, interest rates change, which I forgot to mention. And in the years after the first edition was published, they dropped—from 5 percent to 0.5 percent. I assumed people would run the numbers and realize that the interest rate doesn't really matter much. For example, on a $5,000 balance, that means your monthly interest dropped from $21 to $2. In the grand scheme, not that big of a deal.

But when facing lower interest rates on savings accounts, readers got mad—really mad. And they took their anger out on me. Here are a few emails I got:

- "This book is a scam. Where are the 5% interest rates you talk about??"

- "What bank has 3% interest rates??"

- "Subj: WHERE ARE THE BANKS U WROTE ABOUT"

For the last ten years, I've gotten over twenty of these emails every single day. Never again. On page 84, you'll see my favorite banks. But not their interest rates. WHICH WILL CHANGE, GUYS. In this edition, I've corrected these mistakes. And I've added new material.

1. New tools, new investment options, and new approaches to money.
If you want to get more aggressive about investing, I'll show you how (page 216). What do I think about robo-advisors? I'll tell you (page 116). And what about pre-nups? I share my thoughts (page 302).

2. New money scenarios you'll confront. How do you handle relationships and money? I've added new material (page 286). Once your financial system is set up, I want you to know what to focus on next (page 260). And finally, if you know people who complain about politics and baby boomers to explain why they can't pay off their debt and get ahead, they should read my thoughts on victim culture (page 11).

3. Incredible stories from other IWT readers. I've included tons of new examples, including inspirational success stories from all different kinds of people: men and women in their twenties, thirties, forties, and fifties; people who started from nothing and people who built on success to grow even more. Plus, gut-wrenching stories about people who procrastinated on implementing the material in this book—and what it cost them.

I added new material where appropriate, but I preserved techniques that continue to work. Many people want "new" advice—but the value in this book doesn't come from novelty; it comes from usefulness.

In ten years, I've also changed. I've gotten married, I've grown my business, and I've learned more about money and psychology. Now I get the chance to share what I've learned with you. Amidst the noise, the hype, the apps of the day, the IWT personal finance system *works*. Long-term, low-cost investing *works*. Automation *works*. Use this book to create your own Rich Life, just like thousands of others have.

—Ramit Sethi

WOULD YOU RATHER BE SEXY OR RICH?

I've always wondered why so many people gain weight after college. I'm not talking about people with medical disorders, but regular people who were slim in college and vowed that they would "never, ever" let that happen to them. Yet, little by little, most Americans gain an unhealthy amount of weight.

In the ten years since I wrote my book, weight and health have become such controversial topics that I was advised to delete my references to them. But after my own journeys with nutrition, fitness, and money, I now believe even more in the connections between them—and that you can take control.

Weight gain doesn't happen overnight. If it did, it would be easy for us to see it coming—and to take steps to avoid it. Ounce by ounce, it creeps up on us as we're driving to work and then sitting behind a computer for eight to ten hours a day. It happens when we move into the real world from a college campus populated by bicyclists, runners, and varsity athletes who once inspired us to keep fit. But try talking about post-college weight loss with your friends and see if they say one of these things:

"Avoid carbs!"

"Don't eat before you go to bed, because fat doesn't burn efficiently when you're sleeping."

"Keto is the only real way to lose weight."

"Drinking apple cider vinegar speeds up your metabolism."

I always laugh when I hear these things. Maybe they're correct or maybe they're not, but that's not really the point.

The point is that we love to debate minutiae.

When it comes to weight loss, 99.99 percent of us need to know only two things: Eat less and exercise more. Only elite athletes need to do more. But instead of accepting these simple truths and acting on them, we discuss trans fats, obscure supplements, and Whole30 versus paleo.

WHY ARE MONEY AND FOOD SO SIMILAR?

When it comes to food, we ...	When it comes to personal finance, we ...
don't track calorie intake	don't track spending
eat more than we know	spend more than we realize—or admit
debate minutiae about calories, diets, and workouts	debate minutiae about interest rates and hot stocks
value anecdotal advice over research	listen to friends, our parents, and TV talking heads instead of reading a few good personal-finance books

Most of us fall into one of two camps regarding our money: We either ignore it and feel guilty, or we obsess over financial details by arguing interest rates and geopolitical risks without taking action. Both options yield the same results—none. The truth is that the vast majority of people don't need a financial adviser to help them get rich. We need to set up accounts at solid banks, automate our day-to-day money management (including bills, savings, and, if applicable, debt payoff). We need to know about a few things to invest in, and then we need to let our money grow for thirty years. But that's not as cool or exciting, is it? Instead, we read internet articles from "experts" who make endless predictions about the economy and "this year's hottest stock" without ever being held accountable for their picks (which are wrong more than 50 percent of the time). "It's going up!" "No, down." As long as something is being said, we're drawn to it.

Why? Because we love to debate minutiae.

When we do, we somehow feel satisfied. We might just be spinning our wheels and failing to change anyone's mind, but we feel as if we're really expressing ourselves, and it's a good feeling. We feel like we're getting somewhere. The problem is that this feeling is totally illusory. Think back to the last time you and your friend talked about finances or fitness. Did you go for a run afterward? Did you send money to your savings account? Of course not.

People love to argue minor points, partially because they feel it absolves them from actually having to do anything. You know what? Let the fools debate the details. I decided to learn about money by taking small steps to manage my own spending. Just as you don't have to be a certified nutritionist to lose weight or an automotive engineer to drive a car, you don't have to know everything about personal finance to be rich. I'll repeat myself: You don't have to be an expert to get rich. You do have to know how to cut through all the information and get started—which, incidentally, also helps reduce the guilt.

I knew I should save for retirement, but I didn't really know how, besides "put some money in your 401(k)." I also thought saving was only about NOT spending money. As a result, I felt horribly guilty about spending money on *anything*, even if I had saved up for it. I had also never really thought about asking for a raise and didn't know how to approach it. I had just treated the initial wage I'd been offered as set in stone.

—**ELIZABETH SULLIVAN-BURTON, 30**

Why Is Managing Money So Hard?

People have lots and lots of reasons for not managing their money, some of them valid, but most of them poorly veiled excuses for laziness or not having spent ten minutes on research. Let's look at a few:

Info Glut

The idea that there is too much information is a real and valid concern. "But Ramit," you might say, "that flies in the face of all American culture! We need more information so we can make better decisions! All the experts on TV say this all the time, so it must be true!" Sorry, nope. Look at the actual data and you'll see that an abundance of information can lead to decision paralysis, which is a fancy way of saying that with too much information, we do nothing. Barry Schwartz writes about this in *The Paradox of Choice: Why More Is Less*:

> *As the number of mutual funds in a 401(k) plan offered to employees goes up, the likelihood that they will choose a fund— any fund—goes down. For every 10 funds added to the array of options, the rate of participation drops 2 percent. And for those who do invest, added fund options increase the chances that employees will invest in ultraconservative money market funds.*

You scroll online and see ads about stocks, 401(k)s, Roth IRAs, insurance, 529s, and international investing. Where do you start? Are you already too late? What do you do? Too often, the answer is nothing— and doing nothing is the worst choice you can make. As the table on the next page shows, investing early is the best thing you can do.

Look carefully at the chart on the next page. Smart Sally actually invests less, but ends up with about $80,000 more. She invests $200/ month from age thirty-five to age forty-five and then never touches that money again. Dumb Dan is too preoccupied to worry about money until he's forty-five, at which point he starts investing $200/month until he's sixty-five. In other words, Smart Sally invests for ten years and Dumb Dan for twenty years—but Smart Sally has much more money. And that's with just $200/month! The single most important thing you can do to be rich is to start early.

HOW TO MAKE $60,000 MORE THAN YOUR FRIENDS (WITH LESS WORK)		
	Smart Sally	**Dumb Dan**
When beginning to invest, the person is . . .	35 years old	45 years old
Each person invests $200/month for . . .	10 years	20 years
With an 8 percent rate of return, at age 65, their accounts are worth . . .	$181,469. Voilà—the value of starting early	$118,589. Even though he invested for twice as long, he's behind by $60,000

If you're younger, your money will grow even more. If you're older, don't get discouraged. I recently got a message from a woman in her forties who was unhappy about these numbers. "What's the point of writing that?" she asked. "It makes me feel bad that I'm already too far behind."

I understand how she feels. But we can't hide from the math—so instead of sugarcoating the facts, I believe in showing you the truth, including ways to increase your savings. Yes, the best time to start investing was ten years ago. The second best time is today.

The Media Is Partially to Blame (I Love Casting Blame)

Open the typical financial site and I bet you'll see an article called "10 No-Hassle Frugality Tips for Getting Ahead with Your Finances" or "How Today's Senate Vote Affects Estate Taxes." Reading those headlines, you intuitively know why online columnists wrote them: to get pageviews and sell ads.

We know that because reading yet another frugality article is not going to change anyone's behavior. And the estate tax affects less than 0.2 percent of people. But both of those headlines make people feel good—or angry.

Enough! I don't care about pageviews or stoking rage. If you're like me, you care about knowing where your money's going and redirecting it to go where you want it to go. We want our money to grow automatically, in accounts that don't nickel-and-dime us with fees. We don't want to have to become financial experts to get rich.

The Rise of Victim Culture

There's a group of people—mostly young, disaffected people—who have decided it's easier to be cynical than to improve themselves.

"LOL! Invest? I can't even save enough for pizza."

"LOL! Find a job? What world do you live in . . ."

"Maybe if baby boomers hadn't ruined it for all of us . . ."

People actually *compete* to see who's the bigger victim. Oh, you can't afford a four-bedroom house at the age of 26? *I can't afford to live in a cardboard box!* Oh, you like going to parties to meet new people? *That must be nice, I have social anxiety so I can't do that. (What? No, I didn't see a doctor. I diagnosed myself.)*

You know who's the real victim here?

Me. I'm offended at you being offended. And at the stupidity of this entire victim culture.

I refuse to play into the theatrics of how you can't afford to save even $20 a month. When this book was originally published, I got hundreds of angry emails accusing me of being elitist for encouraging people to save and invest even a modest amount. Those cynics were wrong. They surrounded themselves with other naysayers, bought flimsy arguments, and incurred a staggering cost for their beliefs: They missed out on hundreds of thousands of dollars of gains. Meanwhile, my readers put in the work to create their Rich Lives.

You choose. Be a cynic or carefully evaluate your options, knowing you'll probably make a mistake here or there . . . but you'll grow at each step of the way. I choose to move forward.

I understand this is a complex issue. Yes, socioeconomic policy, access to technology, and pure luck matter. For example, if you start off with two parents and you graduate from college, you're already luckier than most people on this planet.

But we play with the cards we're dealt. I believe in focusing on what I can control.

For example, by the time I entered kindergarten, it was clear I would never be in the NBA—fine. On the other hand, it was clear I would dominate the shit out of my classmates in spelling bees. Also fine.

Then there were the gray areas, like starting a business, becoming more fit, and learning to be better in dating. I had to learn those skills and work really, really hard.

This is where the victim mindset comes in. So many people complain about politicians and sociological problems without looking around at their own behavior. They give up at the first sign of failure. If you want to be a passenger in life, fine—go with the flow. I've found it's a lot more fun to be the captain of my own ship, even if I go off course sometimes.

As you can see, I don't have a lot of sympathy for people who complain about their situation in life but do nothing about it. That's why I wrote this book! I want you to be empowered to take control of your situation, no matter where in life you started from. I want you to have a level playing field against these huge Wall Street firms, mindless articles, and even your own psychology.

Here are a few examples of victim culture when it comes to money:

"I can't save any money." Years ago, when the economy crashed, I launched something called the "Save $1,000 in 30 Days Challenge," where I showed people tactical ways to save money using fresh psychological techniques. Thousands of people joined and worked to save thousands and thousands of dollars.

Except a few people.

While most people were supportive, I was surprised by how many people were actually offended by the very concept of a "Save $1,000 in 30 Days Challenge" because they didn't even earn that much each month, or they found my recommendations to be "too obvious"— even though I defined "saving" as cutting costs, earning more, and optimizing spending.

Here are some examples of their complaints:

- "Doing this is impossible for me . . . I don't make enough to try this exercise."

- "Nice idea, but the current median family income here in Ohio is $58,000/year. After taxes this means a monthly paycheck of about $3,400. Note that this is the median, so fully half of Ohio families

live on less than this! I doubt many of them could save $1,000/
month without selling off their children."

■ "This'd be nice . . . If I even made $1,000 in a month, I might try it.
But I'm in university . . ."

First of all, notice that crazy people have a particular way of writing—
they're always trailing off at the end of a sentence. If someone writes
you and says, "It must be nice . . ." or "That sounds hard . . ." odds are
good that they're a serial killer who will be knocking on your door very
soon, then wearing your skin as a raincoat.

Also, people love to use their particular situation—living in Ohio, or
Malaysia, or not having gone to an Ivy League school—to explain why
they can't get the same results others can. I used to engage and show
them examples of people in their own area who got amazing results.
Their response? "Well, did they have [increasingly obscure criteria:
moved around three times as a kid, eleven fingers, whatever]?" As soon
as I said no, they said, "See? I knew this wouldn't work for me." Cynics
don't want results; they want an excuse to not take action. Ironically,
even if they win their own manufactured argument, they lose overall,
because they're stuck in a prison of their mind.

"The world is against me." Yes, there are lots of societal problems
right now. But when it comes to personal finance, I focus on what I can
control. This idea escapes whiners, whose natural reaction when asked
to actually do something about their situation is to create reasons
why they can't. It used to be personal excuses ("no time"). Now, with
the rise of victim culture, it's more politically correct to point to some
external force, like median earnings or economic policy. Yes, getting
your financial life in order does require some work. But the rewards far
surpass the effort.

The truth is that these whiners miss the point. While saving $1,000
in a month was eminently reasonable, it was also an aspirational goal.
If you couldn't save $1,000, what about $500? Or $200? Finally, the
people who complained about money a year ago are probably still
complaining, while many of the people who took the challenge saved
hundreds and even thousands of dollars.

Other People We Can Blame for Our Money Problems

There are other common excuses for why we don't manage our money. Most of them don't stand up to scrutiny:

- **"Our education system doesn't teach this."** It's easy for people in their twenties to wish that their colleges had offered some personal finance training. Guess what? Most colleges do offer those classes. You just didn't take them!

- **"Credit card companies and banks are out to profit off us."** Yes, they are. So stop complaining and learn how to beat the companies instead of letting them beat you.

- **"I'm afraid of losing money."** That's fair, especially after global crises where front-page articles used words like "tanked" and "lost generation." But you need to take a long-term view: The economy grows and contracts in cycles. If you withdrew your money from the stock market in 2009, you missed out on one of the longest sustained periods of growth in history. Fear is no excuse to do nothing with your money. Remember, you can choose among many different investment options—some aggressive, some conservative. It all depends on how much risk you're willing to take. In fact, by automating your money, you can put yourself in a position to excel when others are scared—by continuing to consistently save and invest. When others are scared, there are bargains to be found.

- **"What if I don't know where to get an extra $100 per month?"** You don't need to earn another penny. I'll show you how to streamline your existing spending to generate that money to invest. Follow my CEO Method: Cut costs, Earn more, and Optimize your existing spending.

- **"I don't want average returns."** Our culture stigmatizes being average. Who wants to have an average relationship? Or an average income? Financial firms have weaponized that fear of average: They suggest it's bad to be average, that it's boring, and that you can do better. There's actually an entire ad campaign based on this idea by a popular robo-advisor whose tagline reads "Be better than average." The truth is, you likely can't beat average returns. In fact, average 8 percent returns are actually very good. Ironically, people who fear "being average" do exactly the things that make them perform *worse* than average: trade frequently, make outlandish bets, incur high taxes, and pay unnecessary fees. Remember: In relationships and work, we want to be better than average. In investing, average is great.

You're not a victim, you're in control. Once you truly internalize that, you can start to go on offense. No more being paralyzed by the thought that you have to get every single part of your personal finances perfectly organized before you can begin to manage your money.

Do you need to be the Iron Chef to cook a grilled-cheese sandwich? No, and once you make your first meal, it's easier to cook something more complicated the next time around. The single most important factor to getting rich is getting started, not being the smartest person in the room.

Put the Excuses Aside

Listen up, crybabies: This isn't your grandma's house and I'm not going to bake you cookies and coddle you. A lot of your financial problems are caused by one person: you. Instead of blaming circumstances and corporate America for your financial situation, you need to focus on what you can change yourself. Just as the diet industry has overwhelmed us with too many choices, personal finance is a confusing mess of overblown hype, myths, outright deception—and us, feeling guilty about not doing enough or not doing it right. If you're not satisfied with your finances and you're willing to take a hard look in the mirror, you'll discover one inescapable truth: The problem, and the solution, is *you*.

Let's put the excuses aside. What if you could consciously decide how to spend your money, rather than say, "I guess that's how much I spent last month"? What if you could build an automatic infrastructure that made all your accounts work together and automated your savings? What if you could invest simply and regularly without fear? Guess what? You can! I'll show you how to take the money you're making and redirect it to the places you want it to go—including substantially growing your money over the long term, no matter what the economy is like.

The Key Messages of
I Will Teach You to Be Rich

I believe in small steps. I want to reduce the number of choices that paralyze us. It's more important to get started than to spend an exhaustive amount of time researching the best fund in the universe. *I Will Teach You to Be Rich* is about taking the first step—understanding the barriers that keep us from managing our money and then tearing them down and putting our money in the right places so we can achieve our goals. Frankly, your goal probably isn't to become a financial expert. It's to live your life and let money serve you. So instead of saying, "How much money do I need to make?" you'll say, "What do I want to do with my life—and how can I use money to do it?" And instead of being driven by fear, you'll be guided by what history has shown us about investing and growth.

I'll keep it simple: Too many books try to cover everything about money, leaving you holding a book that you "should" read but don't because it's overwhelming. I want you to know enough to get started setting up automated accounts and investing, even with just $100. So here are the essential messages of *I Will Teach You to Be Rich*:

The 85 Percent Solution: Getting started is more important than becoming an expert. Too many of us get overwhelmed thinking we need to manage our money perfectly, which leads us to do nothing at all. That's why the easiest way to manage your money is to take it one step at a time—and not worry about being perfect. I'd rather act and get it 85 percent right than do nothing. Think about it: 85 percent of the way is far better than zero percent. Once your money system is good enough—or 85 percent of the way there—you can get on with your life and go do the things you really want to do.

It's okay to make mistakes. It's better to make them now, with a little bit of money, so that when you have more, you'll know what to avoid.

Spend extravagantly on the things you love and cut costs mercilessly on the things you don't. This book isn't about telling you to stop buying lattes. Instead, it's about being able to actually spend more on the things you love by not spending money on all the knucklehead things you don't

The Best Mistake I Ever Made

When I was in high school, my parents told me that if I wanted to go to college, I'd need to pay for it with scholarships. So like a good Indian son, I started applying . . . and applying and applying. In the end, I'd applied for about sixty scholarships and had won hundreds of thousands of dollars.

But my best scholarship was the first one—an award for $2,000. The organization wrote a check directly to me. I took it and invested in the stock market—and immediately lost half my money.

Oops. That's when I decided that I really needed to learn about money. I read the personal-finance books, watched the TV shows, and bought the magazines. After a while, I also started sharing what I'd learned. I taught informal classes to friends at Stanford (even though in the early days, nobody would ever attend). Then, in 2004, I began writing a blog called "I Will Teach You to Be Rich," covering the basics of saving, banking, budgeting, and investing. The rest, as they say, is history.

care about. Look, it's easy to want the best of everything: We want to go out all the time, live in a great apartment, buy new clothes, drive a new car, and travel anytime we want. The truth is, you have to prioritize. My friend Jim once called to tell me that he'd gotten a raise at work. On the same day, he moved into a smaller apartment. Why? Because he doesn't care very much about where he lives, but he loves spending money on camping and biking. That's called conscious spending. (Learn how one of my friends consciously spends $21,000 per year going out on page 132.)

There's a difference between being sexy and being rich. When I hear people talk about the stocks they bought, sold, or shorted last week, I realize that my investment style sounds pretty boring: "Well, I bought a few good funds five years ago and haven't done anything since, except buy more on an automatic schedule." But investment isn't about being sexy—it's about making money, and when you look at investment literature, buy-and-hold investing wins over the long term, every time.

Don't live in the spreadsheet. I encourage you to pick your financial system and move on with your life, which means not "living in the spreadsheet," or obsessing over every tiny change in your spending and in the market. The idea that you could do this might seem far-fetched right now, but by the time you're done with this book you'll be extremely comfortable with your money and investing. I've known too many people who end up tracking every single fluctuation in their net worth, running different scenarios in Excel and modeling out how soon they can retire. Don't do this. You'll turn into a social weirdo and, more important, it's unnecessary. If I do my job right, you'll automate your money and live your Rich Life, which takes place outside the spreadsheet.

Play offense, not defense. Too many of us play defense with our finances. We wait until the end of the month, then look at our spending and shrug: "I guess I spent that much." We accept onerous fees. We don't question complicated advice because it's given to us in a language we don't understand. In this book, I'll teach you to go on offense with your credit cards, your banks, your investments, and even your own money psychology. My goal is for you to craft your own Rich Life by the end of Chapter 9. Get aggressive! No one's going to do it for you.

I Will Teach You to Be Rich *is about using money to design your Rich Life.* I'll teach you how to set up your accounts to create an automatic financial infrastructure that will run smoothly with minimal intervention. You'll also learn what to avoid, some surprising findings from financial literature (is real estate really a good investment?), and how to avoid common financial mistakes. And you'll start taking action instead of debating minutiae. All this will take you just six weeks—then you'll be on the road to being rich. Doesn't that sound good?

Why Do You Want to Be Rich?

I've talked to more than a million people about personal finance over the last fifteen years through my website and speaking engagements. When I do, I always ask two questions:

- *Why do you want to be rich?*

- *What does being rich mean to you?*

Most people never spend even ten minutes thinking through what "rich" means to them. Here's a hint: It's different for everyone, and money is just a small part of being rich. For example, my friends all value different things. Paul loves eating out at Michelin-starred restaurants where a meal might cost $500. Nicole loves traveling. And Nick loves buying clothes. If you don't consciously choose what "rich" means, it's easy to end up mindlessly trying to keep up with your friends. I consider myself rich now that I can do these things:

- Make career decisions because I want to, not because of money

- Help my parents with their retirement, so they don't have to work if they don't want to

- Spend extravagantly on the things I love and be relentlessly frugal about the things I don't (e.g., live in a nice apartment in New York but not own a car)

Every December, I sit down with my wife and we get intentional about the next year. Where do we want to travel? Who do we want to invite with us? What can we imagine doing in the next year that we'll remember for the next fifty years? This planning process—where we get to intentionally design our Rich Lives—is one of the most fun things we do together as a couple.

Before you go further, I encourage you to think about your Rich Life. Why do you want to be rich? What do you want to do with your wealth?

Get really specific. If your Rich Life is "I want to take a taxi instead of a bus," write it down! I realized I live in New York but I hadn't been taking advantage of all the cultural events here, so I decided that once every quarter, I'd go to a museum or Broadway show. Once I set the intention, it became a part of my Rich Life. Don't be embarrassed about how small—or big—your vision is. For example, when I first wrote down my list of a Rich Life, one of the key goals was being able to order appetizers from a restaurant menu, which I never did as a kid. As time went on, my goals got bigger.

When you picture your ideal life, what are you doing in it?

10 Rules for a Rich Life

1. A Rich Life means you can spend extravagantly on the things you love as long as you cut costs mercilessly on the things you don't.

2. Focus on the Big Wins—the five to ten things that get you disproportionate results, including automating your savings and investing, finding a job you love, and negotiating your salary. Get the Big Wins right and you can order as many lattes as you want.

3. Investing should be very boring—and very profitable—over the long term. I get more excited eating tacos than checking my investment returns.

4. There's a limit to how much you can cut, but no limit to how much you can earn. I have readers who earn $50,000/year and ones who earn $750,000/year. They both buy the same loaves of bread. Controlling spending is important, but your earnings become super-linear.

5. Your friends and family will have lots of "tips" once you begin your financial journey. Listen politely, then stick to the program.

6. Build a collection of "spending frameworks" to use when deciding on buying something. Most people default to restrictive rules ("I need to cut back on eating out . . ."), but you can flip it and decide what you'll *always* spend on, like my book-buying rule: If you're thinking about buying a book, just buy it. Don't waste even five seconds debating it. Applying even one new idea from a book is worth it. (Like this one.)

7. Beware of the endless search for "advanced" tips. So many people seek out high-level answers to avoid the real, hard work of improving step by step. It's easier to dream about winning the Boston Marathon than to go out for a ten-minute jog every morning. Sometimes the most advanced thing you can do is the basics, consistently.

8. You're in control. This isn't a Disney movie and nobody's coming to rescue you. Fortunately, you can take control of your finances and build your Rich Life.

9. Part of creating your Rich Life is the willingness to be unapologetically different. Once money isn't a primary constraint, you'll have the freedom

to design your own Rich Life, which will almost certainly be different from the average person's. Embrace it. This is the fun part!

10. Live life outside the spreadsheet. Once you automate your money using the system in this book, you'll see that the most important part of a Rich Life is outside the spreadsheet—it involves relationships, new experiences, and giving back. You earned it.

What You'll Get Out of This Book

Most people think that investing means "buying stocks," as if they should buy and sell random stocks and somehow magically make a profit. Because they've started with a mistaken assumption—that investing means picking stocks—the ones who decide to learn more go down the rabbit hole of fancy terms like "hedge funds," "derivatives," and "call options."

In reality, their fundamental assumption was incorrect. Investing isn't about picking stocks. In fact, your investment plan is actually more important than any individual investment you make. Sadly, most people actually think you need this level of complexity to get rich because they see people talking about this stuff online each day. Guess what? For individual investors like you and me, these options are irrelevant.

It sounds sexy, but when individual investors talk about complicated concepts like this, it's like two elementary school tennis players arguing about the string tension of their racquets. Sure, it might matter a little, but they'd be much better tennis players if they just went outside and hit some balls for a few hours each day.

Simple, long-term investing works. This idea gets nothing but yawns and eye rolls. But you decide: Do you want to sit around impressing others with your sexy vocabulary, or do you want to join me on my gold-lined throne as we're fed grapes and fanned with palm fronds?

I Will Teach You to Be Rich will help you figure out where your money is going and redirect it to where you want it to go. Saving for a vacation to China? A wedding? Just want to make your money grow? Here's the six-week program that will let you tackle it.

SIX WEEKS OF ACTION STEPS

IN WEEK 1, you'll set up your credit cards, pay off debt (if applicable), and learn how to master your credit history and free credit rewards.

IN WEEK 2, you'll set up the right bank accounts.

IN WEEK 3, you'll open a 401(k) and an investment account (even if you have just $100 to start).

IN WEEK 4, you'll figure out how much you're spending. And then you'll figure out how to make your money go where you want it to go.

IN WEEK 5, you'll automate your new infrastructure to make your accounts play together nicely.

IN WEEK 6, you'll learn why investing isn't the same as picking stocks—and how you can get the most out of the market with very little work.

You'll also learn to choose a low-cost automatic portfolio that beats typical Wall Street portfolios, and find out how to maintain your investments by setting up a system that lets you remain as hands-off as possible while your money accumulates automatically. Plus, I provide answers to many specific money questions, including how to buy a car, pay for a wedding, and negotiate your salary.

After reading this book, you'll be better prepared to manage your finances than 99 percent of other people. You'll know what accounts to open up, ways not to pay your bank extra fees, how to invest, how to think about money, and how to see through a lot of the hype that you encounter online every day.

There aren't any secrets to getting rich—it just takes small steps and some discipline, and you can do it with a little bit of work. Now let's get started.

CHAPTER 1

OPTIMIZE YOUR CREDIT CARDS

How to beat the credit card companies at their own game

You'll never see an Indian driving a two-door coupe. Really, think about it. If you have a neighborhood Indian—let's call him Raj—this guy is driving a practical four-door car, usually a Honda Accord or Toyota Camry. However, Indian people aren't just fanatical about driving sensible cars. We're absolutely nuts about hammering down the price to the last penny. Take my dad, for example. He'll bargain for five straight days just to buy one car. I've been along for the ride on these weeklong negotiating sessions with him before. Once, as he was literally about to sign the papers, he stopped, asked them to throw in free floor mats (a $50 value), and walked away when they refused. This, after he'd spent five days bargaining them down. As he dragged me from the dealership, I stared straight ahead, shell-shocked.

As you can imagine, by the time I went to buy my own car, I had been steeped in a rich tradition of negotiating. I knew how to make unreasonable demands with a straight face and never take no for an answer. I took a more modern approach, however: Instead of spending a week going from dealership to dealership, I simply invited seventeen dealers in Northern California to bid against each other for my business while I sat at home and browsed around the internet, calmly reviewing the emails and faxes (yes, really) as they came in. (For more about buying a car, see page 315.) In the end, I found a great deal in Palo Alto and walked in ready to sign the papers. Everything was going smoothly until the dealer went to check my credit. He came back smiling. "You know, you have the best credit of anyone I've ever seen at your age," he said.

"Thanks," I replied, actually wanting to say, "AWWW, YEAH, I KNEW IT." That's because I was a weird twentysomething Indian who chooses a four-door Accord for his dream car and prides himself on his credit score.

Then the dealer said, "Hmm."

"Hmm?" I asked.

"Well," he said, "it looks like you have great credit, but not enough credit sources." The bottom line, he told me, was that they couldn't offer me the low-interest option we had talked about. Instead of 1.9 percent interest, it would be 4.9 percent. That didn't sound like much, but I pulled out a notepad and did a quick calculation. The difference would be more than $2,200 over the life of my car loan. Because I was getting such a great deal on the car, I convinced myself that the higher interest rate was okay, and I signed the papers for the loan. But I was still pissed. Why should I have to pay an extra two grand when I had great credit?

Most people weren't raised like me, so I understand that you probably hate negotiating. Most Americans do. We're not sure what to say, we get nervous about looking cheap, and then we look at ourselves and say, "Is this really worth it?" In a pool of sweaty discomfort, most of us conclude "No"—and we pay full price.

I have a fresh perspective: It's not worth negotiating everything, but there are a few areas of life where negotiation is a Big Win. In this chapter, I'm going to show you how to go on offense and squeeze as many rewards and benefits out of your credit cards as possible. You're going to start winning against them. And for the first time, negotiating is going to be fun.

The Usual Credit Card Scare Tactics

Virtually every section on credit cards in every book starts with these three scare tactics.

Scary stats. According to the Prosperity Now Scorecard, the median US household credit card debt is $2,241, and the median student loan debt is $17,711. The Fed Reserve notes that "Four in 10 adults in 2017 would have to either borrow money, sell something, or simply not be able to pay if faced with a $400 emergency expense."

Scary headlines. "The looming debt crisis will hurt these Americans the most," reports CNBC. Or this one from the *Washington Post*: "A debt crisis is on the horizon." *Business Insider* reports that "America's student debt crisis is worse than we thought."

Scary emotions. Confusion, anxiety, and lies—the media knows that if they employ these, they'll sell pageviews and ads.

Reading these scare tactics, how do you feel? Most of us respond by shutting down and ignoring the problem.

Debt was about fear. I didn't talk about it, I didn't look at the whole picture, I avoided any conversation or thought about it.

—WARREN KOPP, 36

Debt was always at the back of my mind. I couldn't enjoy spending the money I had because it haunted me.

—CHRIS BEHRENS, 45

I remember feeling embarrassed when I would apply for a credit card and get turned down . . . When debt collectors would call, I would feel embarrassed and stressed about ignoring the call, because I owed money, but couldn't afford to pay it off.

—ALLISON REYNOLDS, 28

The media thrives on creating fear and anxiety around debt, as if it's inescapable and crippling. And they rarely suggest solutions—

when they do, they're along the lines of "eat out less." Thanks, guys.

The result is a tornado of negative emotions. We feel helpless. We feel outraged. Who should get the blame? I don't know, but somebody should.

Most of all, we do nothing. This is how "outrage culture" works—it makes you feel angry and exhausted . . . and then you go back to doing nothing.

I have a different approach.

The Way I See It

Credit cards give you thousands of dollars worth of perks. If you pay your bill on time, they're a free short-term loan. They can help you keep track of your spending much more easily than cash, and they let you download your transaction history for free. Most offer free warranty extensions on your purchases and free rental car insurance. Many offer rewards and points worth hundreds or even thousands of dollars.

Credit cards are also convenient enemies. Almost everyone has a bad story about late fees, unauthorized charges, or overspending. Not surprisingly, many pundits have a knee-jerk reaction to credit cards: "Using credit cards is the worst financial decision you can make," they shout. "Cut them all up!" What an easy battle cry for people who want simple solutions and don't realize the benefits of multiple sources of credit.

The truth about credit cards lies somewhere between these two extremes. As long as you manage them well, they're worth having. But if you don't completely pay off your bill at the end of the month, you'll owe an enormous amount of interest on the remainder, usually about 14 percent. This is what's known as the annual percentage rate, or APR. Credit card companies also tack on a whopping fee every time you miss a payment—usually around $35. It's also easy to overuse credit cards and find yourself in debt, as many American credit card users have done.

This isn't meant to scare you away from using credit cards. In fact, instead of playing defense by avoiding credit cards altogether, I want you to play offense by using credit cards responsibly and getting as many benefits out of them as possible. To do so, you need to optimize your credit card(s) and use them as a spearhead to improve your overall credit. By the end of this chapter, you'll know how to squeeze the credit card companies for everything they're worth—without paying unnecessary fees—and you'll know how to use your cards to boost your all-important credit score. I'll show you how to negotiate with credit card companies and reveal secret perks that nobody talks about. And I'll show you exactly how I maximize my credit cards for perks and cash back, including examples of how I use points for free flights and high-end hotel stays.

When I was traveling with my fiancée to see her family in Dubai, I surprised her with a three-night stay at a resort in the desert that could only be described as 7-star. We had a private villa in traditional bedouin style overlooking the Dubai desert with a private pool, and all meals at the resort were provided. The whole experience easily would have cost $2,000-plus a night, but I did the whole thing for free with points.

—NATHAN LACHENMYER, 29

I recently booked 2 round-trip tickets from San Francisco to Italy for a 2-week vacation this fall. The flights were completely free with credit card points!

—JANE PHILIPPS, 30

In the past year I've flown business class to Spain and stayed at luxury hotels for a week, flown round-trip business class with my girlfriend to Thailand, and flown my mother to Germany business class to visit for her father's 80th birthday. I'm also about to redeem miles to go to Budapest next spring!

—JORDAN PETIT, 27

Student loans can be a great decision. Journalists love to write about the student debt "crisis." Yet a student loan can be one of the best investments you ever make, with the average bachelor's degree holder earning over $1 million more than people with only a high school diploma. Yes, debt sucks, and yes, many predatory colleges and graduate schools actively lie to young Americans about the actual value of their degree—a problem that's completely inexcusable and supported by an educational-industrial complex. Many earnest but naive students were misled by their counselors, colleges, and even their parents about incurring student loan debt on degrees that will never pay off.

But you can pay off your debt faster than you thought possible (to see how, flip to page 284). And your college degree was almost certainly worth it—even if you're only considering the financial return on investment and not including the benefits of making lifelong friends, building priceless habits of discipline, and exposing yourself to new ideas as an educated citizen. Ignore the scare tactics of the student loan "crisis." If you have student loan debt, use the material in this book to create a repayment plan.

Most people are playing the game wrong. I've spoken to literally thousands of people who are in debt. Some of them have had tough situations—unexpected illnesses, elderly parents who need support, surprise expenses. But, candidly, some of them are simply playing the game wrong. They've never spent a weekend reading a book on personal finance. They don't even know how much they owe! Instead of doing the work to aggressively win at the game of debt, they complain. It's like watching a four-year-old trying to play Monopoly, then realizing they can't understand the rules (which they've never read), getting angry, and flipping the board over. I'll show you how to win.

Bank of America Hates Me

Bank of America, one of the world's shittiest banks, hates me because I've named them as one of the worst banks out there. Good news! Ten years later, they're still on my list for screwing over my readers repeatedly. (Wells Fargo is also on my list.) I don't cut deals with banks—I don't need their money—and I call out the best, and worst, financial companies for my readers.

As you can imagine, the worst companies don't like being named in a *New York Times* bestselling book. I discovered Bank of America hates me because one of my friends works in their corporate office. One day, she reached out to me and said, "Did you know you're on a Bank of America influencer list?" I was surprised. Me? Little old me?

Then she added: "It's a *negative* influencer list."

I have never been so proud.

When it comes to student loans and credit cards, my goal is for you to stop playing defense. I'm going to show you how to play offense instead. For student loans, make an aggressive plan and minimize the amount of interest you pay. For credit cards, I squeeze every single benefit out of them. Basically I want the credit card companies to hate you, as they hate me.

The best part is how fast you can change your financial life once you switch from playing defense to playing offense with your money.

In the 3½ years since I read the book, I paid off $14,000 in credit card debt and $8,000 in student loan debt.

—RYAN HEALEY, 27

In the past year since I started this book, I opened a 401(k) and a Roth IRA, understand how they work, and have funded $7,200 toward my retirement. I also opened 2 credit cards to build my utilization and boost my credit score and am 100 percent a deadbeat customer who pays on time every month in full.

—JEFF COLLINS, 35

I learned how to automate my credit card payments, set up flexible spending, and start investing in index funds. Today I have amassed over $40,000 in my "net worth," having been out of school for less than 2 years. Thanks for the advice!

—EMILY BAUMAN, 24

Playing Offense: Use Credit to Accelerate Your Rich Life

People love to pick sexy investments and use fancy terms like "distressed securities" and "EBITDA" when they focus on getting rich. But they often ignore something that is so simple, so basic, that it just doesn't seem important: their credit. Ironically, credit is one of the most vital factors in getting rich, but because it's hard to wrap our minds around it, we often overlook it entirely. It's time to wake up and pay attention to it, because establishing good credit is the first step in building an infrastructure for getting rich. Think about it: Our largest purchases are almost always made on credit, and people with good credit save tens of thousands of dollars on these purchases. Credit has a far greater impact on your finances than saving a few dollars a day on a cup of coffee.

There are two main components to your credit (also known as your credit history): your credit report and your credit score. These boring terms can actually save you tens of thousands of dollars over your lifetime, so listen up. This is an example of a Big Win—worth paying attention to.

Your **credit report** gives potential lenders basic information about you, your accounts, and your payment history. It tracks all credit-related activities (e.g., credit cards and loans), although recent activities are given higher weight.

Your **credit score** (often called your FICO score because it was created by the Fair Isaac Corporation) is a single, easy-to-read number between 300 and 850 that represents your credit risk to lenders. It's like an SAT score for the credit industry (higher is better). The lenders take this number and, with a few other pieces of information, such as your salary and age, decide if they'll lend you money for credit like a credit card, mortgage, or car loan. They'll charge you more or less for the loan depending on your score, which signifies how risky you are.

It's ridiculously easy to check your credit score and credit report— and you should do it right now. Once a year, by law, you're allowed to obtain your credit report for free at annualcreditreport.com. It includes basic information about all your accounts and payment history.

Lots of people use Credit Karma (creditkarma.com) to get a free credit score, but I prefer the official credit score from MyFico (myfico. com), which is more accurate even though it has a small fee.

Why are your credit report and credit score important? Because a good credit score can save you hundreds of thousands of dollars in interest charges. How? Well, if you have good credit, it makes you less risky to lenders, meaning they can offer you a better interest rate on loans. Maybe you don't need a loan today, but in three or four years, you might need to start thinking about a car or a house. So please don't scoff at or dismiss what you just read. One of the key differences

CREDIT SCORE VS. CREDIT REPORT

What your credit score is based on:	What your credit report includes:
35% payment history (How reliable you are. Late payments hurt you.)	■ Basic identification information
30% amounts owed (How much you owe and how much credit you have available, aka your credit utilization rate)	■ A list of all your credit accounts
15% length of history (How long you've had credit)	■ Your credit history, or whom you've paid, how consistently, and any late payments
10% new credit (Older accounts are better, because they show you're reliable.)	■ Amount of loans
10% types of credit (For example, credit cards, student loans. Varied is better.)	■ Credit inquiries, or who else has requested your credit info (other lenders)
Get your credit score at myfico.com for a small fee.	■ Get your free credit report once a year at annualcreditreport.com

between rich people and everyone else is that rich people plan before they need to plan.

If you doubt that a loan's interest rate really makes that much of a difference, check out the table on the next page. Look at the differences in what you'd pay for a 30-year mortgage based on your credit score.

As you can see, a high credit score can save you tens of thousands of dollars over your lifetime (or more if you live in a high-cost-of-living area). While other people spend many hours cutting coupons, agonizing over generic brands at the grocery store, or beating themselves up over a morning latte, they're failing to see the bigger picture. It's fine to keep a close eye on your expenses, but you should focus on spending time on the things that matter, the Big Wins. So let's dig into tactics for improving your credit, which is quantifiably worth much more than any advice about frugality.

HOW CREDIT SCORES AFFECT WHAT YOU PAY

On a $200,000 30-year mortgage, if your FICO score is . . .	. . . your APR* (interest rate) will be . . .	. . . with interest, you'll pay a total of . . .
760–850	4.279%	$355,420
700–759	4.501%	$364,856
680–699	4.678%	$372,468
660–679	4.892%	$381,773
640–659	5.322%	$400,804
620–639	5.868%	$425,585

*APR calculated in August 2018.

My credit mistake was I opened my account too late, I very quickly started using my card to stay out of my bank overdraft, and it got out of hand. Then I forgot I had to make a payment and missed a payment. I wish I'd understood how a credit card would help my credit score a decade ago, because then I would've already made, learned from, and recovered from my daft mistakes with it.

—JC, 29

Building Credit with Credit Cards

Credit comes in many forms (car loans, mortgages, and so on), but we're going to start with credit cards because almost all of us have one, and most important, they're the fastest and most concrete way to optimize your credit. Most people are making at least one or two major mistakes with their credit cards. The good news is that it's incredibly easy to fix this by learning a little bit about how credit cards work.

GUESS HOW MUCH AN IPHONE COSTS IF YOU FINANCE IT WITH A CREDIT CARD?

One of the biggest problems with credit cards is the hidden cost of using them. It may be incredibly convenient to swipe your card at every retailer, but if you don't pay your bill every month, you'll end up owing way more than you realize.

Let's say you buy this . . .	Paying minimum payments, it will take this long to pay it off . . .	You'll pay this much in interest
$1,000 iPhone	9 years, 2 months	$732.76
$1,500 computer	13 years, 3 months	$1,432.19
$10,000 furniture	32 years, 2 months	$13,332.06

Assumes 14% APR and 2% minimum payment

   If you paid only the minimum monthly balance on your $10,000 purchase, it would take you more than 32 years and cost you more than $13,000 in interest alone, more than the purchase price itself. Remember, this doesn't even factor in your "opportunity cost": Instead of paying off a $10,000 sofa for over 30 years, if you'd invested the same amount and earned 8 percent, it would've turned into about $27,000! Try calculating how much your own purchases really cost at bankrate.com/brm/calc/minpayment.asp.

Getting a New Card

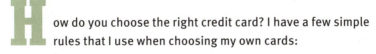

How do you choose the right credit card? I have a few simple rules that I use when choosing my own cards:

- Don't accept credit card offers that come in the mail or from retail stores like Gap or Nordstrom.

- Squeeze every reward you can out of your credit cards.

- Pick a good one, then move on with your life.

Now here's how to do it.

Get rewarded for your spending. There are different levels of rewards cards. Some are very basic, while others offer hundreds of dollars in annual benefits—or even thousands, depending on how much you spend.

First, decide what you want to get rewarded with—cash back or travel. I recommend cash back because it's straightforward, there are excellent cash back cards, and it's simpler than travel rewards, which require more sophistication to truly maximize. (For more on maximizing travel rewards, look up forums on "credit card churning.")

Once you decide on the primary reward you want, use a site like bankrate.com to sort through your options.

Most of the best rewards cards have fees. Are they worth it? You should run the numbers to decide, which takes less than 5 minutes. Here's a quick rule of thumb: If you spend thousands per month on your credit card, the rewards are usually worth it. But if you spend more modestly or you're not sure whether you want to pay a fee, spend a few minutes doing a quick analysis by searching for "credit card rewards calculator." Plug in your numbers and you'll quickly see which rewards cards are worth it for you.

Bottom line: It's almost always worth getting a rewards card. Be sure to do your homework and pick one where you value the rewards.

Don't sign up for retail store credit cards. These cards might as well have "You Screwed Yourself" written on them in thirty-six-point type. I can't count how many times I've been in line and seen someone buying $40 of socks or a cheap T-shirt or two. I just wait for the conversation I know is about to happen. "Would you like to open a credit card?" the salesperson asks, praying he meets his commission goal for the month. "You'll save ten percent."

Yup! There it is! Between clenched teeth, it's me muttering, "Shut your mouth, Ramit. Don't say anything. They don't want your unsolicit—"

Person at the register: "Hmm . . . sure, I'll open that card. Why not? It couldn't hurt."

Two points for our friend who decided to open a retail credit card:

1. As a general rule, whenever you say, "It couldn't hurt," IT VERY MUCH COULD HURT. Every single time I've said that in my life, I've proceeded to make a huge mistake.

2. This person just opened one of the most predatory cards out there to save $4. Jesus. You might as well reach into a dirty gutter to find a few

Searching for Credit Cards Online

A secret of the credit card industry: When you compare credit cards online, you're entering a murky world of SEO and affiliate fees where nearly all credit card listings are compensated. This means that virtually every site is being paid for showing you their "recommended" cards, and it's not easy to see why certain cards are being recommended. You can usually find very good cards on these sites. But if you're a high spender, be sure to take a few extra minutes searching around. For example, when I was beginning to plan my wedding, I looked for the best cash back card. Buried at the bottom of some forum post, I found a cash back credit card from Alliant Credit Union that paid 3 percent for the first year of spending, then 2 percent afterward. That was the best cash back reward on the market, but the card never showed up in my original searches.

pennies. That would be cheaper than the financial beating you're going to eventually take.

Get some standards, people. You wouldn't marry the first person who touched your elbow. Why would you sign up for a retail store card that has high fees, near-extortionate interest rates, and terrible rewards?

As for the credit card offers that come in the mail, generally you can find better options by researching online. (Sidenote: If you find yourself getting a ton of credit card offers and other junk mail, go to optoutprescreen.com to get off their marketing lists.)

I forgot to pay a stupid $25 Gap bill. It was a big PITA over 25 bucks. They dinged my credit and almost sent it to collections. I followed the process to challenge it 6 months later. Told them it was a one-time mistake. I believe the phone agent gave me an address to send a letter. I did and a couple months later the remark was gone from my account.

—**PAUL FRAZIER, 30**

The Exact Credit Cards I Use

Years ago, I decided to optimize my credit card rewards. I knew I was about 95 percent of the way there—I had cash back and travel cards for my business and personal spending—but I wanted to get truly dialed in for that last 5 percent. As my business had grown to dozens of employees, my spending had increased considerably. These rewards started to become meaningful and I wanted to be sure I was getting every benefit available.

For example, at a certain point, we were spending over $40,000 on ads *every month*. I know most people don't need to maximize points at this level. But I think it's fascinating, and I want to share what I learned.

I wanted to know:

- Am I squeezing out every possible reward from my spending?

- How should I handle large spending events, like a wedding or a team retreat?

- When should I use a cash back card versus a travel card?

Most important, what am I missing? What are all the cool things I *should* be asking for that I don't even know about?

Finding answers was harder than I thought. First, I posted on Facebook, asking if anyone knew an expert who could audit my spending and give me feedback on the cards I was using. Most of the people I initially talked to were focused on maximizing points for frugal traveling. That's cool, but it's not really my thing.

Then I had an unusual call with a guy named Chris.

"I had my credit cards in pretty good shape," Chris told me. "But then I wanted to get *really good*. And I know guys like you and me don't have a lot of time to play the credit card games of opening and closing cards all the time."

I was listening.

Chris told me how he set up his cards to maximize rewards to the tune of millions of points. I was interested, but I wanted to see if he really knew what he was talking about. Then he said this.

CHRIS: You want to know what I do to really squeeze the points out of my credit cards?

RAMIT: YES!

CHRIS: Some hotels will give you five hundred points for every night you waive housekeeping. So if I'm traveling alone, I get a room with two beds. I switch beds, switch towels, and I get my five hundred points.

When I heard this, I was sold.

He was so detailed, so fanatical, that he had optimized down to the level of towel usage. I had met my hero.

Chris Hutchins is a friend who happens to be extremely skilled in optimizing travel rewards.

My goal was to build a "playbook" of how to use credit cards to maximize rewards for my personal and business lives. My assistant, Jill, spent weeks working with Chris, analyzing my spending and upcoming expenses. The goal was to boil it down to a simplified "playbook" that Jill could use when making purchase decisions. The entire document is 15 pages long. But here is the key takeaway:

If you're booking travel or eating out, use a travel card to maximize rewards. For everything else, use a cash back card.

The card I use for travel and eating out is the Chase Sapphire Reserve. For everything else, I use an Alliant cash back card. And for business, I use a Capital One cash back business card. For extra benefits, I have an Amex Platinum card.

The result of this is thousands of dollars in cash back each year, millions of rewards points, and a new life motto: MBWOSIS.

My Body Will Only Sleep in Suites.

Don't go card crazy. Now that you're in the market, you might be tempted by any number of card offers. But don't overdo it. There's no magic number of cards you should have, but each additional card you get means added complexity for your personal finance system: more to keep track of and more places for things to go wrong. Two or three is a good rule of thumb. (The average American has four credit cards.)

My online business profile didn't have my latest address so I never received statements. For 34 months, my bank account got charged $60. I ignored it and didn't investigate it, hoping it would go away. I was cocky I could force them to waive these charges because of the relationship. Then I finally willed myself to look into it, visited branches, called 5 different departments. No bid. Once all was said and done, I ended up paying ~$2,000 for a $3,000 initial balance. It completely smoked my confidence. I closed down all 11 of my cards except my CSP. Technically I'm still "ahead" but the thought of having paid $2,000 when I *didn't have to* and it was *100% avoidable and in my control* was too much.

—HASSAN AHMED, 36

Remember, there are other sources of credit besides credit cards. These include installment loans (such as auto loans), personal lines of credit, home equity lines of credit, and service credit (such as utilities). Your credit score is based on your overall sources of credit. "Take it slow," Craig Watts of Fair Isaac Corporation says, cautioning against prescribing a specific number of credit sources. "It depends on how long you've been managing credit. The less information in your credit report, the higher the prominence of each new report. For example, if . . . you only have one credit card in your name, when you open another account, the weight of that action is more than it would be ten years down the line." In short, pick two or three great cards, maximize rewards sensibly, and remember that these cards are just one part of your overall financial infrastructure.

The Six Commandments of Credit Cards

Now it's time to go on offense and take full advantage of your cards. You'll improve your credit while automatically being rewarded for the purchases you're already making. Optimizing your credit is a multistep process. One of the most important factors is getting out of debt, which we'll tackle at the end of the chapter. But first, we'll set up automatic credit card payments so you never miss a payment again. Then, we'll see how to cut fees, get better rewards, and take everything you can from the credit card companies.

1. Pay off your credit card regularly. Yeah, we've all heard it, but what you may not know is that your debt payment history represents 35 percent of your credit score—the largest chunk. In fact, the single most important thing you can do to improve your credit is to pay your bills on time. Whether you're paying the full amount of your credit card bill or risking my wrath by paying just part of it, pay it on time. Lenders like prompt payers, so don't give your credit card company the opportunity to raise your rates and lower your credit score by being a few days late with your payment. This is a great example of focusing on what will get you rich, not on what's sexy. Think about your friends who search every single website to get the best deals on travel or clothes. They might be thrilled after saving $10—and they can brag to everyone about all the special deals they get—but you'll quietly save thousands by understanding the invisible importance of credit, paying your bills on time, and having a better credit score.

Today, most people pay their credit card bills online, but if you haven't set up automatic payment yet, log on to your credit card's website to do

Awful Consequences

f you miss even one payment on your credit card, here are four terrible, horrible, no good, very bad results you may face:

1. Your credit score can drop more than 100 points, which would add $227/month to an average 30-year fixed-rate mortgage.

2. Your APR can go up to 30 percent.

3. You'll be charged a late fee, usually around $35.

4. Your late payment can trigger rate increases on your other credit cards as well, even if you've never been late on them. (I find this fact amazing.)

Don't get too freaked out: You can recover from the hit to your credit score, usually within a few months. In fact, if you're just a few days late with your payment, you may incur a fee, but it generally won't be reported to the credit bureaus. See page 42 to find out what to do if you miss a payment.

so now. Note: Don't worry if you don't always have enough money in your checking account to pay off the full amount on your credit card. You'll get a statement from your card company each month before the payment goes through so that you can adjust your payment as needed.

I totally forgot the due date for my credit card. So not only did they charge me a late fee, but they charged me interest on that month's and the previous month's purchases. I called up the customer service line of the card and told them that I had been a good customer in the past and asked if they could do anything for me with the fees. The representative removed the late fee and refunded $20 of the interest charge back to my account. They returned a total of $59 to me with one phone call.

—ERIC HENRY, 25

---

2. Try to get fees on your cards waived. This can be a great way to optimize your credit cards, because your credit card companies will do all the work for you. Call them using the phone number on the back of the card and ask if you're paying any fees, including annual fees or service charges. It should go a little something like this:

YOU: Hi, I'd like to confirm that I'm not paying any fees on my credit card.

CREDIT CARD REP: *Well, it looks like you have an annual fee of $100. That's actually one of our better rates.*

YOU: I'd rather pay no fees. Can you waive this year's annual fee?

Earlier I mentioned that it can be worth paying annual fees for rewards cards. This is true—but why not ask? Remember, credit card companies compete ferociously with each other, which can benefit you. Call them a month before your new annual fee kicks in and ask them to waive it. Sometimes it works, sometimes not.

If you decide that your credit card fee isn't worth it, ask your credit card company what they'll do for you. If they waive your fees, great! If not, switch to a no-fee card. I suggest you do this at the same credit card company to simplify your life—and so you don't have to close one account and open another, which will temporarily affect your credit score.

3. Negotiate a lower APR. Your APR, or annual percentage rate, is the interest rate your credit card company charges you. APRs fluctuate, but in general, they hover around 13 to 16 percent. That is very high! This makes it extremely expensive if you carry a balance on your card. Put another way, since you can make an average of about 8 percent in the stock market, your credit card is getting a great deal by lending you money. If you could get a 14 percent return, you'd be thrilled. You want to avoid the black hole of credit card interest payments so you can earn money, not give it to the credit card companies.

So, call your credit card company and ask them to lower your APR. If they ask why, tell them you've been paying your bill in full on time for the last few months, and you know there are a number of credit cards offering better rates than you're currently getting. (See page 64 for a sample script.) In my experience, this works about half the time.

It's important to note that your APR doesn't technically matter if you're paying your bills in full every month—you could have a 2 percent APR or 80 percent APR and it would be irrelevant, since you don't pay interest if you pay your total bill each month. But this is a quick and easy way to pick the low-hanging fruit with one phone call.

Reading IWT, I've probably saved $15,000 to $25,000 in interest alone. I've negotiated car loans, student loans, home loans, etc.
—LYLA NUTT, 30

4. Keep your main cards for a long time, and keep them active—but also keep them simple. Lenders like to see a long history of credit, which means that the longer you hold an account, the more valuable it is for your credit score. Don't get suckered by introductory offers and low APRs—if you're happy with your card, keep it. Some credit card companies will cancel your account after a certain period of inactivity. To avoid having a card you rarely use shut down, set up an automatic payment on it. For example, I set it up so that one of my credit cards pays a $12.95 monthly subscription through my checking account each month, which requires zero intervention on my part. But my credit report reflects that I've had the card for more than five years, which improves my credit score. Play it safe: If you have a credit card, keep it active

What to Do If You Miss a Payment

Nobody's perfect. Despite my warnings, I understand that accidents happen and you might miss a payment at some point. When this happens, I use my Indian heritage to beat the companies by negotiating with them, and you can, too:

YOU: Hi, I noticed I missed a payment, and I wanted to confirm that this won't affect my credit score.

CREDIT CARD REP: *Let me check on that. No, the late fee will be applied, but it won't affect your credit score.*

(Note: If you pay within a few days of your missed bill, it usually won't be reported to the credit agencies. But ask to be sure.)

YOU: Thank you! I'm really happy to hear that. Now, about that fee . . . I understand I was late, but I'd like to have it waived.

CREDIT CARD REP: *Why?*

YOU: It was a mistake. It won't happen again, so I'd like to have the fee removed.

(Note: Always end your sentence with strength. Don't say, "Can you remove this?" Say, "I'd like to have this removed.") At this point, you have a better-than-50-percent chance of getting the fee credited to your account. But just in case you get an especially tough rep, try this.

CREDIT CARD REP: *I'm very sorry, but we can't refund that fee. I can try to get you our latest blah blah marketing pitch blah blah . . .*

YOU: I'm sorry, but I've been a customer for four years and I'd hate for this one fee to drive me away from your service. What can you do to remove the late fee?

CREDIT CARD REP: *Hmm . . . Let me check on that . . . Yes, I was able to remove the fee this time. It's been credited to your account.*

You don't believe me that it can be so simple? It is. Anyone can do it.

using an automatic payment at least once every three months.

Now the one tricky part: If you decide to get a new card, should you close your old card? I've changed my view here over the years. The typical advice is to keep cards open for as long as possible, which is generally smart. But if you have lots of cards that you never use, reconsider this. Some of my readers have opened over twenty-plus cards to "churn" rewards, and now they can't keep track of all their cards. This is where you have to make a decision on risk versus reward and simplicity versus complexity. There's lots of advice warning against closing credit cards, but as long as you're paying your balances on time and have good credit, closing an old card will not have a major long-term impact on your credit score.

Think balance: For most people, having two or three credit cards is perfect. If you have a special reason to have more cards—for example, if you own a business or are intentionally maximizing temporary sign-up rewards—great. But if you find yourself swamped with the number of cards you have, close the inactive ones. As long as you have good credit, the long-term impact will be minimal and you'll sleep easier at night with a simple financial system you can easily keep track of.

5. Get more credit. (Warning! Do this only if you have no debt.) This one is counterintuitive, and to explain it, I have to reach into personal finance lessons of yore. Many people don't realize this, but in the classic '80s Salt-N-Pepa song "Push It," when they say that the dance isn't for everybody—"only the sexy people"—they are actually detailing a sound personal finance strategy.

Before I explain, I want to first acknowledge that, yes, I did just quote Salt-N-Pepa in an actual, published book. Anyway, when Salt-N-Pepa talk about "only the sexy people," what they really mean is "This tip is only for the financially responsible people." I'm serious about this warning: This tip is only for people who have no credit card debt and pay their bills in full each month. It's not for anyone else.

It involves getting more credit to improve something called your credit utilization rate, which is simply how much you owe divided by your available credit. This makes up 30 percent of your credit score. For example, if you owe $4,000 and have $4,000 in total available credit, your ratio is 100 percent (($4,000/$4,000) x 100), which is bad. If, however, you owe only $1,000 but have $4,000 in available credit, your credit utilization rate is a much better 25 percent (($1,000 / $4,000) x 100). Lower is preferred because lenders don't want you regularly spending all the money you have available through credit—it's too likely that you'll default and not pay them anything.

To improve your credit utilization rate, you have two choices: Stop carrying so much debt on your credit cards (even if you pay it off each month) or increase your total available credit. Because we've already established that if you're doing this, you're debt-free, all that remains for you to do is to increase your available credit.

Here's how: Call up your card company and ask for a credit increase.

YOU: Hi, I'd like to request a credit increase. I currently have five thousand dollars available, and I'd like ten thousand.

CREDIT CARD REP: *Why are you requesting a credit increase?*

YOU: I've been paying my bill in full for the last eighteen months and I have some upcoming purchases. I'd like a credit limit of ten thousand dollars. Can you approve my request?

REP: *Sure. I've put in a request for this increase. It should be activated in about seven days.*

I request a credit-limit increase every six to twelve months. Remember, 30 percent of your credit score is represented by your credit utilization rate. To improve it, the first thing you should do is pay off your debt. Only after you've already paid off your debt should you try to increase your available credit. Sorry to repeat myself, but this is important!

When my husband and I were in college, we got a free T-shirt or something and got credit cards with reasonable limits ($500). Sure, I had no income, but that didn't seem important at the time. Wouldn't you know it, I was responsible enough to have my limit raised to $2,000 after a very short period of time! Except that I wasn't actually responsible, and I paid thousands of dollars in interest and late fees and wrecked my credit rating for several years. It took many years for us to clear up this debt. I can't name one purchase that was truly necessary.

—MICHELE MILLER, 38

---

6. Use your credit card's secret perks! Before I get into rewards programs, let me say this: Just like with car insurance, you can get great deals on your credit when you're a responsible customer. In fact, there are lots of tips for people who have very good credit. If you fall in this category, you should call your credit cards and lenders once a year to ask them what advantages you're eligible for. Often, they can waive fees, extend credit, and give you private promotions that others don't have access to. Call them up and use this line:

"Hi there. I checked my credit and noticed that I have a 750 credit score, which is pretty good. I've been a customer of yours for the last four years, so I'm wondering what special promotions and offers you have for me . . . I'm thinking of fee waivers and special offers that you use for customer retention."

As discussed, credit cards also offer rewards programs that give you cash back, airline tickets, and other benefits, but most people don't take advantage of all the free stuff they can get. For example, when I had to fly to a wedding in an obscure town in Wisconsin, I redeemed my credit card's travel reward to save more than $600 on the flight. That's an easy example, but there are even more rewards: Did you know that credit cards automatically give you amazing consumer protection? Here are a few examples you might not know about:

- Automatic warranty doubling: Most cards extend the warranty on your purchases. So if you buy an iPhone and it breaks after Apple's warranty expires, your credit card will still cover it up to an additional year. This is true for nearly every credit card for nearly every purchase, automatically.

- Car rental insurance: If you rent a car, don't let them sell you on getting the extra collision insurance. It's completely worthless! You already have coverage through your existing car insurance, plus your credit card will usually back you up to $50,000.

- Trip-cancellation insurance: If you book tickets for a vacation and then get sick and can't travel, your airline will charge you hefty fees to rebook your ticket. Just call your credit card and ask for the trip-cancellation insurance to kick in, and they'll cover those change fees—usually between $3,000 to $10,000 per trip.

■ Concierge services: When I couldn't find LA Philharmonic tickets, I called my credit card and asked the concierge to try to find some. He called me back in two days with tickets. They charged me (a lot, actually), but he was able to get them when nobody else could.

Most important, your credit card automatically tracks your spending, making it easy for software to download and categorize your expenses. For these reasons, I put almost all my purchases on a credit card— especially the large ones.

Your key takeaway: Call your credit card company and ask them to send you a full list of all their rewards. Then use them!

We paid for our entire 3-week honeymoon using points, including first-class, round-trip direct flights from NYC to Vegas, luxury suite at the Venetian, luxury car rental and all other accommodations, attractions, and food (yeah, even food). We literally didn't spend a penny (and came home with +$200. Thanks, blackjack!).

—TE ROMEO, 34

My honey and I go to Hawaii and Italy/Europe each year almost entirely on points. It looks like we are living large and lavish, but our last 9-day trip to Italy cost us $350, and that was only because our favorite hotel in Sienna doesn't take any points.

—ROBYN GINNEY, 45

Mistakes to Avoid

Think ahead before closing accounts. If you're applying for a major loan—for a car, home, or education—don't close any accounts within six months of filing the loan application. You want as much credit as possible when you apply.

However, if you know that an open account will entice you to spend and you want to close your credit card to prevent that, you should do it. You may take a slight hit on your credit score, but over time, it will recover—and that's better than overspending.

Always Track Your Calls to Financial Companies

Unfortunately for you, credit card companies are very good at using BS late fees to increase their revenues. Unfortunately for them, I'm giving you a script for getting these fees reversed (see page 42). One of the best ways to improve your chances of having fees waived is by keeping track of every call to your financial institutions, including credit card companies, banks, and investment companies. When I call to dispute anything, I open a spreadsheet that details the last time I called them, who I spoke with, and what was resolved. If only criminals were as diligent as I am.

Create a spreadsheet that looks like this:

The Pocket Tracker for Tracking Credit Card Calls

Call Date	Time	Name of Rep	Rep's ID#	Comments

Whenever you make a call regarding a dispute on your bill, you wouldn't believe how powerful it is to refer back to the last time you called—citing the rep's name, the date of the conversation, and your call notes. Most credit card reps you talk to will simply give in because they know you came to play in the big leagues.

When you use this to confront a credit card company or bank with data from your last calls, you'll be more prepared than 99 percent of other people—and chances are, you'll get what you want.

Disputing a Charge: How to Mobilize Your Credit Card's Army for You

Once, when I canceled my cell phone service, they told me my account had a $160 charge. "For what?" I asked. Wait for it . . .

"An early cancellation fee."

Yeah, right. I knew I didn't have a contract, and I had negotiated out of an early cancellation fee a long time before that. (Cell phone companies make a lot of money from trying these shady moves, hoping customers will get frustrated, give up, and just pay.) But I'm not the one to try this on: Ever since the company had started trying to rip me off three years before, I had kept records of every phone conversation I'd had with them. The customer service rep was very polite, but insisted she couldn't do anything to erase the charge.

Really? I'd heard this tune before, so I pulled out the notes I had taken the previous year and politely read them aloud to her.

As soon as I read them, I experienced a miraculous change in her ability to waive the fee. Within two minutes, my account was cleared and I was off the phone. Amazing!!!!! Thank you, madam!!!

Wouldn't it be great if that were the end of the story? I wish. They told me they wouldn't charge me . . . and they did it anyway. By this point, I was so fed up that I called in the big guns.

Many people don't know that credit cards offer excellent consumer protection. This is one reason I encourage everyone to make major purchases on their credit card (and not use cash or a debit card).

I called my credit card company and told them I wanted to dispute a charge. They said, "Sure, what's your address and what's the amount?" When I told them about my experience with the cell phone company, they instantly gave me a temporary credit for the amount and told me to mail in a form with my complaint, which I did.

Two weeks later, the complaint was resolved in my favor.

What happens in disputes like this is the credit card company fights the merchant for you. This works with all credit cards. Keep this in mind for future purchases that go wrong.

Manage debt to avoid damaging your credit score. "If you close an account but pay off enough debt to keep your credit utilization score the same," says Craig Watts of FICO, "your score won't be affected." For example, if you carry $1,000 debt on two credit cards with a credit limit of $2,500 on each, your credit utilization rate is 20 percent ($1,000 debt, $5,000 total credit available). If you close one of the cards, suddenly your credit utilization rate jumps to 40 percent ($1,000, $2,500). But if you pay off $500 in debt, your utilization rate would be 20 percent ($500, $2,500), and your score would not change.

Don't play the zero percent transfer game. Some people have started playing the zero percent transfer game to profit off credit cards by making balance transfers or taking cash advances. They take the introductory zero percent APR that you get when you open many credit cards (which usually only lasts for six months). Then they borrow money from the card at this low rate and stick it in a high-interest savings account, which allows them to profit off the interest. Some actually invest the money in short-term CDs or even stocks. At the end, they plan to return the money and keep the interest. I find these zero percent credit card games to be a huge waste of time. Sure, you can make a few bucks a year, or maybe even a few hundred, but the time, risk of

Oh No! My Credit Score Dropped

Some of my type A readers worry too much about their credit scores. If your credit score suddenly drops, first you should figure out why by getting a copy of your credit report and score (see page 30). Then what's important is how you deal with it going forward. Your credit score can start recovering immediately as more positive information is reported, like that you've been paying your bills on time. So work to manage your credit wisely and consistently. As FICO's Craig Watts notes, "The natural movement of these scores is to slowly grow. How do you think people end up with scores in the mid-800s? It's through years and years of consistently boring credit management."

mismanaging the process, and possibility of screwing up your credit score just aren't worth it. Most important, this is a distraction that gets you only short-term results. You're much better off building a personal finance infrastructure that focuses on long-term growth, not on getting a few bucks here or there. Dave Ramsey, a popular personal finance author and radio host, specializes in helping people get out of debt.

Rate Chasers: Wasting Time Earning $25/Month

One of my blog readers, a guy named Mike, wrote in to tell me about his rate chasing. In this case, it was savings accounts, not credit cards, but they're very similar: It's just moving money around from one account to another to eke out a few additional percentage points.

Mike admitted, "I'm one of those rate chasers, so [with $40,000 in emergency savings] I've consistently been earning anywhere between 0.65 and 0.85 percent higher than my operating money market account . . . That's an extra $300/year in interest, which is definitely worth changing banks every four to six months for me."

My response: "Mike, if you were smart enough to sock away $40,000 in an emergency fund (which is really impressive, by the way), I bet you're smart enough to spend your time doing something better than earning $300/year—something that will let you earn much more sustainably. You're only earning $0.82/day doing that! How about spending the same time optimizing your asset allocation? (See page 226.) That step alone is probably worth thousands per year. Or starting a side business? Or even spending those few hours with your family? I don't know what you value, but in my eyes, any of those things would produce more value than $300/year . . . especially for someone who's so far ahead of everyone else, like you are. This is just my two cents . . . about 1/40th of what you earned today (sorry, couldn't resist)."

Focus on the Big Wins to get the big results. They may not be as obvious or sexy as jumping from account to account and getting a few extra bucks, but the Big Wins will make you rich over the long term.

He says, "I have met with thousands of millionaires in my years as a financial counselor, and I have never met one who said he made it all with Discover card bonus points."

Debt, Debt, Debt

Statistically speaking, being in debt is "normal." And yet, think about it: Is it really normal to owe more than you have? Maybe for certain things, like a house or an education, but what about for random purchases on a credit card?

Some people differentiate debts by calling them "good debt" and "bad debt," depending on if the debt appreciates (education) or depreciates (car) over time. Others despise debt altogether. Whatever the case, most of us have a lot of it. And it doesn't feel good.

I want to talk about student loans and credit card debt, the two largest types of debt facing most people. To do that, let's start by tackling the obvious: We already know debt is bad. In fact, we already know what to do about it. So what's stopping us? The answer isn't just "money," it's psychology.

We Know What to Do. So Why Don't We Do It?

I can give you all the information on earth about credit, but until you master your money psychology, none of it makes a difference. That's why so many people "know" all of this information, but they're still drowning in debt or sticking with poor cards that cost them thousands in fees and lost rewards.

What's stopping them? It's not knowledge—it's something else. Dr. Brad Klontz (yourmentalwealth.com), a professor in financial psychology, coined the term "invisible money scripts" to describe "typically unconscious, trans-generational beliefs about money" that are developed in childhood and drive your behavior today.

These beliefs are incredibly powerful, and once you recognize them in yourselves, you might understand your own behavior better.

Here are some of the most common invisible money scripts around debt.

Credit Card and Debt Scripts

Invisible script	What it means
"It's not so bad. Everyone has credit card debt. At least I don't have as much debt as Michelle."	Humans are wired to compare themselves to others. Interestingly, the worse situation we're in, the more we look for others to reassure us that we're not really *that bad*. It doesn't change our situation, but we feel better about ourselves.
"I probably shouldn't buy this, but $100 is just a drop in the bucket compared to how much I owe. Oh well . . ."	Once the problem is sufficiently large, we rationalize any single change as "not enough" (when in reality, real change happens through small, consistent steps). There are lots of similarities here between the decision making of those in serious debt and those who are overweight.
"Paying interest is just like any other fee."	This is "normalization," or the idea that paying interest on your debt is actually not that bad. I've never met one person who says this and understands the math of 14 percent interest rates.
"These credit card companies just try to trap you."	This is the surrendering of responsibility for personal decisions. It's very common among people who are surrounded by friends and family who are also in debt. Yes, credit card companies do want you to pay lots of fees—but it's also your responsibility for making the decisions that got you into debt in the first place. Until you take responsibility, the credit card companies will be a convenient enemy.
"I don't even know how much I owe."	Notice the transition to a more hopeless script. In my estimation, over 75 percent of people in debt do not know how much they actually owe. The truth would be too painful, so they ignore it. But there is power in acknowledging the problem and making a plan.
"I'm just trying to do my best."	The most hopeless of all. This person is effectively saying, "I have no control over my finances" and "Life happens to me" rather than acknowledging their own agency. Once someone says this, it's very difficult for them to ever change.

Damn, that got depressing. But I included these examples to show you how insidious and powerful these invisible money scripts are.

These invisible money scripts turn into very peculiar behaviors. People "know" they're not handling their money the right way, but they continue doing what they've done for years on end. To the outside observer, this can seem puzzling: "You're in debt! Why are you spending $800 on that weekend trip?"

But people are not purely rational. In fact, these invisible money

People Don't Know How Much Debt They're In

"It would appear that Americans don't even know how much they owe," Binyamin Appelbaum of the *New York Times* wrote. "Only 50 percent of households reported any credit card debt, while credit card companies reported that 76 percent of households owed them money."

It seems hard to believe, but in my experience, most people have no idea how much they actually owe. I get dozens of emails every day from people in debt. When I ask them how much they owe, fewer than 25 percent know. When I ask what their debt payoff date is, 95 percent of people don't know.

I have a lot of compassion for people in debt. Some are in tough life situations. Some don't understand how credit cards work. Some people have debt spread out over multiple credit cards and student loan accounts. Almost everyone is trying to do their best.

But I have no sympathy for people who complain without a plan. And a plan means that if you're in debt, you should know how much you owe and the exact day your debt will be paid off. Almost nobody does.

A plan turns debt from a "hot" emotional topic to a "cool" math problem. As I say in the business class I teach, "It's not magic, it's math." Same for building a business, same for paying off debt.

Most of all, a plan gives you control. It might take you three months to pay off your debt. It might be ten years! But once you have a plan, and you use the rest of this book to automate your plan, you'll know you're on track to live a Rich Life. I'll show you how.

scripts explain why so many people in debt avoid opening their mail. You might say, "JUST OPEN YOUR BILLS! PAY IT OFF! It's not that hard!" But if your invisible money scripts have been honed and sharpened by the stories you tell yourself over more than twenty years ("bills = bad"), it can be hard to change. My goal with this book is to show you that you *can* change your money stories.

What are the stories you've told yourself about debt?

The Burden of Student Loans

I'm not going to lie to you: Getting rid of student loan debt is hard. The average student graduates with about $30,000 of debt, but lots of my friends have graduated with more than $100,000 in loans. Unfortunately, it's not like you can just wave a magic wand and make it disappear. In fact, even if you declare bankruptcy, you'll still have to pay your student loans. However, even if you have huge student debt, I want you to pay attention to how much money you're putting toward the monthly payments. Because the loan amounts are so large, even an extra $100/month can save you years of payments.

Let's look at an example. My friend Tony has $30,000 in student loan debt. If he pays off the loan over ten years, his monthly payment will be about $345.24/month, meaning he'll pay just over $11,428.97 in interest. But if he pays just $100 more/month, he'll have to pay only $7,897.77 in interest—and he'll pay off his loan in 7.2 years.

Most of us accept our student debt as is. We get a bill each month, we pay it, and we shrug, frustrated about the burden of our loans but not really sure if we can do anything. Guess what: You can change your student loan payments.

First, to inspire you to take action on paying off your student debt, play with the financial calculators at bankrate.com. You'll be able to see how paying different amounts changes the total amount you'll owe.

Second, I want to encourage you to put at least $50 more each month toward any debt you have. Not only is it a psychological victory to know that you're consciously working to pay off your debt, but you'll also be able to focus on investing sooner. Make sure this is automatic, drawing right out of your checking account, so you don't even see the money. (I describe automatic payments in Chapter 5.)

The Most Common Internet Comments About Saving and Debt

'**ve seen this conversation happen a million times on some internet forum.**

Someone posts an article about how much money the average person should have saved at 35 years old, 40 years old, and 50 years old.

It gets 8,000 comments bemoaning capitalism, geopolitics, and baby boomers.

Helpful Commenter: "Well, you can save 10% and start investi—"

500 Angry Commenters: "LOL! Save? I live in a cardboard box! There's no way any of us can save." (2,000,000 likes)

Helpful Commenter: "Well, you can start with even $20/month."

Angry Commenters: "Maybe YOU can save $20/month. I can't even spare 50 cents per year."

Helpful Commenter: "I'm sorry to hear that. Anyway, when I started saving a little bit, I took some of it and invested. If you assume 8%, that means after a few year—"

Angry Commenters: "8%??? LOL! Yeah, I'd looove to get 8%. I invested in a landfill and got 0.0000023% over the last nine years. Haha, 8%, yeah right."

Helpful Commenter: "Um, the S&P 500 has returned an average of 8%, including inflation. And you can invest directly in the market with index funds."

Angry Commenters: "What? Really? Can you send me a link for where I can find out more about that?"

These people spend their time complaining on internet forums and spend *decades* paying thousands of dollars in interest. But they've never read a single book about personal finance. You can do better.

Finally, if you find that, no matter how you run the numbers, you're not going to be able to pay your loan off in any reasonable amount of time, it's time to call your lender. Look at the phone number on that monthly bill you keep ignoring. Call them up and ask them for their advice. I can't emphasize this enough: Call them. Your lenders have heard it all, from "I can't pay this month" to "I have five different loans and want to consolidate them." You'll want to ask them the following:

- "What would happen if I paid $100 more per month?" (Substitute in the right amount for you.)

- "What would happen if I changed the timeline of the loan from five years to fifteen years?"

- If you're looking for a job, you might ask, "What if I'm looking for a job and can't afford to pay for the next three months?"

Your lender has answers to all these questions—and chances are they can help you find a better way to structure your payment. Typically, they'll help you by changing the monthly payment or the timeline. Just think: With that one call, you could save thousands of dollars.

I refinanced $10,000 in private student loans, reducing the interest rates from 8% to 6%, which will save me about $2,000 over the life of the loan.

—DAN BULLMAN, 28

I called in to Navient and changed my student loans from 20-year to 10-year loans. I had no idea the difference, and it ended up saving me over $10,000 . . . just by paying an extra $50 a month.

LYLA NUTT, 30

When Credit Cards Go Bad

Most people don't get into serious credit card debt overnight. Instead, things go wrong little by little until they realize they've got a serious problem. If you've ended up in credit card debt, it can seem overwhelming. When you watch *Dr. Phil*, you wonder why those people can't figure out

"The Moment I Realized I Could Pay Off My Debt"

I asked my readers about the moment when they realized they could pay off their debt. Here's what just a handful of them said.

The major turning point for me was when I got serious with my girlfriend. She made about a third of what I made, but she had about a year's salary saved up. I was ashamed to have $40,000 in debt, so I started applying the IWT principles to pay down debt and accomplished that inside two years.

—SEAN WILKINS, 39

Debt was something I had got "used to"—my lifestyle was short-term and reactive rather than planned. I was so used to living paycheck to paycheck, I hadn't experienced the freedom of being able to make conscious financial choices. Now money is a tool, not my slave master.

—DAVE VINTON, 34

Oh man, debt absolutely SUCKED. I remember crying about it (multiple times). I had debt for all of in-state college, my $9,000 boob job, my $3,000 mattress, and my daily mall shopping spree habits. I was so unhappy and clueless. When I chose to turn my life around, your book was one of the first I bought, and it really woke me the hell up. I felt wealth coming into my life just by reading it, haha. I am now completely debt-free and started a Roth IRA.

—STEPHANIE GANOWSKI, 27

I lacked confidence and felt like it was holding me back from taking advantage of all life has to offer. After reading IWT (and now living debt-free!), I have more confidence and spend money on experiences, people, and possessions that I value.

—JUSTINE CARR, 28

how to solve their problems when the answers are so clear: "Yes, you should leave him! He hasn't had a job for the last eight years! And he looks like a rat. Are you blind?" But when we have our own problems, the answers don't seem so simple. What should you do? How do you manage your day-to-day finances? And why do things keep getting worse? The good news is that credit card debt is almost always manageable if you have a plan and take disciplined steps to reduce it.

Now, almost nothing makes people feel guiltier than having credit card debt. Seventy-five percent of Americans claim they don't make major purchases on their credit card unless they can pay it off immediately. Yet from looking at actual spending behaviors, over 70 percent of Americans carry a balance, and fewer than half are willing to reveal their credit card debt to a friend. Those numbers are an indication that American consumers are ashamed of their debt levels, says Greg McBride, senior vice president, chief financial analyst at Bankrate. He told me, "They are more willing to give their name, age, and even details of their sex lives than provide the amount of their credit card debt."

Really? Their sex lives? If this is you, let me know. I have a few single friends who'd like to meet you.

This shame means that those in debt often don't educate themselves on how to stop the madness. Instead, they fall victim to the credit card companies' nefarious practices, which prey on the uninformed—and the undisciplined. These companies have become very good at extracting more money from us, and we've become very bad at knowing when to say no.

For instance, the number one mistake people make with their credit cards is carrying a balance, or not paying it off every month. Astonishingly, of the 125 million Americans who carry a monthly credit card balance, half of them pay only their minimum monthly payments. Sure, it's tempting to think that you can buy something and pay it off little by little, but because of credit cards' insanely high interest rates, that's a critical mistake.

Let's say it again: The key to using credit cards effectively is to pay off your credit card in full every month. I know I said that casually, in the same way someone would ask you to pass the salt, but it's important. Ask your friend with $12,000 in credit card debt how it happened. Chances are he'll shrug and tell you he decided to "just pay the minimum" every month.

I used my credit cards for everything and paid the monthly minimums. That plan left me with maxed-out cards. I opened new 0% balance transfers to try to pay down the debts. Since I was so far over my head and didn't have any emergency cash funds, I used the credit cards I had to pay for things I truly needed. I wound up owing pretty much every major creditor you can think of, and still do.

The interest on my debt crushed me. Just because you have room on the card doesn't mean you have room in your budget!!!!

—DAVID THOMAS, 32

I'm not going to belabor the point, but you would be shocked by how many people I talk to who charge purchases without knowing how much they'll actually end up paying once interest is figured in. Paying the minimum amount on your credit card is the grown-up equivalent of a little boy letting the school bully take his lunch money on the first day of school, then coming back with his pockets jingling every single day afterward. Not only are you going to get your ass kicked, but it's going to happen again and again. By learning how the system works, though, you can figure out how to avoid the card companies' traps and get out of debt more quickly.

Pay Your Debt Off Aggressively

If you've found yourself in credit card debt—whether it's a lot or a little—you have a triple whammy working against you:

- First, you're paying tons of high interest on the balance you're carrying.

- Second, your credit score suffers—30 percent of your credit score is based on how much debt you have—putting you into a downward spiral of trying to get credit to get a house, car, or apartment and having to pay even more because of your poor credit.

- Third, and potentially most damaging, debt can affect you emotionally. It can overwhelm you, leading you to avoid opening your bills, causing more late payments and more debt, in a vicious circle of doom.

It's time to make sacrifices to pay off your debt quickly. Otherwise, you're costing yourself more and more every day. Don't put it off, because there's not going to be a magic day when you win a million dollars or "have enough time" to figure out your finances. You said that three years ago! Managing your money has to be a priority if you ever want to be in a better situation than you are in today.

Think about it: Credit cards' high interest rates mean you're likely paying a tremendous amount of interest on any balance you're carrying. Let's assume someone has $5,000 in debt on a card with 14 percent APR. If Dumb Dan pays the 2 percent monthly minimum payment, it will take him more than twenty-five years to pay off this debt. No, that's not a typo—it's really twenty-five years! Over the entire process, he'll pay over $6,000 in interest, more than the original amount he spent. And that's assuming he doesn't rack up more debt, which you know he will.

If you're outraged, you should be: This is how people can spend their entire lives in credit card debt. You can do better.

Smart Sally, by contrast, is sick of her debt and decides to get aggressive about paying it off. She has a few options: If she pays a fixed amount of $100 per month, she'll pay about $2,500 in interest, making her debt-free in six years and 4 months. This shows why you should always pay more than the minimum on your credit card. There's also an added benefit to doing that: It fits in beautifully to your automation system, explained in Chapter 5.

Or maybe Smart Sally decides to pay a little more — let's say $200 per month. Now it takes her 2.5 years to pay off her debt, including about $950 in interest payments. All from a tweak to her payments. Or what if Smart Sally gets truly aggressive and pays $400 per month? Now she'll pay off her debt in one year and two months, totaling just over $400 in interest payments.

That's just from paying $100 or $200 more per month. Don't have $200 extra? How about $50? Or even $20? Even a tiny increase in how much you pay every month can dramatically shorten your time to being debt free.

If you set up automatic payments (which I discuss on page 39) and work your debt down, you won't pay fees anymore. You won't pay finance charges. You'll be free to grow your money by looking ahead. In the credit card companies' eyes, you'll be a "deadbeat," a curious nickname they actually use for customers who pay on time every month and therefore produce virtually no revenue. You'll be worthless in their eyes, which is perfect in mine. But to beat them, you have to prioritize paying off whatever you already owe.

I spent four years in college racking up debt that I was certain I'd pay off easily once I started working. I spring-breaked in Las Vegas, Mexico, and Miami. I bought Manolo Blahnik shoes. I went out several nights a week. I had no idea then that I'd spend five post-college years paying that debt off—five years in which I could not vacation, could not buy fancy shoes, and could not go out very much at all. So on the day when I sent my final payment to my credit card company, I decided that that payment would be my last. I promised myself that I would never go back into debt again.

—JULIE NGUYEN, 26

DUMB DAN VS. SMART SALLY: PAYING OFF $5,000 CREDIT CARD DEBT AT 14% APR

Dumb Dan pays the minimum monthly payment.

His monthly payment starts at . . .	Time it will take to pay off . . .	Total amount of interest paid is . . .
$100*	25+ years	$6,322.22

Smart Sally pays a fixed amount.

Her monthly payment is . . .	Time it will take to pay off . . .	Total amount of interest paid is . . .
$100**	6 years, 4 months	$2,547.85

Super Smart Sally pays double the fixed amount.

Her monthly payment is . . .	It will take this long to pay off . . .	Total amount of interest she pays is . . .
$200**	2 years, 6 months	$946.20

*This minimum is a variable amount that decreases as your balance goes down (e.g., when your balance is $4,000, your payment will be $80). Because your minimum payment will decrease, your payments will stretch out, which costs you more. Bottom line: Always pay more than the minimum on your credit card debt.

**This is a fixed amount. As your balance decreases, you continue to pay the fixed amount, which speeds your debt payoff, costing you less.

Five Steps to Getting Rid of Credit Card Debt

Now that you see the benefits of climbing out of debt as quickly as possible, let's look at some concrete steps you can take to get started. *I Will Teach You to Be Rich* is a six-week program, but obviously paying off your loans will take longer than that. Even if you're carrying debt, you should still read the rest of the book now, because there are important lessons on automating your finances and getting conscious about your spending. Just keep in mind that you won't be able to invest as aggressively as I recommend until you pay off your debt. Yeah, it sucks, but that's a reasonable cost to pay for incurring your debt. Now, here's what to do.

1. Figure out how much debt you have. You wouldn't believe how many people don't do this and continue blindly paying off any bills that come in with no strategic plan. This is exactly what the credit card companies want, because you're essentially just dumping money into their pockets. You can't make a plan to pay off your debt until you know exactly how much you owe. It might be painful to learn the truth, but you have to bite the bullet. Then you'll see that it's not hard to end this bad habit. In fact, you can get the credit card companies to help you: Look at the back of your credit cards for their numbers, call them, and put their answers into a simple spreadsheet like this one.

HOW MUCH DO YOU OWE?			
Name of credit card	Total amount of debt	APR	Minimum monthly payment

Congratulations! The first step is the hardest. Now you have a definitive list of exactly how much you owe.

2. Decide what to pay off first. Not all debts are created equal. Different cards charge you different interest rates, which can affect what you decide to pay off first. There are two schools of thought on how to go about this. In the standard method, you pay the minimums on all cards, but pay more money to the card with the highest APR, because it's costing you the most. In the Dave Ramsey snowball method, you pay the minimums on all cards, but pay more money to the card with the lowest balance first—the one that will allow you to pay it off first.

PRIORITIZING YOUR DEBT		
	Snowball method: lowest balance first	**Standard method: highest APR first**
How it works	Pay the minimum on all cards, but pay more on the card with the lowest balance. Once you pay off the first card, repeat with the next-lowest balance.	Pay the minimum on all cards, but pay more on the card with the highest interest. Once you pay off the first card, repeat with the next-highest-APR card.
Why it works	This is all about psychology and small wins. Once you pay off the first card, you're more motivated to pay off the next one.	Mathematically, you want to pay off the credit card that's costing you the most first.

This is a source of fierce debate in credit card circles. Technically, the snowball method isn't necessarily the most efficient approach, because the card with the lowest balance doesn't necessarily have the highest APR. But on a psychological level, it's enormously rewarding to see one credit card paid off, which in turn can motivate you to pay off others more quickly. Bottom line: Don't spend more than five minutes deciding. Just pick one method and do it. The goal is not to optimize your payoff method, but to get started paying off your debt.

> I've saved over $3,000 and paid off over $3,000 in credit card debt. The idea of snowballing payments from the smallest card to the largest had the greatest impact on my mentality toward paying off the debt.
>
> **—SEAN STEWART, 31**

3. Negotiate down the APR. I'm a huge fan of taking fifty-fifty odds if the upside is big and it takes only five minutes of my time. Accordingly, try negotiating down your APR. It works surprisingly often, and if it doesn't, so what? Just call your card companies and follow this script:

YOU: Hi. I'm going to be paying off my credit card debt more aggressively beginning next week, and I'd like a lower APR.

CREDIT CARD REP: *Uh, why?*

YOU: I've decided to be more aggressive about paying off my debt, and that's why I'd like a lower APR. Other cards are offering me rates at half of what you're offering. Can you lower my rate by 50 percent, or only 40 percent?

CREDIT CARD REP: *Hmm . . . After reviewing your account, I'm afraid we can't offer you a lower APR. We can offer you a credit limit increase, however.*

YOU: No, that won't work for me. Like I mentioned, other credit cards are offering me zero percent introductory rates for twelve months, as well as APRs of half what you're offering. I've been a customer for X years, and I'd prefer not to switch my balance over to a low-interest card. Can you match the other credit card rates, or can you go lower?

CREDIT CARD REP: *I see . . . Hmm, let me pull something up here. Fortunately, the system is suddenly letting me offer you a reduced APR. That is effective immediately.*

It doesn't work every time, but when it does, you can save a significant amount of money with a five-minute conversation. Make the call, and if you're successful, don't forget to recalculate the figures in your debt spreadsheet.

I literally called my credit card company in the bookstore at the airport BEFORE buying the book, read the script, and was able to negotiate a better APR. And they even credited the interest for the last few years back to my account (only a few hundred bucks, but STILL). I bought the book seconds after hanging up.

—CHRIS COLETTI, 33

That first week I practiced my script, then called up my credit cards and had my rate dropped from 18 percent to 11 percent.

—CHARLOTTE S., 35

Debt was awful. It felt like a cloud over me at all times. I started contributing $100 more than the minimums and crushed that shit. I still have my 'paid in full' notices saved.

—MATT GROVES, 31

4. Decide where the money to pay off your credit cards will come from.

One common barrier to paying off debt is wondering where the money should come from. Balance transfers? Should you use your 401(k) money or your savings account? How much should you be paying off every month? These questions can be daunting, but don't let them stop you.

- **Balance transfers.** Many people begin by considering a balance transfer to a card with a lower APR. I'm not a fan of these. Yes, it can help for a few months and save you some money, particularly on large balances. But this is just a Band-Aid for a larger problem (usually your spending behavior, when it comes to credit card debt), so changing the interest rate isn't going to address that. Plus, balance transfers are a confusing process fraught with tricks by credit card companies to trap you into paying more, and the people I've known who do this end up spending more time researching the best balance transfers than actually paying their debt off. As we just discussed, a better option is to call and negotiate the APR down on your current accounts.

- **Taking money from a 401(k) or home equity line of credit (heloc).** I don't recommend either of these options. You're trying to reduce complexity, not increase it, even if it costs slightly more. Again, there's the behavioral problem: People with credit card debt often find it difficult to reduce spending and end up getting back into debt after tapping their 401(k) or HELOC. If you use your HELOC money to pay off credit cards, you'll risk losing your home if you run up more debt.

- **Reducing spending and prioritizing debt.** The most sustainable way to pay off credit card debt is also the least sexy. Unlike balance transfers or HELOC borrowing, it's not very exciting to tell people you decided to spend less on other things so you could pay off your debt. But it works.

Let me ask you a question. Right now, for every $100 you earn, how much of it goes to debt? Two dollars? Maybe $5? What if you paid $10 toward your debt? You'd be surprised that many people don't even have to cut much spending to pay off debt quickly. They just have to stop spending on random items, get conscious about making debt a priority, and set up aggressive automatic transfers to pay off their credit card debt. I don't want to make this sound easy, because paying off your credit card debt is challenging. But millions of others have done it.

As you read the rest of this book, think of yourself as being on a little treasure hunt to figure out where to get the money to pay off your credit card debt. Pay special attention to these discussions:

- "The Next $100" concept on page 171.

- Figuring out how much you can afford to put toward your debt using the Conscious Spending Plan on page 139.

- The "Save $1,000 in 30 Days" Challenge on page 12.

- Setting up automatic payments on page 175.

- My bonus resources at iwillteachyoutoberich.com/bonus

You'll notice that I haven't offered you a simple secret or cute sound bite about how to pay off your debt with no work. That's because there isn't one. If there were, I would be the first to tell you. But truthfully, paying off debt just takes a plan and the patience to execute it. It may seem like pure agony for the first few weeks, but imagine the relief you'll feel when you see your debt growing smaller and smaller with each passing month. And sometime after that, you'll be debt-free! Then you can focus all your energy on getting ahead, investing, and living your Rich Life.

5. Get started. Within the coming week, you should start paying more money toward your debt. If you find yourself taking more time than that to get started, you're overthinking it. Remember the philosophy behind the 85 Percent Solution: The goal is not to research every last corner to decide where the money will come from; it's action. Figure out how much debt you have, decide how you want to pay it down, negotiate your rates, and get started. You can always fine-tune your plan and amount later. I'll cover more on your Conscious Spending Plan in Chapter 4.

Being in debt means giving up choices, means staying at a job you hate because it pays good money, means not being able to build a decent savings account. My biggest mistake was not thinking about the future and using credit cards to live beyond my means. I got myself into debt in my midtwenties by spending, spending, spending—and on stupid things like clothes, eating out, movies, etc. I learned my lesson and am now living within my means on a strict budget that will allow me to be debt-free in two years. All of my debt is now on cards with APRs between zero and 4.99 percent. I have a small but growing savings account, a 401(k), and a plan to achieve financial freedom.

—MELISSA BROWN, 28

ACTION STEPS

WEEK ONE

1 **Get your credit score and credit report (one hour).** Check them to make sure there are no errors and to get familiar with your credit. You can access your report and score at myfico.com. (As I mentioned, lots of people use Credit Karma to get a free credit score, but I prefer the official credit score from MyFico, which is more accurate even though it has a small fee.) In addition to your credit score, get your free credit report from annualcreditreport.com.

2 **Set up your credit card (two hours).** If you already have one, call and make sure it's a no-fee card. If you want to get a new credit card, check out bankrate.com to find the best one for you.

3 **Make sure you're handling your credit cards effectively (three hours).** Set up automatic payments so your credit card bill is paid off in full every month. (If you're in debt, set up an automatic payment for the largest amount you can afford.) Get your fees waived. Apply for more credit, if you're debt-free. Make sure you're getting the most out of your cards.

4 **If you have debt, start paying it off (one week to plan, then start paying more).** Not tomorrow, not next week, today: Give yourself one week to figure out how much you owe, call the lender to negotiate down the APR or restructure your payments (in the case of student loans), and set up your automatic payment with more money than you're paying now. Getting out of debt quickly will be the best financial decision you ever make.

That's it! You've mastered improving your credit by using your credit card. You've waived your card fees, negotiated your rates down, and even set up automatic payments. And if you have debt, you've taken the first steps toward paying it all off. Congratulations! In the next chapter, we're going to optimize your bank accounts. You'll earn more interest, pay no fees, and upgrade to better accounts than the worthless checking and savings accounts we grew up with. Once you've tackled your credit card and bank accounts, you'll be ready to start investing—and growing your money significantly.

CHAPTER 2

BEAT THE BANKS

Open high-interest, low-hassle accounts and negotiate fees like an Indian

L ast week, you got your credit cards organized. Now, in Week 2, we're going to get your bank accounts set up right. Since they're the backbone of your personal finance infrastructure, we're going to spend a little time picking the right ones, optimizing them, and making sure you're not paying unnecessary fees. The good news is that this can be done in just a few hours over the next week, and once you do it, your accounts will basically run themselves. The bad news is that the bank account you have—probably from your neighborhood Big Bank—is most likely a big fat rip-off with fees and minimums that you don't need to be paying. See, banks love average customers, because we don't really want to switch banks, and they think we don't know any better about things like monthly fees and overdraft protection. With this chapter, that's going to change. I'll show you how to pick the best bank and the best accounts so you can earn the maximum amount of interest.

In any ordinary business, you'd think that the better they treat customers, the better they would perform. Right?

It's a reasonable assumption. Amazon CEO Jeff Bezos once said this: "If you do build a great experience, customers tell each other about that. Word of mouth is very powerful." Amazon grew explosively into one of the most successful companies in the history of the world.

But then there are exceptions—companies that seem to cosmically defy the rule that "helping customers is good for business." Can you think of a company like this?

Here, let me help with an example. Imagine a company that treats customers poorly. They levy onerous fees. They have terrible customer service. They even illegally open accounts on behalf of millions of their customers. What kind of company could this be?

The answer? Banks.

I hate banks as a matter of practice. I find them scammy, dishonest, and selective with their information. Their "advice" is always what's in their best interest, not the customer's. I had a bank bounce my rent check because they seized money from my checking account to pay an overdraft in my savings account caused by a bullshit fee they charged me. It was $5. I had another bank accuse me of elder abuse when I was trying to manage my grandfather's affairs while he was dying of cancer. There is a special place in hell for that bank teller.

—JAMIE B., 36

I want you to go on offense and choose the right accounts. It's easy to do: Just look at the banks' past behavior. The good ones simply offer better services and no fees.

The bad ones offer ever-increasing fees and unnecessary products, and devise even more ingenious ways to screw you out of your money.

But guess what? People already know this. They just don't care.

People claim they want good customer service, but really, they just stick with the same old horrible banks for decades.

The 30-Second Test

I have a theory that the first thirty seconds in a restaurant tell you everything you need to know.

I was waiting for a train in the Philadelphia Amtrak station and I was starving, so I went into a deli. The employee at the door pretended he didn't see me and looked away. The guy at the sandwich counter walked into the back and didn't reappear. And I caught a glimpse of a third employee sitting in an office watching TV.

Three employees, a customer walks in, and they all vanish.

Here's my theory: If your first thirty seconds in a restaurant are bad, it never gets better. This is the moment when restaurants put their friendliest, most charismatic staff out front to greet you. If they fail at that, who knows what's going on in the kitchen?

The real lesson is: *When companies—and people—show you who they truly are, believe them.*

Wells Fargo committed fraud and was fined $1 billion by federal regulators. Believe that they are a shitty bank that will screw you at the first chance they get.

TIAA used to be a trustworthy investment firm—I even recommended them in the last version of this book—but after lawsuits surfaced alleging they imposed heavy sales quotas and pushed unnecessary products, I stripped them from my recommendations.

On the other hand, there are companies that consistently demonstrate excellent values.

Schwab rolled out a phenomenal high-interest checking account years ago that offered unrivaled benefits for free. They've honored it and improved it over time. I trust them and have a checking account with them.

Vanguard has consistently demonstrated a long-term focus on low costs and putting their clients first. They actually *lower* fees proactively. I trust them and invest with them.

I share this because I want you to become discerning about the companies you work with. This is *your money*—it's important. You should judge the companies you work with on their values and how they treat you.

In my experience, if you are poor or just getting started, banks are basically out to screw you over. I remember tracking my balance down to the nearest dollar to avoid overdraft fees. I'm now able to keep a healthy buffer in my checking account, but starting out it was a constant source of anxiety to make sure I didn't get hit with double whammy fees. An example is an overdraft that hit for less than $5, but I was then charged EACH time my account was pinged. Ended up with $100 in overdraft fees for going over $5.

—NATHAN P., 35

I hate Wells Fargo. I had a passbook savings account as a kid, and as a destitute young adult I remembered that $16. I could use it to buy groceries. Turns out they had absorbed the entire amount through fees after I turned 18 and then closed the account. Robbed a child's piggy bank, stole a young person's grocery bag, and lost a high-income customer for life over $16. Nice work, Wells Fargo.

—JESSICA DENHAM, 42

While I was on a trip Bank of America charged me overdraft fees when my account wasn't overdrawn and kept going until $800 in fees were accumulated, then attempted to sue me over the money.

—ALLEN NASH, 28

You already know that these Big Banks are trying to screw you for all the money they can get out of you. Not only do they levy fee after fee, they launch marketing campaigns to trick customers into signing up for services they don't need and which, if they understood the terms, they would never agree to. Shit, Wells Fargo fraudulently opened accounts for 3.5 million people!

In fact, as *Forbes* reported, "Wells employees opened 1,534,280 unauthorized deposit accounts, 85,000 of which accrued a total of $2 million in fees."

Those fake accounts didn't just hurt customers' credit scores. CNN reported, "Wells Fargo admitted to forcing up to 570,000 borrowers into unneeded auto insurance. About 20,000 of those customers may have had their cars repossessed due to these unnecessary insurance costs."

How Banks Rake It In

Fundamentally, banks earn money by lending the money you deposit to other people. For example, if you deposit $1,000, a Big Bank pays you a small amount in interest to hold on to that money, then turns around and lends it out at a much higher percent for a home loan. Assuming that everyone repays their loans in full, the bank makes a huge return on their money for simple arbitrage. But here's how they really make tons more money.

FEES, FEES, FEES. In 2017, banks made more than $34 billion from overdraft fees alone. For example, if you're using a debit card and accidentally buy something for more money than you have in your checking account, you'd expect your bank to decline the charge, right? Nope. They let the transaction go through, and then helpfully charge you around $30 for an overdraft fee. Even worse, banks can charge you multiple overdraft fees in one day, leading to horror stories of more than $100 in fees levied in a single day.

NO MORE OVERDRAFTS. One overdraft fee wipes out your interest for the entire year and makes you hate your bank more than you already do, if that's even possible. More than half the people I've spoken to during my personal finance talks have had at least one overdraft. One night, I was out for dinner and my friend—let's call her Elizabeth—started asking me questions about overdrafts. They got increasingly complex, which weirded me out because I wondered how she knew so much about them. I asked her a simple question: "How many overdrafts have you had?" She got quiet, which of course made me want to interrogate her more (welcome to my twisted mind). I learned that she'd incurred more than $400 in overdraft fees over four years of college by simply not paying attention to how much money she had in her account. The sad thing is that she could have negotiated her way out of the first few fees and then set up a system so that it never happened again. For more on negotiating bank fees, see page 88.

Remember, your bank's fees can be more important than the interest rate it offers: If you have $1,000 and another bank has a 1 percent higher interest rate, that's a difference of $10 per year. Just one overdraft fee equals three times that amount. Costs matter.

Just imagine the type of people who had their cars repo'd because Wells Fargo screwed them over. We're not talking about hedge fund titans living in Manhattan—we're talking about ordinary people.

Bank of America institutes new fees for what seems to be no reason, sometimes unexpectedly. Like $5 maintenance fee on savings accounts? It's not like the interest offered is even worth it. Not to mention their $12 fee for checking accounts that don't have deposits of $250 or more. I know the amounts seem small but I know for some people $5 to $12 is a lot of money and can be the difference in paying bills. It always seems like those with the lowest balances end up paying the price."

—BRIDGETTE SALLEY, 26

This infuriates me. I absolutely hate when sophisticated financial firms take advantage of people who don't understand the complexity of these financial products. That's why I wrote this book and why I share these stories with you.

And people *still* stick with banks who have proven bad patterns of behavior.

I asked some of my readers who'd chosen to stay with horrible banks like Wells Fargo or Bank of America—why? Their answers:

I've been with Wells Fargo for like 20 years . . . so it's just one of those things where "it's always been that way" and I don't think about it.
—[NAME REDACTED]

I have 8 accounts with WF, and although I hate them and what they stand for, the idea of moving those accounts seems like a gigantic, annoying time suck.
—[NAME REDACTED]

I've changed banks before, but it was a struggle to get the ball rolling. It's almost like an emotional attachment.
—[NAME REDACTED]

No matter how many times I say to switch to a better bank, most of my readers don't give a shit. It's fine! Stay with the bank that's going to open fake accounts under your name, charge you near-extortionate fees, and figure out a way to screw you today—or five years from now. God.

On the other hand, the people who did follow my recommendations in this chapter universally loved it.

I've been with Schwab for years thanks to your recommendation. Service is always great—the few problems I've had are always cleared up. **—RICK MCCLELLAND, 27**

I switched to Schwab YEARS ago based on your recommendation and haven't looked back. **—RAIHAN ANWAR, 29**

On your recommendation, I moved to Schwab. I've used them all over the world (including in Pakistan at what claims to be the world's highest ATM). **—SAAD GUL, 42**

WHY HAVEN'T YOU SWITCHED BANKS YET?

Invisible money script	What it means
"It's a headache to switch banks."	Honestly, I get it. You've got your account set up and it works. Why not just stay? My analysis: You don't have to switch, but if you spend about one day doing it, you'll ensure that the foundation of your financial system is solid. The banks I recommend are more convenient, cheaper, and offer better rewards than Big Banks. As you grow your income, you'll know you're working with the best.
"I don't know where else I would go."	This is irrelevant. Just read the rest of this chapter and I'll tell you the best banks.
"This was my first bank ever."	I've only heard this once, but it was so ridiculous I had to include it. Do you have a lifelong love of your first thumbtack? What about your first garden hose? No? So why are we talking about how you cuddle up with your "first bank ever"? GTFO.

The Nuts and Bolts

Now that I've got my bank rants out of the way, let's go over a few account basics. You may think you know all this stuff (and a lot of it you probably do), but bear with me.

Checking Accounts

Your checking account is the backbone of your financial system. It's where your money will first go before it's "filtered" to different parts of your system, like your savings account, your investing account, and your guilt-free spending. That's why I believe in picking the best account, then moving on.

As you know, checking accounts let you deposit money and withdraw money using debit cards, checks, and online transfers. I think of my checking account like an email inbox: All my money goes in my checking account, and then I regularly apportion it out to appropriate accounts, like savings and investing, using automatic transfers. I pay most of my bills through my credit card, but the bills that I can't pay with my card—like rent or my car payment—I pay directly from my checking account using automatic transfers. (In Chapter 5, I'll show you how to make these transfers and bill paying work automatically.) Checking accounts are the number one place where unnecessary fees are levied, and we're going to fix that.

Savings Accounts

Think of savings accounts as places for short-term (one month) to mid-term savings (five years). You want to use your savings account to save up for things like vacations and holiday gifts, or even longer-term items, like a wedding or the down payment on a house. The key difference between checking and savings accounts is this: Savings accounts technically pay more interest. I say "technically" because on a practical level, the interest on your savings account is essentially meaningless.

In the last edition of this book, I included a chart that showed what you earned in interest at Big Banks—a paltry amount—versus online banks, which offer higher rates.

Then, because interest rates change, I proceeded to get thousands of emails over ten years frantically asking where the interest rates from the book were.

Guys, I have learned two things from this: First, I am never, ever including interest rates in a book again.

Second, I failed to explain why the interest rate on your savings account is not all that important. Let's assume you have $5,000 sitting in a savings account as part of your emergency fund (covered on page 277).

If your bank offers you a 3 percent interest rate, that's $150 per year, or $12.50 a month. If it's a 0.5 percent interest rate, that's $25 per year, or $2.08 per month. In short, who cares? $12.50 vs. $2 is not a huge difference when we're talking about hundreds of thousands of dollars over our lives.

Before I read IWT, my personal finances were in shambles, and all my money was escaping me through late fees, overdraft fees, credit card annual fees. After reading the book, I was able to automate my finances to eliminate overdraft and late fees. By applying your strategies I moved into a better place and doubled the amount I pay toward my debt every month.

—JOE LARA, 29

(Interestingly, if we're getting technical, many people lose money every day their money is in savings, since inflation erodes the real purchasing power of your cash. That's why the bulk of your wealth will be made from investing, which I cover in Chapter 7.)

If you learn only one thing from this book, it should be to turn your attention from the micro to the macro. Stop focusing on picking up pennies and instead focus on the Big Wins to craft your Rich Life. Now that I've set up my investing accounts and automated them, the amount I earn from one year of investing is worth more than 500 years of interest in a savings account. You heard that right. Don't worry about micro-optimizing your bank account interest rates. Just pick great bank accounts and move on.

Before reading your book I had all my savings lumped into one Chase savings account and no investments. The burden of choice was holding me back from opening any new accounts and starting to invest.

—JONATHAN BAZ, 24

Why You Need Both a Savings Account and a Checking Account

The most important practical difference between checking accounts and savings accounts is that you withdraw money regularly from your checking account—but you rarely withdraw from your savings account. Checking accounts are built for frequent withdrawals: They have debit cards and ATMs for your convenience. But your savings account is really a "goals" account, where every dollar is assigned to a specific item you're saving up for, like a house, a vacation, or an emergency fund.

You might think I'd encourage you to have your checking account and savings account at the same place. Surprisingly, I recommend two different accounts at two *separate* banks. Here's why: Having your money in two separate accounts—and banks—uses psychology to keep your savings growing. One basic way of looking at it is that your savings account is where you deposit money, whereas your checking account is where you withdraw money. In other words, if your friends want to go out on Friday night, you're not going to say, "Hold on, guys, I need three business days to transfer money to my checking account." If you don't have the money available in your discretionary (checking) account because you've spent your "going out" money, you'll know it. Having a separate savings account forces you to keep your long-term goals in mind instead of just blowing them off to have a few rounds of drinks. Finally, in my experience, banks that try to offer checking and saving and investing tend to be mediocre at all of them. I want the best checking account, the best savings account, and the best investment account—no matter where they are.

Before, all my money went to shopping, paying my debt, and my credit card. I never saved. I always felt that I wasn't making enough and maybe, just maybe, if I earned more I would start saving and be in a good financial situation. But I was wrong—no matter how much money I made, if I didn't have a plan, I would always feel like I had insufficient money. Four months later, no debt for me. I have a savings account and I also started investing. I feel so much better and I can focus on improving my life in general since one of the most important pillars in my life is on a good track.

—ROXANA VALENTINA, 27

Right now, you might be saying to yourself, "Why should I bother with a savings account? I only have $300." I hear this all the time. It's true, the interest you'll be earning on that kind of money isn't really that much.

But it's not just about your immediate earnings—it's about developing the right habits. I remember once asking my readers why they hadn't yet made certain decisions, like switching bank accounts or automating their investments. One guy told me that his amounts were so small, it didn't really matter.

To me, that's the perfect time to start: when the stakes are low. Build the right habits when the amounts are small—with the right accounts, with automatic saving and investing—so that when your income increases, your habits are rock-solid.

We're cutting our teeth with small amounts of money, sure. But as our savings accounts increase from $5,000 and $10,000 to $100,000 to $1 million and beyond, the habits really start to matter. Start now so that when you do have a lot of money, you'll know what to do with it.

Finding the Perfect Account Setup

I'll tell you my favorite accounts in a few pages. But before you go about finding the specific banks and accounts you want to use, take a minute to consider the bigger picture. You want to pick accounts that work well with your personality. You have to know yourself: Do you value simplicity? Or are you the kind of person who wants to spend your time building a complicated system for a slightly larger payout? For most people, another option—"basic option + small optimization"—is perfect.

Most basic option (good for lazy people): A checking account and a savings account at any local bank. This is the bare minimum. Even if you already have these accounts, it's worth talking to your bank to be sure you're not paying fees.

Basic option + small optimization (recommended for most people): This option means opening accounts at two separate institutions: a no-fee checking account at your local bank and a high-yield online savings account. With the checking account, you'll have immediate access to your money and free cash transfers to your high-interest online savings account. You can also deposit cash through your local bank. If you already have this setup, great! Just call to make sure you're not paying unnecessary fees.

How My Bank Accounts Work

Here are the accounts I use and how I've set them up to work together.

MY ACCOUNTS. All of my money goes through my interest-bearing Schwab online checking account. Deposits happen through direct deposit or by taking a photo of a check and depositing it through the Schwab app.

MY SYSTEM. My finances work on a monthly cycle, and my system automatically disburses money where it needs to go. I've set up accounts to draw from my checking account. For example, my Capital One 360 savings account automatically withdraws a certain amount every month from my checking account, as does my investment account (more about these in Chapter 3). For rewards, tracking, and consumer protection, I pay my bills using my credit card. The credit card is automatically paid in full every month by my online checking account. For cash expenses, I use the Schwab ATM card to withdraw money at any ATM nationwide. All ATM charges are automatically reimbursed at the end of the month. Generally, I use my Capital One 360 account as a receiver, not a sender: I rarely transfer money out of there unless I need to cover a temporary shortage in my checking account or want to spend savings money on something important, like a vacation . . .

And that's how I do it.

Advanced setup + full optimization (perfect for people who read things like Lifehacker *and* The 4-Hour Workweek*):* This setup consists of maintaining several checking accounts and savings accounts at different banks, usually to eke out the most interest and services that various banks have to offer. For example, I have an interest-bearing checking account at an online bank and a savings account at a different online bank. Although you can set up automatic online transfers, having multiple banks means multiple websites, multiple customer-service numbers, and multiple passwords. Some people find this overly complicated—if you're one of them, stick to a more basic setup, unless it's very important to you to fully optimize your bank accounts. (Personally, I think this option is awesome.)

So Many Choices, So Little Time

Depending on what accounts you already have and what setup you've opted to go with, getting this part of your financial infrastructure squared away may be as easy as making small changes to accounts you've had for a while. Or you may need to open new accounts, which can be pretty overwhelming.

As usual with financial decisions, we have too many options, leading most of us to make less-than-ideal choices—like opening a bank account in college and then staying with that bank forever. There are some good accounts out there, but of course banks don't always make these deals easy to find.

Most traditional banks offer different checking and savings accounts to serve customers with different needs and amounts of money. They start at student accounts, which are bare-bones accounts with no fees, no minimums, and few value-added services. These are usually perfect for young people. Next, they offer accounts that have nominal monthly fees. They also offer ways for you to get these fees waived, like using direct deposit (where your paycheck is automatically sent to your bank every month) or maintaining a minimum balance. If your employer offers direct deposit, these accounts might be a good choice. Finally,

What About Credit Unions?

I used to be a big fan of credit unions. I love their mission and I recommended them in the first edition of this book. I even spoke at a national credit union conference years ago.

Credit unions are like local banks, but they're not-for-profit and are owned by their customers (or, in credit union parlance, "members"). Theoretically, this means they offer better service.

Unfortunately, I've changed my opinion. Their constant navel-gazing ("Let me give you a painstaking explanation of why being member-owned is better . . . wait . . . come back") instead of delivering solutions and features that my readers actually care about is a disappointment. Credit unions squandered a generational opportunity to position themselves against predatory and scammy banks like Bank of America and Wells Fargo. I hope this changes.

banks offer higher-end accounts with higher minimums—often $5,000 or $10,000—and more services, like commission-free brokerage trades (which you should avoid, since banks are the last place you should invest), "bonus" interest rates, and discounts on home loans. These accounts are worthless. Avoid them. If you have that much money lying around, I'll show you how to put it to work in Chapter 7 and earn more than any bank could give you.

Five Shiny Marketing Tactics Banks Use to Trick You

1. TEASER RATES ("6 percent for the first two months!"). Don't get sucked in by this trick—your first two months don't matter. You want to pick a good bank that you can stick with for years—one that offers overall great service, not a promo rate that will earn you only $25 (or, more likely, $3). Banks that offer teaser rates are, by definition, to be avoided.

2. REQUIRING MINIMUM BALANCES to get "free" services like checking and bill paying. No, I'm not going to agree to a minimum amount. I'll just go somewhere else.

3. UP-SELLS to expensive accounts ("Expedited customer service! Wow!"). Most of these "value-added accounts" are designed to charge you for worthless services. I can't wait to have kids one day so my three-year-old can walk into a Wells Fargo, throw his lollipop at the bank manager, and say "THIS ACCOUNT IS CLEARLY A RIP-OFF!" Good job, little Raj.

4. HOLDING OUT by telling you that the no-fee, no-minimum accounts aren't available anymore. They are. Banks will resist giving you a no-fee, no-minimum account at first, but if you're firm, they'll give you the account you want. If they don't, find another bank. There are many, many choices, and it's a buyer's market.

5. BUNDLING A CREDIT CARD with your bank account. If you didn't walk in specifically wanting the bank credit card, don't get it.

You should research the options at a few different banks. You can compare these banks in less than an hour by going to their websites, or you can just use the banks I use (see page 84).

Beyond just the type of accounts offered, there's more to consider when choosing your bank(s). I look for three things: trust, convenience, and features.

Trust. For years, I had a Wells Fargo account because their ATMs were convenient, but I don't trust Big Banks anymore. I'm not the only one. Perhaps it's because they secretly insert fees, like the filthy double charges for using another bank's ATM, then count on our inaction to make money off us. There are still some good banks out there, though. The best way to find one is to ask friends if they have a bank they love. You should also browse the major bank websites. Within about five minutes, you should be able to tell which banks are trustworthy and which are not by seeing how straightforward they are with their accounts and fees. Your bank shouldn't nickel-and-dime you through minimums and fees. It should have a website with clear descriptions of different services, an easy setup process, and 24/7 customer service available by phone. Another thing: Ask them if they send you promotional material every damn week. I don't want more junk mail! I don't need more cross-sells! I actually switched my car insurance because they would not stop sending me mail three times a week. Go to hell, 21st Century Insurance.

Convenience. If your bank isn't convenient, it doesn't matter how much interest you're earning—you're not going to use it. Since a bank is the first line of defense in managing your money, it needs to be easy to put money in, get money out, and transfer money around. This means its website has to work, and you need to be able to get help when you need it—whether by email or by phone.

Features. The bank's interest rate should be competitive. Transferring money around should be easy and free, because you'll be doing a lot of it, and you should have free bill paying. Their app or website should be something you enjoy using.

Don't Be a Rate Chaser

Do me a favor: If your bank account offers one rate and another bank starts offering a slightly higher rate, don't change accounts. Half the time, those rates are simply introductory teaser rates that will drop after six months. I'd rather take a slightly lower interest rate if it's at a bank I can trust to give me great service over the long term. But there are a lot of dorks who spend every waking hour online digging up the best interest rate and switching to it immediately. "OMG!!!!" they say. "Ally Bank increased its rate from 2.25 percent to 2.75 percent!! Now it's 0.02 percent higher than Capital One 360! I'm going to switch accounts right now!!!" If you do this, you are a moron.

Do you really want to spend each month figuring out which bank is offering a slightly better rate? That's a colossal waste of time for most of us, since a 0.5 percent difference equals just a few dollars per month more in interest. Plus, interest rates change over time, so rate chasing doesn't even make sense. I plan on sticking with my bank for the next few decades, and I'm sure you have better things to do with your time. So focus on the Big Wins, not on rate chasing.

The Best Accounts (Including the Ones I Use)

As we've seen, a lot goes into finding the right accounts. Here are a few options that I've found work well for many people—along with my own personal picks.

Checking Accounts
Schwab Bank Investor Checking with Schwab One Brokerage Account (schwab.com/banking): This is the checking account I use. In my opinion, this is the single best checking account available. Schwab offers a stunningly good account with no fees, no minimums, no-fee overdraft protection, free bill pay, free checks, an ATM card, automatic

transfers, and—best of all—unlimited reimbursement of any ATM usage. That means you can withdraw from any ATM and you'll pay no fees. When I saw this account, I wanted to marry it.

Although you need to open a Schwab brokerage (investment) account to get all fees waived, you don't actually need to use the investment account. It can just sit there, empty, as you use the magnificent features in the checking account. You can deposit money by transfer, direct deposit, or mobile check deposit. Important note: You cannot deposit physical cash through this account, so if depositing cash is important, you'll need to pair this checking account with another checking account. (In my case, I rarely use cash and when I do, I'm withdrawing it, not depositing it. If I have extra cash, it's just sitting in my bedroom drawer. Please don't rob me.) Also, Schwab may do a credit pull if you're opening a new account. In the long term, this is a minor issue, but if you're monitoring your credit closely (e.g., for an upcoming house purchase), you should be aware of this since your credit score may temporarily decrease.

Your local bank checking account with no fees and no minimums. For the rare person who needs to deposit physical cash regularly, you should read this section. Otherwise, I honestly have no idea why you would use your local bank for checking. When I asked my readers, they told me "convenience" and "Schwab doesn't accept cash deposits." If you really want a checking account at your local bank, you can typically get no-fee and no-minimum accounts with one of these criteria: if you're a student, if you set up direct deposit, or if you agree to maintain a certain minimum balance. They'll almost always throw in free bill pay, new checks, and an ATM card. These accounts pay little or no interest, but because you won't be storing much money here, that's no big deal. Using the criteria I laid out on the last few pages, you can find a local bank that you'll be happy with.

Savings Accounts

I would not encourage anyone to use a standard Big Bank savings account. Online savings accounts let you earn more interest with lower hassle. And because you'll be primarily sending money there, not withdrawing it, what does it matter if it takes three days to get your money?

Capital One 360 Savings (capitalone.com/bank): This is the savings account I use. It lets you create virtual sub-savings accounts, in which you can specify savings goals like an emergency fund, wedding, or down payment for a house. You can also set up automatic transfers to other accounts ("Transfer $100 on the 1st of every month from my checking account to my savings account, and send $20 to my investment account on the 5th of every month"). There are no fees, no minimums, and no tricky up-sells or annoying promotions. It's not always the highest interest rate, but it's close. Capital One 360 Savings is just a simple savings account that works.

Ally Online Savings Account (ally.com/bank): Also recommended. This no-fee savings account also lets you create multiple savings accounts, which will help your automation system. It has solid interest rates and works great.

Other savings accounts to consider: Marcus by Goldman Sachs and American Express Personal Savings.

Banks to consider	Banks to avoid
Ally Bank: ally.com	Bank of America
CapitalOne360: capitalone.com	Wells Fargo
Schwab: schwab.com	
Marcus by Goldman Sachs: marcus.com	
American Express Personal Savings: americanexpress.com/personalsavings/home	

Now you've got all the information you need to open a new checking or savings account. It shouldn't take more than three hours of research and two hours to open each account and fund it. If you need to transfer money from an old account to a new one, your new bank will help you arrange the transfer. I recommend you keep your old account open with a small amount of money in it in case you have any automatic transfers that are still trying to draw from your old account. Set a 60-day calendar reminder to close the old account. And we're off to our next step!

I didn't know how to put money toward my goals. I had one savings account and would constantly reallocate my money in my mind. After reading the book, I opened different accounts to put money toward the things I wanted to spend money on—not just emergency savings and retirement, but travel and giving to others. **—EMILY CRAWFORD, 33**

Optimizing Your Bank Accounts

Whether they're accounts you just opened or accounts you already had, you need to optimize your checking and savings accounts. This means you shouldn't be paying fees or minimums. The key to optimizing an account is talking to an actual customer service rep, either in person or on the phone. Yes, nerds, you might actually have to pick up the phone. For some reason, half of my friends are afraid of talking to people on the phone. I have a friend who recently lost his bank password and, for security reasons, had to call the bank to prove who he was. He turned into a Stockholm syndrome victim in front of my eyes, muttering, "It's not that important. They're right. I'll just wait until I go into the bank" over and over. He didn't get his password for four months! What the hell is wrong with people? You may not like to talk on the phone, but most of the special deals I'll show you how to get require talking to someone in person or on the phone.

Avoiding Monthly Fees

Maybe I'm too demanding, but if I'm lending a bank my money to relend out, I don't believe I should have to pay them additional fees. Think about it: If your Big Bank charges you a $5 monthly fee, that basically wipes out any interest you earn. This is why I'm fanatical about my savings and checking accounts having no fees of any kind, including monthly fees, overdraft fees, or setup fees. If you already have an account at a bank you like but they are charging a monthly fee, try to get them to waive it. They will often do this if you set up direct deposit,

When They Say "We Don't Have No-Fee Accounts"

Say you realize your current checking account charges you fees and you want to switch. When you call, they tell you they can't offer a no-fee account. Are you going to accept that? Hell no. Go on offense. Here's what to say.

YOU: Hi. I noticed that my current checking account has fees. I'd like my account to have no annual fees, free checking, and no minimum balance, please.

BANK REP: *I'm really sorry, but we don't offer that kind of account anymore.*

YOU: Really? That's interesting, because [competitor] is offering me that exact deal right now. Could you check again and tell me which comparable accounts you offer?

(Eighty percent of the time, you'll get a great account at this point. If not, ask for a supervisor.)

SUPERVISOR: *Hi, how can I help you?*

YOU: (Repeat argument from the beginning. If the supervisor doesn't give you an option, add this:) Look, I've been a customer for X years, and I want to find a way to make this work. Plus, I know that your customer-acquisition cost runs hundreds of dollars. What can you do to help me stay a customer?

SUPERVISOR: *What an astounding coincidence. My computer is suddenly allowing me to offer the exact account you asked for!*

YOU: Why, thank you, kind sir. (Sip Darjeeling tea.)

The bank has already spent a lot of money to land you as a customer and doesn't want to lose you over something as small as a $5 monthly fee. Use this knowledge as leverage whenever you contact any financial company.

which lets your employer deposit your paycheck directly into your account every month. Banks will also try to trick you by demanding "minimums," which refer to minimum amounts you must have in your account to avoid fees or to get "free" services like bill pay. These are BS. Imagine if a bank required you to keep $1,000 sitting in its low-interest checking account. You could be earning twenty times that much by investing it.

If you can't do direct deposit because your job doesn't offer it or if you can't get the bank to waive a "minimum," I strongly recommend that you switch to an online high-interest account that has no fees and no minimums.

Note: Certain charges are okay—for example, when it comes to services like money orders and reordering checks. Please don't run into your bank screaming, "BUT RAMIT TOLD ME NO FEES!!!!" when you're trying to order more checks. If you do, though, send me the video on Instagram or Twitter (@ramit).

Almost All Bank Fees Are Negotiable

The most painful and expensive fees are usually overdraft fees—which is the fee your bank charges you if you don't have enough money in your checking account to cover a purchase. Of course, the best way to avoid overdraft fees is to not let them happen in the first place. Set up automatic transfers and keep a cash cushion in your account (I keep about $1,000 in my checking at all times). But mistakes do happen. Most banks understand that people are occasionally forgetful, and they'll waive a first-time fee if you ask. After the first time, it gets harder, but can still be done if you have a good excuse. Remember: They want to keep you as their customer. A well-executed phone call can often make a difference. But when calling, keep in mind that you should have a clear goal (to get your fee erased) and should not make it easy for companies to say no to you.

Here's how I negotiated my way out of a $20 overdraft fee and a $27.10 finance charge from Wells Fargo (back when I had an account there).

I had transferred money from my savings account to my checking account to cover a temporary shortage, and the transfer arrived one day late. I saw the overdraft fee, sighed, and called the bank to get it waived.

RAMIT: Hi. I just saw this bank charge for overdrafting, and I'd like to have it waived.

BANK REP: *I see that fee . . . hmm . . . Let me just see here. Unfortunately, sir, we're not able to waive that fee. It was [some BS excuse about how it's not waivable].*

Bad things to say here:

"Are you sure?"
Don't make it easy for the rep to say no to your request.

"Is there anything else I can do?"
Again, imagine if you were a customer service rep and someone said this. It would make your life easier to just say no. As a customer, don't make it easy for companies to say no.

"Well, this Indian author told me I could. Have you read his book? It's called I Will Teach You to Be Rich, *and I love it because . . ."*
Nobody cares. But it would be cool if a thousand customers called their banks and said this.

"Okay."
Don't give up here. It's easy to walk away, but there's a better way.

Try this instead:

RAMIT: Well, I see the fee here, and I'd really like to get it waived. What else can you do to help me? (Repeat your complaint and ask them how to constructively fix it.)

At this point, about 85 percent of people will get their fees refunded. I have hundreds of comments from people on my blog who have taken this advice and saved thousands of dollars in fees. But in case the rep is obstinate, here's what you can do.

BANK REP: *I'm sorry, sir, we can't refund that fee.*

RAMIT: I understand it's difficult, but take a look at my history. I've been a customer for more than three years, and I'd like to keep the relationship going. Now, I'd like to get this waived—it was a mistake, and it won't happen again. What can you do to help?

BANK REP: *Hmm, one second, please. I see that you're a really good customer . . . I'm going to check with my supervisor. Can you hold for a second?*

(Being a long-term customer increases your value to them, which is one reason you want to pick a bank you can stick with for the long term. And the fact that you didn't back down at the first "no" makes you different from 99 percent of other customers.)

BANK REP: *Sir, I was able to check with my supervisor and waive the fee. Is there anything else I can help you with today?*

That's all I had to do! This doesn't just work for overdraft fees—it can also work for certain processing fees, late fees, and even ATM fees. I learned this lesson the hard way. I lived in New York for a summer when I was doing an internship. I decided not to open a bank account while I was there, because it would take time and I was lazy. So I just used those ATMs left and right and ate the $3 charges ($1.50 from my bank, $1.50 from the ATM) each time. Now I feel dumb, because I just talked to a friend who recently moved to New York for a few months. She didn't want to open a bank account for such a short time either, but instead of just shrugging and saying, "Oh, well," she actually called her bank. She just asked them if they would waive the ATM fees while she was there. "No problem," they said. She saved more than $250 just by making a phone call! Remember, with a customer-acquisition cost of more than $100, banks want to keep you as their customer. So use this information to your advantage and make the call next time you see any fees levied on your account.

While many bank fees are ridiculous, I find that they are quite willing to wipe them for a good customer. I bounced a check because I stupidly wrote a check out of the wrong account. I'd been a customer for about five years, and I simply walked into the bank and asked them to waive it. They did it right there on the spot. I didn't have to do any convincing or anything.

—ADAM FERGUSON, 22

ACTION STEPS

WEEK TWO

1 **Open a checking account or assess the one you already have (one hour).** Find an account that works for you, call the bank (or go in), and open the account. If you've already got one, make absolutely sure it is a no-fee, no-minimum account. How? Open up your last bank statement or, if you don't have that, call your bank and say, "I'd like to confirm that my bank account has no fees and no minimums whatsoever. Can you confirm that?" If you discover you've been paying fees, use the negotiating tactic on page 88 to get your account switched to a no-fee, no-minimum account. Be aggressive in threatening to leave if they don't switch you.

2 **Open an online high-interest savings account (three hours).** You'll earn higher interest, and it's psychologically powerful to have your savings account separate from your checking: You'll be much less likely to dip into your savings if it's not immediately reachable through your normal banking. Spend a couple of hours looking over the banks I recommended on page 84. To see a more comprehensive list, compare banks at bankrate .com or check my website to see what my blog readers think of different bank accounts.

2a **Optional: Open an online checking account (two hours).** This isn't absolutely necessary, but if you're ready to be more advanced about your checking and earn a higher interest rate, go ahead and open up an online checking account. Remember, the main benefits of an online checking account are a high interest rate and fewer tricky fees. If you don't love your checking account, switch! It doesn't take that long, and having the right checking account means the rest of your financial system will run smoothly for years to come.

3 **Fund your online savings account (one hour).** Leave one and a half months of living expenses in your checking account, or as close to it as you can manage. (The little extra prevents overdrafts as you're getting used to transferring money between accounts. Remember, most transfers take a day or two.) Transfer the rest to your savings account—even if it's only $30.

Congratulations! Now that you've got the backbone of your personal financial infrastructure up and running, we're going to open your investment account.

GET READY TO INVEST

Open your 401(k) and Roth IRA—even with just $50

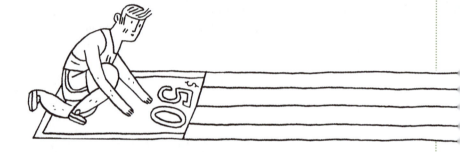

There's something special about Indian parents. To understand what I mean, ask any Indian kid you know what happened when he excitedly brought home his straight-A report card. His parents probably gleamed with pride, gave him a huge hug, and then immediately frowned. "Vijay, this is very good! But what happened? Why did you get this A minus?" they said. As you can imagine, this approach tends to promote a slightly warped view of the world for Indian children. I can't wait to do this to my future kids someday. They're not even born yet and I'm already disappointed in them.

Perhaps the fact that I grew up with this worldview explains why, when people finally start thinking about their finances, I congratulate them for approximately six seconds before I secretly judge them because I know they're not doing enough. Michael Batnick, author of *Big Mistakes: The Best Investors and Their Worst Investments,* writes: "The median retirement balance in the United States for people ages 56–61 is $25,000. This could have been accomplished by investing $6 a month since 1980 into a 60/40 portfolio." Guys, it is so easy to win at this game. By the end of this chapter, you will. In the last chapter we talked about saving, and

I'm happy you've opened up a high-interest savings account. I really am. But it's not enough! Saving a little money here and there is not enough, despite what you read in the myriad books and blogs filled with tips and tales of frugality. "Buy 200 cases of orange juice," these fantastic articles say, "and you can save 6 percent! Amazing!"

Get a life. The sad fact is, if you do only the bare minimum—for example, if you get frugal and save $100 a month in an online savings account—the results will not be especially impressive.

Even if you're earning a solid rate in a high-interest savings account, it will take you a long, long time to get a substantial return. Put simply, saving is not enough. You need a way to put that money to work for you so it earns more than even the highest-yielding savings account, and investing is the first and best way to do it. "Compounding," Albert Einstein said, "is mankind's greatest invention because it allows for the reliable, systematic accumulation of wealth."

Rather than earning a little interest, like most people do in their savings accounts, you can earn around 8 percent per year over the long term by investing: Over the twentieth century, the average annual stock market return was 11 percent, minus 3 percent for inflation, giving us 8 percent. To put that in perspective, let's assume that you have $1,000 at age 35 to put somewhere. Let's also assume that your savings account returns 3 percent on average, and that you can get 8 percent returns, net of inflation, over the long term in your investments.

Now watch this.

If you just dropped that money into a savings account, what would it be worth thirty years later? While that $1,000 would have grown to $2,427 on paper, inflation would have also "dragged" your returns down. So while it appears you did well, when you factor in inflation your money has the same purchasing power as it did thirty years ago. Not good.

But there's a twist. If you'd *invested* your money, it would be worth over $10,000—*ten times more!*—eclipsing the drag of inflation and giving you incredible results. And that's just from a one-time investment.

Investing may seem intimidating, but it's actually quite painless. I'll walk you through it, and by the end of this chapter, you'll have opened an investment account. You don't actually have to worry about choosing where to invest yet—that comes in Chapter 7. For now, we'll set up the right accounts so that when you're ready, you can simply "turn on" automatic transfers to funnel cash there each month.

I read the book more than 6 years ago. One of my biggest accomplishments was setting up my retirement account when I was only 18 years old. I have a smile on my face every day knowing that I have enough money in that account. It's liberating, and has allowed me to be more adventurous in other areas of my life, such as pursuing entrepreneurship in a more aggressive manner and being able to spend money on things knowing that we could almost never save a dime again and be better off than 99 percent of people.

—**ALEX CRAIG, 25**

Why Your Friends Probably Haven't Invested a Cent Yet

Before we go any further, let's take a minute to understand why young people are not investing. This will help you do what most millennials specialize in: judging other people.

Ask any of your friends how much they've invested and they'll say things like, "Huh?" or "I don't earn enough to invest." Most of them will say, "I don't know how to pick stocks," which is ironic because

Three Startling Stats About People and 401(k)s

Remember, a 401(k) is just a type of investment account—one that offers huge benefits that I'll cover on page 105. Here's what's stunning:

- Only one-third of people participate in a 401(k).

- Among people earning under $50,000 a year, 96 percent fail to contribute the maximum amount into their 401(k).

- And, astonishingly, only 1 in 5 contributes enough to get the full company match. The company match is literally free money, so 80 percent of people are losing thousands of dollars per year.

INVESTING ISN'T ABOUT PICKING STOCKS. Although it's true that some of them might participate in a 401(k)—a type of retirement account— that's probably the extent of their investments. And yet these are the most important investing years of our lives!

Another reason people don't invest is that they're scared of losing money. It's ironic that people are afraid of "possibly" losing money in the stock market, when they will *certainly* run out of money if they don't invest. The *Washington Post* noted that "Polls show that most older people are more worried about running out of money than dying." The haunting article continues: "As a result, many older workers are hitting the road as work campers—also called 'workampers'—those who shed costly lifestyles, purchase RVs, and travel the nation picking up seasonal jobs that typically offer hourly wages and few or no benefits."

People have peculiar beliefs about risk. We worry about dying from a shark bite (when we should really worry about heart disease). When there's a sale on eggs or chicken, we're happy—but when the stock market gets cheaper, we think it's bad. (Long-term investors should love when the market drops: You can buy more shares for the same price.)

OLDER PEOPLE REGRET NOT INVESTING

They regret it but you don't have to. My thoughts below.

Age of employee	Median balance of their 401(k)	My comment
Under 25	$1,325	Too busy watching a cooking show of things they will never cook.
25–34	$8,192	These people have just started dabbling in saving money, but still don't see the value in it.
35–44	$23,491	These people have realized that perhaps saving money is important.
45–54	$43,467	These older folks are wishing they could go back in time and beat themselves for not saving more, like Biff in *Back to the Future Part II*.

Source: Vanguard report

Remember, knowing how to invest isn't obvious. And that's the problem. When it comes to money, it's actually very easy to end up like most other people: You just . . . do nothing. After years of talking to young people about money, I have come to a couple of conclusions: First, I pretty much hate everyone. Second, I believe there are three categories of people: the As, the Bs, and the Cs. The As are already managing their money and want to optimize what they're doing. The Bs, the largest group of people, are not doing anything but could be persuaded to change that if you figure out what motivates them. The Cs are an unwashed mass of people who are a lost cause. Theoretically, they could be motivated, but it's impossibly hard to get through their knuckleheaded reasons and excuses for putting money management so far down their list of priorities.

Although some people are limited by circumstances, most people will never get rich simply because they have poor attitudes and behaviors about money. In fact, most people in their twenties are Bs: not great, but not bad. There's a lot of time left for them to set aggressive investment goals, but if they don't take any action, they end up inevitably drifting toward being a C. Don't let this happen to you!

I didn't start investing in my 401(k) at my first job out of grad school for almost 2 years. I left thousands on the table.

—**TE ROMEO, 34**

I didn't open a 401(k) when I started my first job out of college because my ex said it wasn't a good investment. What I regret the most is listening to his poor advice and not following my gut. Five years later I did open one, but I still think about how much that relationship cost me. —**YVETTE BATISTA, 37**

I didn't work for an employer who offered a 401(k) until I was 35. I wish someone told me when I was 20 to look for an employer who was established enough to offer this, but I was cheap, and insecure, and desperate for experience. Now I feel like I lost out on a good 10 to 15 years' worth of opportunity. —**ROBYN GINNEY, 45**

INVISIBLE INVESTING SCRIPTS

Invisible script	What It Means
"There are so many stocks out there, so many ways to buy and sell stocks, and so many people giving different advice. It feels overwhelming."	This is code for "I want to hide behind complexity." Any new topic is overwhelming: diets or workout regimens, learning how to dress better, parenting. The answer isn't to avoid it—it's to pick a source of information and start learning.
"I feel like I'm always buying at the highs, and I don't want to be the person who buys into the market when it peaks."	This person intellectually "knows" that you can't time the market . . . but they don't really understand it. They should be automatically investing each month so this problem disappears.
"I haven't invested in anything because there are so many different options to put my money in over the long term (real estate, stocks, crypto, commodities, etc.). I know I should invest but stocks don't 'feel' controllable."	The great irony is that this person believes "control" will help their investment returns, when in reality, they'd actually get better returns by doing less. The less control they have, the better. Data clearly indicates that the average investor buys high, sells low, and trades frequently (which incurs taxes), and all of this cuts their returns by huge amounts. You think you want control but really, you don't. Just let go already.
"Due to my lack of knowledge/experience in it, I don't want to lose my hard-earned money."	Ironically, every day you don't invest, you actually *are* losing money—due to inflation. You will never realize this until you're in your 70s, at which point it will be too late. (I'm fun at parties.)
"Fees are a big part of it. When you only have a small amount to invest, trading fees can make a big dent in your returns."	It is totally mystifying how people think "investing = trading stocks." Oh wait, no it isn't—every stupid commercial and app pushes this agenda. When you follow my advice, your investment fees are extremely low.
"Ordered a small coffee instead of a large, so I'm saving X dollars a day. Am I adulting?"	You will die alone.

Why do so many of us have such poor attitudes toward money? You could make a convincing case for not enough education, too much information, confusing messages from the media, or simply a lack of interest. Whatever the reason, it's clear young people aren't investing enough.

One thing I've learned in the self-development business: We all have lots of reasons why we aren't doing something we "should," like investing, flossing, or starting a business. No time, no money, not sure where to start, etc. Sometimes the truth is simpler: We just don't want to.

If you don't want to learn how money works, nothing I can tell you will help. You could hire someone to help you (often at a hidden cost of hundreds of thousands of dollars, thanks to their commissions and the larded-up funds they'd recommend for you). You could just do what your parents did. Or you can do the time-tested American hallmark: Just ignore the problem and hope it goes away. I don't recommend this.

Financial institutions have noticed an interesting phenomenon: When people enter their forties, they suddenly realize that they should have been saving money all along. As a result, the number one financial concern Americans have is not having enough money for retirement. According to a recent Gallup poll, over half of Americans are "very" or "moderately" worried about not having enough money for retirement.

To bring this close to home, ask your parents what they worry about most. I'll bet you their answer is, simply, "Money." Yet we're not paying much more attention to our finances than our parents did.

Boring but True

Although it's easy to "plan" on winning the lottery to get rich, the real way to do it is actually much simpler: Of America's millionaires, two-thirds are self-made, meaning their parents weren't rich. They collected their significant wealth through controlling their spending, regular investing, and, in some cases, entrepreneurship. Not as sexy as winning the lottery, but much more realistic.

According to a recent survey of millionaires done by US Trust, "83% of the wealthy say their largest investment gains have come from smaller wins over time rather than taking big risks." (Note: This doesn't mean cutting back on coffee. It means consistent, *meaningful* behaviors like disciplined saving and investing, rather than massive speculative risks.)

Their wealth isn't measured by the amount they make each year, but by how much they've saved and invested over time. In other words, a project manager could earn $50,000 per year and have a higher net worth than a doctor earning $250,000 per year—if the project manager saves and invests more over time.

American culture doesn't help us think about investing our money. We see celebrities and Instagram posts that show us the results of being rich, not how to get there. Not surprisingly, as this form of entertainment has become more popular, our attitudes have changed.

The American Psychological Association reports that Americans today, compared to the 1950s, seem less happy, even though we eat out twice as much and own two times as many cars. We have so many more toys, like big-screen TVs, smartphones, and microwaves. But that isn't leading to a more satisfying life.

A FIFTH OF YOUNG PEOPLE THINK THEY'LL GET RICH THROUGH THE LOTTERY

Percentage of young people	Who believe they'll get rich	My comment
21%	By winning the lottery	I hate you.
11%	Through an inheritance	I hate you.
3%	Via an insurance settlement	How about the insurance of doing some actual work to learn about your money?

Despite this preoccupation with material goods and a dizzying array of information sources—including 24/7 financial news channels, countless pundits, and millions of online financial sites—we're not managing our money better. If anything, we're more anxious. Even higher-income earners don't handle their money well: About one in four people who make $100,000-plus a year still report living paycheck to paycheck, according to a SunTrust survey.

What do we do? We berate ourselves and promise to do better by making New Year's pledges. We download new apps (as if an app is really going to solve the problem). We talk about "education" being the solution, like people don't already know they should save more and invest for the future.

Information alone is not enough—you already "know" about compound interest, and if you simply needed information, you would have already found it. The real problem, and the solution, is you. Your psychology, your emotions, your invisible scripts . . . all of it. Without understanding why you behave the way you do with money— and deciding why you want to change—any information is just meaningless drivel.

Notice the dark belief that the deck is totally stacked against us. How many people have you heard complaining that there's no way to save money, much less invest? In a way, this learned helplessness can become addictive. "LOL! Invest? Not possible. There's nothing I can do! Baby boomers really screwed me." In reality, give me ten minutes with your calendar and your spending, and I'll show you your actual priorities—and how to fix them.

Even though lots of people have naive and often delusional ideas about money, you don't need to be one of them. I'm going to help you confront reality, take control, and realize that, yes, you *can* invest. Maybe it's $50/month. Maybe it's $5,000/month. I've been at both levels, and I can show you what it takes. Ten years from now—hell, maybe even three months from now—you'll see an investment account full of money that is automatically added to each month. You'll be earning while you sleep. And instead of waiting for a magical lottery win, you'll consciously use your investment account to get rich.

Investing Is the Single Most Effective Way to Get Rich

By opening an investment account, you give yourself access to the biggest money-making vehicle in the history of the world: the stock market. Setting up an account is an excellent first step toward actually investing, and you don't have to be rich to open one. Many account providers will waive minimums (the amount required to open an account) if you set up an automatic monthly transfer.

INVEST NOW . . .
YOU'RE NOT GETTING ANY YOUNGER

What if you had started investing $10 per week five years ago? Guess how much you'd have. It turns out that by now, you'd have thousands of dollars—all from investing a little more than $1 per day. Think about that $10 a week—where did it go, anyway? If you're like most people, it probably slipped through your fingers on random things like Ubers and lunches. Despite wild rides in the stock market, the best thing you can do is think long-term and start investing early.

If you invest this much per week . . .	After 1 year, you'll have . . .	After 5 years, you'll have . . .	After 10 years, you'll have . . .
$10	$541	$3,173	$7,836
$20	$1,082	$6,347	$15,672
$50	$2,705	$15,867	$39,181

Assumes 8% returns.

This isn't just theoretical. Look at how investing changed these IWT readers' lives.

I've invested $70,000 since reading the book, maxed out my Roth IRA, contributed 19 percent of my paycheck to my 401(k), and don't lose a moment's sleep over active trading. I set my allocation once per year, forget it, and live my life. It's an amazing feeling to have conquered the ignorance I had about money, which is such a source of stress and anxiety for others. Since I know I am on the right track, I don't have to worry, which frees up my mind and time to make more money.

—SAM HATHAWAY, 29

I've been investing in my Roth IRA, 401(k), and HSA for years and finally cracked $100,000 in savings. I'm 28. At this rate, I will be able to retire by my mid-fifties at the LATEST. If I avoid lifestyle creep, I can move that up to early to mid-forties. And I don't feel deprived at all. I'm living a Rich Life.

—MIKE KELLY, 28

Your book helped me set up a basic account infrastructure for my finances. I graduated college in 2010, read it around 2010–2011-ish, and am maxing my 403(b) [a retirement plan often used by teachers] and Roth IRA every year now. I started off putting 8–10 percent in my 403(b) initially and marched it up over the years. I turn 31 in August and currently have $135,000 in my 403(b), $18,000-ish in my Roth IRA, maybe $12,000 in checking/savings and $60,000-ish in other investments like single stocks and crypto. I am absolutely loving making my money for me and not being a slave to it.

—ROSS WHITE, 30

The Ladder of Personal Finance

These are the six systematic steps you should take to invest. Each step builds on the previous one, so when you finish the first, go on to the second. If you can't get to number 6, don't worry—do your best for now. In Chapter 5, I'll show you how to make this automatic so your system can run itself with just a few hours of work per year—but remember, opening these accounts and getting started is the most important step.

Rung 1: If your employer offers a 401(k) match, invest to take full advantage of it and contribute just enough to get 100 percent of the match. A "401(k) match" means that for every dollar you contribute to your 401(k), your company will "match" your contribution up to a certain amount. For example, for easy math, let's assume you make $100,000 and that your employer will 100 percent match your contribution up to 5 percent of your salary. This means that you'll contribute $5,000 and your company will match it with $5,000. This is free money, and there is, quite simply, no better deal.

Rung 2: Pay off your credit card and any other debt. The average credit card APR is 14 percent, and many APRs are higher. Whatever your card company charges, paying off your debt will give you a significant instant return. For the best ways to do this, see page 62 in Chapter 1.

Rung 3: Open up a Roth IRA (see page 111) and contribute as much money as possible to it. (As long as your income is $120,000 or less, you're allowed to contribute up to $5,500 in 2018. For current contribution limits, search for "Roth IRA contribution limits.")

Rung 4: If you have money left over, go back to your 401(k) and contribute as much as possible to it (this time above and beyond your employer match). The current limit is $19,000. For current contribution limits, search for "401(k) contribution limits."

Rung 5: HSA: If you have access to a Health Savings Account (HSA), it can also double as an investment account with incredible tax features that few people know about. For more on HSAs, see page 120. If you've completed Rung 4 and you still have money left over, take advantage of this account.

Rung 6: If you still have money left to invest, open a regular non-retirement ("taxable") investment account and put as much as possible there. For more about this, see Chapter 7. Also, pay extra on any mortgage debt you have, and consider investing in yourself: Whether it's starting a company or getting an additional degree, there's often no better investment than your own career.

Remember, the Ladder of Personal Finance only shows you what accounts to open. In Chapter 7, I'll show you what to invest in.

Mastering Your 401(k)

I f I wanted to create the single worst name for something that could potentially change the lives of tens of millions of people, here's what I would do:

1. Go find the most boring document ever written. Let's say, the IRS tax code.

2. Open up to a random page. Maybe . . . I don't know, section 401(k).

3. LOOK AROUND YOUR OFFICE ONCE, SHRUG, AND DECIDE TO USE THAT AS THE NAME OF THIS LIFE-CHANGING ACCOUNT.

The name sucks, but the account is awesome.

A 401(k) plan is a type of retirement account that many companies offer to their employees. (Note: Ask your HR representative if your company offers a 401(k). If it doesn't, skip ahead to the section on Roth IRAs on page 111.) It's a "retirement" account because it gives you large tax advantages if you agree not to withdraw your money from the account until you reach the retirement age of 59½. (You don't actually have to start withdrawing your money until you're 70½ years old, and even then there's an exception if you're still working. But don't worry about that now.)

To set up your 401(k), you fill out a form authorizing part of each paycheck—you decide how much—to be sent to your account each month. The money goes straight from your employer to your 401(k), so you never see it in your paycheck. When you set the account up, you choose among some simple investment options, then let your money accumulate over time.

Let's dig deeper into the benefits of your 401(k).

401(k) Benefit #1: Using Pretax Money Means an Instant 25 Percent Accelerator. Retirement accounts offer you a deal: You promise to invest your money for the long term, and in exchange, they give you huge tax advantages. Because the money you're contributing isn't taxed until you withdraw it many years later (that's why it's called "pre-tax money"), you have much more money to invest for compound growth—usually 25 to 40 percent more.

Let's look at a regular investment account (a "non-retirement account") first. If you open one of these at any investment brokerage, you don't get many tax advantages: For every $100 you make, you'll be able to invest only about $75 of it, because, depending on your tax rate, about 25 percent goes to pay income taxes.

A 401(k) is different. It's "tax-deferred," meaning you can invest the entire $100 and let it grow for about thirty-plus years. Sure, you'll pay taxes when you withdraw your money later, but that extra 25 percent turns out to make a huge difference as it gets compounded more and more.

401(k) Benefit #2: Your Employer Match Means Free Money. In many cases, your employer will match part of your contribution, meaning you get automatic free money for investing—a win-win situation. To find out if your company offers a 401(k) match, just ask your HR rep what the matching policy is.

How exactly does matching work? Here's an example: Again, say your company offers a 1:1 ("one-to-one") match up to 5 percent. This means your company will match every dollar you invest up to 5 percent of your salary. If you make $60,000 per year and you contribute $3,000 per year (5 percent of your salary), your employer then matches the $3,000, so your actual investment is $6,000 per year.

If you start at age thirty-five and earn 8 percent on your money, you'll have more than $730,000 with the 401(k) match when you retire— or just over $367,000 with no match. A 5 percent match can *double* your returns. And each year you invest, the difference grows larger.

HOW A 401(K) GROWS		
Age	Balance without employer match	Balance with employer match
35	$3,240.00	$6,480.00
40	$19,007.79	$38,015.57
45	$46,936.46	$93,872.92
50	$87,972.85	$175,945.70
55	$148,268.76	$296,537.53
60	$236,863.25	$473,726.49
65	$367,037.60	$734,075.21

Assumes 8% returns. To be conservative, I assumed you received no salary increases.

401(k) Benefit #3: Automatic Investing. With a 401(k), your money is sent into your investment account without you having to do anything. If you don't see the money in your paycheck because it's automatically sent to your 401(k), you'll learn to live without it. This is an excellent example of using psychology to trick yourself into investing. In fact, there's an emerging body of literature on how powerful these effects are.

For example, some companies have begun offering "opt-out" 401(k)s rather than those that require you to opt in, meaning that you're automatically enrolled by default to contribute a certain percentage of your income. Sure, you're given the freedom to opt out, but automatic enrollment takes advantage of the fact that most people don't do anything active with their money. The results are dramatic: 401(k) participation was initially 40 percent in the companies that were studied, but after automatic enrollment, it soared to more than 90 percent.

Common Concerns About 401(k)s

What happens if I really need my money? A 401(k) is a retirement account for long-term investments, not a checking or savings account. If you withdraw money before you're 59½ years old, you incur severe penalties, including income taxes and an early-withdrawal penalty of 10 percent. These punishments are intentional: This money is for your retirement, not for your yoga trip to Tulum. That said, there are allowances for "hardship withdrawals," including paying medical expenses, buying a primary residence, paying educational costs, and the like. These are subject to income tax and the 10 percent early-withdrawal penalty, so they're not a great option (I'd avoid raiding your 401(k) unless you're truly desperate), but they do exist. Remember, the biggest problem most people have is not saving and investing at all, so don't let worrying about how you'll get your money out stop you. Once you've saved and invested money, you can always figure out a way to withdraw it if you really need to.

Will I have to pay taxes when I withdraw my money? Yes. Although your 401(k) is tax-deferred, it's not tax-free: When you start withdrawing after age 59½, you'll have to pay taxes. But don't feel bad about paying these taxes, since your money will have been compounding at an accelerated rate for the last thirty to forty years. Because you agreed to invest your money in a 401(k), you were able to put in about 25 percent more money to grow for you.

What if I switch jobs? The money in your 401(k) is yours, so if you move to another company, don't worry. You can take it with you. Here's how:

1. Move it to an IRA. This option is preferred. It lets you "roll over" your 401(k) money into an IRA, which is great, because an IRA gives you more control over where you invest your money, including lifecycle funds and index funds, which we'll cover in Chapter 7. Call your discount brokerage, such as Vanguard, Fidelity, or Schwab (you'll be signed up with one of these by the end of the chapter), and ask for their help with a 401(k) rollover, including converting to a Roth IRA. It should take about ten minutes, and it's free. Note that there may be a time limit on transferring the money to a new provider, so when you change jobs, you need to call your discount broker right away and ask them how to handle a rollover.

2. Roll your money from the old company's 401(k) to the new company's 401(k). This is fine, but if you've already had a 401(k), you've probably noticed that their investing choices are limited. Plus, the main reason to contribute to a 401(k) is to take advantage of your employer's match, which won't apply to funds you roll into the new account. So I prefer rolling 401(k) money into an IRA. If you really want to roll it over to the new 401(k), ask the HR person at your new employer for help.

3. Leave it at your current company. This is almost always a bad move, because you'll forget about it and certainly won't stay up to date on the investment options and changes offered through the plan.

4. Cash out the money and pay taxes and a 10 percent early-withdrawal penalty. This is the worst thing you could possibly do. Yet here's an astonishing fact: 50 percent of twentysomethings cash out their 401(k)s when they leave their jobs, taking a huge hit on taxes and fees. Don't do it!

What about a Roth 401(k)? Some companies now offer a Roth 401(k), which allows you to contribute after-tax money to a 401(k) instead of pre-tax money like a traditional 401(k). Why would you do this? If you expect your tax rates to be higher later in life, a Roth 401(k) is a great option for you. Two unexpected benefits here: If you use a Roth 401(k), there are no income restrictions, so if you earn too much to contribute to a Roth IRA, a Roth 401(k) is a great way to get after-tax benefits. Also, you can take any Roth 401(k) money and roll it over to a Roth IRA, tax-free, which will give you even more investment options.

Summary of 401(k) Advantages

We've covered this, but it bears repeating: 401(k)s are great because with virtually no effort on your part you get to put pre-tax money to work. (Or, in the case of a Roth 401(k), after-tax money.) What this means is that since you haven't paid taxes on the money yet, there's more of it to compound over time. On top of this, your company might offer a very lucrative 401(k) match, which amounts to free money that you'd be insane not to take. Remember to be aggressive with how much you contribute to your 401(k), because every dollar you invest now will likely be worth many more times that in the future.

Do It Now: Setting Up Your 401(k)

To set up your 401(k), call your HR administrator and get the paperwork to open the account, which should take about thirty minutes to fill out. The forms will ask you to choose which funds you want to invest in. Before you make your choices, read through Chapter 7, where I cover your investment plan.

If you do have an employer match, calculate how much you need to contribute to your 401(k) to get the full match, and then have it automatically deducted from your paycheck. (The 401(k) paperwork you fill out will let you specify this.) For example, if your employer matches 5 percent of your salary and you make $50,000/year, you need to contribute about $208/month (that's $50,000 multiplied by 5 percent divided by twelve months). If that amount was automatically taken out of your paycheck and you never saw it, could you still live? Answer: Yes. If not, adjust the amount down until you're comfortable. Remember, investing 85 percent of the way is better than not doing it at all.

If your employer offers a 401(k) but doesn't offer a match, open up the 401(k) anyway (assuming there are no monthly fees), but don't contribute any money for now. Follow Rungs 2 and 3 of the Ladder of Personal Finance to pay off debt and max out your Roth IRA. Once that's done, continue onto Rung 4 of the Ladder of Personal Finance and invest in your 401(k).

Crush Your Debt

The second step on the Ladder of Personal Finance is addressing your debt. If you don't have any credit card debt, awesome—skip this step and jump to the section on the next page. (If you're wondering why student loan debt is okay to have while you move on to investing, here's why: Student loan debt tends to have lower interest rates than credit card debt. It also tends to be large. That means you can set up a payment schedule, but also invest at the same time.)

If you do have non–student loan debt, it's time to pay it off. I know it's not sexy—or easy. Especially when we're talking about investing. It's a funny thing: Once people get their first taste of investing, setting up new accounts and learning phrases like "asset allocation" become way more exciting than paying off tired old debt. They say, "Why do we have to talk about debt? I'll make more from investing than from paying off debt!" Because I want you to crush all the barriers that keep you from being rich, I encourage you to focus on paying off your loans, especially your credit card debt, which often comes with exorbitant interest rates. For the best ways to get rid of debt, revisit page 62.

The Beauty of Roth IRAs

Once you've set up your 401(k) and tackled your debt, it's time to climb to Rung 3 and start funding a Roth IRA. A Roth IRA is another type of retirement account with significant tax advantages. It's not employer sponsored—you contribute money on your own. Every young person should have a Roth IRA, even if you're also contributing to a 401(k). It's simply the best deal I've found for long-term investing.

HOW MUCH WILL A ROTH IRA SAVE YOU?

Assumptions: 25 percent tax rate (now and at retirement), 8 percent annual rate of return, yearly contribution of $5,000 (that's $417/month). Notice how much taxes eat out of your returns.

	Roth IRA	Regular taxable investment account	Doing nothing
5 years	$31,680	$29,877	$0
10 years	$78,227	$69,858	$0
15 years	$146,621	$123,363	$0
20 years	$247,115	$194,964	$0
25 years	$394,772	$290,782	$0
30 years	$611,729	$419,008	$0

One of the benefits is that it lets you invest in whatever you want. Whereas a 401(k) has an array of funds that you must choose from, a Roth IRA lets you invest in anything you want: index funds, individual stocks, anything. A second difference has to do with taxes: Remember how your 401(k) uses pre-tax dollars and you pay taxes only when you withdraw money at retirement? Well, a Roth IRA uses after-tax dollars to give you an even better deal. With a Roth, you invest already-taxed income and you don't pay any tax when you withdraw it.

Let me put that into perspective: If Roth IRAs had been around in 1972 and you'd invested $10,000 after-tax dollars in LUV, Southwest Airlines' stock, you'd have hit a grand slam. Not only would the money have turned into about $10 million, but when you withdrew the money some thirty years later, you'd have paid no taxes. Although way back in 1972 you would have paid taxes on your initial $10,000 investment, the $9,990,000 you earned in the Roth IRA would have been tax-free. That's unbeatable.

Think about it. In a Roth IRA, you pay taxes on the amounts you contribute, but not the earnings. And if you invest well over thirty years, that is a stunningly good deal, as you can see in the chart on the previous page.

Roth IRA Restrictions

As with a 401(k), you're expected to treat a Roth IRA as a long-term investment vehicle, and you're penalized if you withdraw your earnings before you're 59½ years old. Notice that I said "earnings." Most people don't know this, but you can withdraw your principal (the amount you actually invested from your pocket) penalty-free. There are also exceptions for down payments on a home, funding education for you or your partner/children/grandchildren, and some other emergency reasons.

Important note: You qualify for these exceptions only if your Roth IRA has been open for five years or more. This reason alone is enough for you to open your Roth IRA this week. At present, the maximum you're allowed to invest in your Roth IRA is $6,000 a year, but you can find the most current amount by searching "Roth IRA contribution limits."

One other important thing to know is that if you make more than $135,000 per year, there are restrictions on how much you can contribute to a Roth IRA (and over a certain income, you're not eligible to open one at all). These limits change each year, and you can find the most current numbers by searching "Roth IRA income limits."

How to Open a Roth IRA

I don't care where you get the money to contribute to your Roth IRA, but get it (for ideas on reducing spending and increasing earnings so you can fund it, see Chapter 4). Contributing as much as possible is almost as important as starting early. I'm not going to belabor the point, but every dollar you invest now is worth much, much more later. Even waiting two years can cost you tens of thousands of dollars. I want you to do your research and open your Roth IRA by the end of the week.

To start a Roth IRA, you're first going to open an investment brokerage account with a trusted investment company (see the table on the next page). Think of the "investment brokerage account" as your house and the Roth IRA as one of the rooms. Although this account will probably hold only your Roth IRA for now, you can expand it to host other accounts (such as taxable investment accounts or additional Roth IRAs for your future spouse and kids) as your needs change.

If this sounds complicated, don't worry. We're not going to pick the actual investments today—that comes in Chapter 7—but we are going to open your account and fund it with a little money so that when you're ready to invest, you can.

Growth vs. Access

Q: *I DON'T WANT TO LOCK MY MONEY UP IN A RETIREMENT ACCOUNT—I MIGHT NEED IT SOON. WHAT SHOULD I DO?*

A: Many people think of a retirement account as "locking" the money up, which is not entirely accurate. Remember that if you contribute to a Roth IRA, you can always withdraw the money you contribute ("the principal") penalty-free. With both Roths and 401(k)s, you can also access your money, penalty-free, in certain cases of real need (like to pay medical expenses, prevent foreclosure, cover tuition, pay funeral expenses, and so on—the IRS covers this under "Hardship Distributions"). Nevertheless, unless you really have no other recourse, you should not withdraw money from your retirement account.

If you know you'll need your money in fewer than five years, put it in a high-interest savings account. But don't make the mistake of keeping your money in a savings account just because you're too lazy to take the time to learn how to invest it. If you'd invested ten years ago, wouldn't it feel good to have a lot more money right now? Well, the next best time to invest is today.

We'll focus on discount brokerages like Vanguard because they charge dramatically smaller fees than full-service brokerages like Morgan Stanley. Full-service brokerages offer so-called "comprehensive services," but they basically just charge you a lot of money to sell you useless research and let you talk to salespeople. Discount brokerages, on the other hand, let you make the choices, charge only small fees, and offer online access. Don't get fooled by smooth-talking salespeople: You can easily manage your investment account by yourself.

RECOMMENDED DISCOUNT BROKERAGES

Brokerage name	Things to know
Vanguard vanguard.com	My personal recommendation is Vanguard. They're great because of their relentless focus on low-cost funds. Vanguard is the primary company I invest through (see page 146).
Schwab schwab.com	Schwab is also a solid option. If you set up a high-interest Schwab checking account (see page 84), Schwab will automatically link a brokerage account to it. Handy for automatic investing.
Fidelity fidelity.com	Fidelity has also gone low cost. Keep an eye on the expense ratios of their funds, though.

Factors to Consider When Choosing Your Investment Brokerage

Frankly, most discount brokerages are pretty much the same.

Minimums. Before you open your investment account, you'll want to compare minimum required investments. For example, some full-service brokerages will require you to have a hefty minimum amount to open an account. When I recently called Morgan Stanley, the rep I spoke to recommended a minimum balance of $50,000. "Technically, you could open an account with $5,000," she told me, "but the fees would kill you." This is why you use a discount brokerage. Most do require a minimum contribution of $1,000–$3,000 to open a Roth IRA, but they'll often waive it if you set up an automatic transfer. Even if it doesn't waive any minimums, I recommend setting up a monthly automatic transfer so your money will grow without you having to think about it. More on this in Chapter 5.

Features. You can also investigate the features your brokerage offers, but frankly most of these are now commodities, so what used to be differentiators—24/7 customer service, apps, easy-to-use websites—are now standard.

And that's it. Yes, you could spend hundreds of hours doing a detailed comparison of the total number of funds offered, frequency of mailings, and alternative-investment accounts available, but more is lost from indecision than bad decisions. As Benjamin Franklin said, "Don't put off until tomorrow what you can do today." And as Ramit Sethi said, "Let others debate minutiae—all you need to do is open an investment account at a discount brokerage. BOOM."

Signing up should take about an hour. You can do it entirely online, or you can call the companies and they'll mail or email you the necessary documents. Remember to tell them that you want to open a Roth IRA so they give you the right paperwork. There will be a way to connect your checking account to your investment account so that you can regularly automatically transfer money to be invested. Later, when we start investing in Chapter 7, I'll show you more about how companies waive minimum investing fees if you agree to automatically send $50 or

$100 per month. But opening a Roth IRA is free. Ideally you will be able to increase that amount—you'll learn exactly how much you're able to invest monthly after reading the next chapter.

What About Robo-Advisors?

You may have heard about "robo-advisors" like Betterment and Wealthfront. Robo-advisors are investment firms that use computer algorithms to invest your money ("robo" refers to a computer investing for you versus an expensive adviser).

Robo-advisors took the elite financial planning services offered to clients of financial advisers and full-service investment firms like Fidelity and made them accessible to the average person. You know how Uber made private cars more accessible and convenient than taxis? That's sort of what robo-advisors have done to the investment industry.

Robo-advisors implemented new technology to offer investment recommendations for low fees. They improved the user interface so you can sign up online, answer a few questions, and know exactly where to invest your money in a few minutes. And they personalized the experience so you can add in your goals—like when you want to buy a home—and automatically allocate money aside for it.

I have a strong opinion on robo-advisors: While they are good options, I don't think they are worth the costs and I believe there are better options. As an example, I specifically chose Vanguard and have stuck with them for many years.

Let me explain the pros and cons of robo-advisors so you can make your own decision.

In the last few years, robo-advisors have become increasingly popular for three reasons:

- **Ease of use.** They have beautiful interfaces on the web and on your phone. They offer low minimums and make it easy to transfer your money over and get started investing.

- **Low fees.** In general, their fees started off lower than those of full-featured investment firms like Fidelity and Schwab. (Those firms quickly realized their competition and lowered their fees accordingly, while the fees at low-cost firms like Vanguard have always been low.)

- **Marketing claims.** Robo-advisors make lots of marketing claims. Some are true, such as their ease of use. Some are disingenuous, bordering on absurd, like their focus on "tax-loss harvesting."

As you've probably realized, I'm a huge proponent of anything that expands the use of low-cost investing to ordinary people. Long-term investing is a critical part of living a Rich Life, so if companies can strip away complexity and make it easier to get started—even charging a generally low fee—I'm a fan. These robo-advisors have added phenomenal features that are genuinely helpful, including planning for medium-term goals like buying a house and long-term goals like retirement.

What's more, you can often tell how good something is by who hates it. For example, Bank of America hates me because I publicly call them on their bullshit. Good! In the case of robo-advisors, commission-based financial advisers generally hate them because they use technology to achieve what many advisers were doing—but cheaper. Advisers' logic on this is not especially compelling. Financial advisers essentially say that everyone is different and they need individual help, not one-size-fits-all advice (untrue—when it comes to their finances, most people are mostly the same). Robo-advisors have responded by adding financial advisers you can talk to over the phone. Traditional financial advisers say their advice provides value beyond the mere returns. (My response: Fine, then charge by the hour, not as a percentage of assets under management.)

Robo-advisors emerged to serve an audience that was previously ignored: young people who are digitally savvy, upwardly affluent, and don't want to sit in a stuffy office getting lectured by a random financial adviser. Think of an employee at Google who doesn't know what to do with their money, which is just sitting in a checking account. Robo-advisors have done a good job of appealing to that audience.

But the real issue here is "Are they worth it?" My answer is no—their fees don't justify what they offer. The most popular robo-advisors have superb user interfaces, but I'm not willing to pay for that. Since they opened, many robo-advisors have dropped their fees, sometimes even lower than Vanguard. But there are two problems with that: In order to run a sustainable business on fees lower than 0.4 percent, they have

Keep Track of All Your Accounts

One thing that drives me insane is searching for the login information for all my different accounts. To help me keep track of all my accounts, I use a password-management tool called LastPass. It securely stores the URLs, passwords, and details of every account, and it works on my laptop and phone. This is an important part of my financial system because it's essential to have all your information in one place so you can seamlessly log in when you need to.

to offer new, more expensive features and manage massive amounts of money—we're talking trillions of dollars. As an example, Vanguard currently manages nine times more than Betterment and ten times more assets than Wealthfront. That sheer, massive scale is a huge competitive advantage to Vanguard, which built itself over decades to sustain on tiny fraction-of-a-percentage fees. New robo-advisors can't sustain on those low fees unless they grow their business rapidly, which is unlikely. Instead, they've raised money from venture capital investors, who want rapid growth.

In order to attract more customers, robo-advisors have begun using marketing gimmicks like highlighting a minuscule part of investing, "tax-loss harvesting"—which is basically selling an investment that's down to offset tax gains—that they blew up into a seemingly critically important part of an account. (This would be like a car manufacturer spending millions of dollars marketing a triple coat of paint as one of the most important parts of buying a car. Sure, tax-loss harvesting might save you a little money over the long term . . . but not a lot. And in many cases, it's unnecessary. It's a "nice to have" feature, but hardly something on which you should base the important decision of choosing what firm to invest your money with.)

Some robo-advisors have also begun offering products with higher fees, as the *Wall Street Journal* reported in 2018.

Wealthfront added a higher-cost fund of its own. The offering uses derivatives to replicate a popular hedge fund strategy known as "risk-parity."

Some clients—joined by consumer advocates and rivals—quickly took to online forums to criticize the fund's costs and complexity. They also took Wealthfront to task for automatically enrolling certain customers in the fund.

"I just looked at my account & it's true. There was money moved into your 'Risk Parity' fund without my consent," Wealthfront customer Cheryl Ferraro, 57 years old, of San Juan Capistrano, California, recently posted on Twitter.

"I had to go into my account and tell them I wanted my money moved out of that fund. It shook my confidence in them for sure," Ms. Ferraro said in an interview.

This is the predictable outcome when a low-cost provider raises venture capital and needs to grow rapidly. It either finds more customers or finds a way to make more money from each customer.

I believe Vanguard has the edge, and I invest through them. But realize this: By the time you've narrowed down your investing decision to a low-cost provider like Vanguard or a robo-advisor, you've already made the most important choice of all: to start growing your money in long-term, low-cost investments. Whether you choose a robo-advisor or Vanguard or another low-fee brokerage is a minor detail. Pick one and move on.

Feed Your Investment Account

Okay, you have an investment account. Excellent! Since most of you set up automatic monthly contributions to waive the minimum, your money will be regularly sent to your Roth IRA. It will patiently wait for you to decide exactly how to invest it, which we'll cover in Chapter 7. If you didn't set up automatic contributions, do so now, even if it's just $50/month. It's a good habit to get into and will help you accrue any necessary minimum.

Hungry for Even More?

Let's say you've been kicking ass and you've maxed out your employer 401(k) match, paid off your credit card debt, and gotten your Roth IRA going. If you still have money to invest, you have great options.

First, ascend to Rung 4 and look again at your 401(k). In 2019 the maximum amount you could invest in a 401(k) was $19,000 a year (to find the latest number, search "401(k) contribution limits"). So far, you have only invested enough to get your employer match, so you likely still have the ability to invest more in a 401(k) and reap the huge tax benefits. Cool thing to note: Your employer match isn't counted toward your contribution limit, so if you contribute $5,000 and your employer matches $5,000, you can still contribute another $14,000 for a total of $24,000 annually in your 401(k).

What should you do? Calculate how much you need to contribute each year: $19,000 minus the contribution you figured out on page 104. That gives you the amount you can still contribute. To break this amount down into a monthly contribution, divide that number by twelve. Again, set your contributions so they happen automatically and you never even have to see the money.

Next, an unlikely tax-advantaged account that few people know about.

HSAs: Your Secret Investing Weapon

If you offered me the choice to sit in a fiery hell listening to Ariana Grande remixes for 10,000 years or to write about health insurance, I would sigh and reluctantly start bopping my head to "Side to Side." Everyone hates talking about health insurance—which is why I'm not going to write about it here.

What I *am* going to show you is a shortcut that can earn you hundreds of thousands of dollars by turning something called a Health Savings Account into a supercharged account for growing your money. HSAs let you set aside pre-tax money to pay for qualified medical expenses, including deductibles, copayments, coinsurance, and some other health-related expenses. The cool thing is you can invest the money you put in it.

HSAs get ignored for three reasons:

- First, anything with the word "insurance" means we want to stop thinking about it as quickly as possible. Nobody ever got excited about cell phone bills. Same for health insurance.

- Second, HSAs are only available to people with high-deductible insurance plans. Since most of us would rather eat bags of sand for breakfast than figure out what kind of health insurance plan we have, we skip it.

- Finally, the rare person who has access to an HSA and even uses it still doesn't understand the intricacies of how to use it to make money.

The truth is that an HSA can be an incredibly powerful investment account because you can contribute tax-free money, take a tax deduction, and then grow it tax-free—it's a triple whammy. If you use this account correctly, you will earn hundreds of thousands of dollars.

Does Investing in an HSA Make Sense for Me?

Before you get excited about investing through your HSA, you should find out if you're even eligible. If not, don't waste your time—skip this section and move on to page 124.

1. Have you already completed at least the first three rungs of the Ladder of Personal Finance: investing in a 401(k) match, paying off any credit card debt, and maxing out your Roth IRA? If so, read on. If not, skip this section—you're not ready to invest in an HSA yet.

2. Do you have a high-deductible health plan? Call your insurance provider or benefits manager (ugh, I know) and ask them this simple question: "Do I have a high-deductible health plan?" If they say no, I give you permission to curse me out for forcing you to make such a call. (Before you hang up, though, ask them if you're eligible for a high-deductible plan. You may want to consider it, especially if you're young and generally healthy.) On the other hand, if they say yes, you do have a high-deductible plan, ask them if you can pair an HSA with your account.

If the answer to both of these questions is yes, you may be ready for an HSA account. I use an account called Navia Benefits, but you can search around and compare options. The most important factor for me was the investment options and fees: Do they have good funds with low fees?

How an HSA Works

1. You contribute money to your HSA account. This money sits in your HSA, which effectively functions like another checking account—with a few special exceptions.

2. You get a debit card that you can use for "qualified medical expenses," including bandages, chiropractors, eye exams and glasses, and prescriptions. (This is just a small handful of the health-related expenses you can pay for with your HSA card. To see them all, search for "HSA eligible expenses.")

3. Why does this matter? Because the money in your HSA is tax-free, meaning you get to spend money *before* you pay taxes on it—which can be a discount of 20 percent or more.

For example, let's say you earn $100,000. And let's say you take your credit card and spend $5,000 on a pregnancy test, lab fees, a DEXA body scan, and laser eye surgery. Okay, that's an eclectic set of choices, but hey—you do you. You might think that those treatments cost you $5,000, but in reality, since you've already paid taxes on that money, they actually cost you $6,000.

But with an HSA, since you're using tax-free money, you're saving whatever you would have normally paid on taxes.

4. The real benefit of an HSA comes when you treat it as an investment vehicle. Think about it: If you're contributing thousands of dollars to your HSA but you're not actually getting body scans and new glasses every year, then what are you doing with that money? Most people think it just sits there. *But you can invest it.* You're taking tax-free money and investing it, and it grows. Tax-free. This is incredible.

I'll show you what I mean with a few examples. For easy math, let's assume you have $3,000 per year to invest (or $2,250 after taxes).

FIRST EXAMPLE: You're reading this book half paying attention while watching Netflix, and you skip all my awesome research on investing. You have $3,000 of pre-tax income that you want to save per year. It's taxed at 25 percent, leaving you $2,250 per year to invest. Instead of putting it into your 401(k) and Roth IRA, you just dump it in a normal savings account. Let's assume 1 percent interest for easy math. After twenty years, you end up with $49,453. After applying taxes to your growth, you're left with $48,355. Basically, you lost money due to inflation, but you will never realize it. The lesson: Saving alone is not enough.

SECOND EXAMPLE: You take the same amount—$3,000 of pre-tax income taxed at 25 percent, leaving you $2,250 per year to invest. But this time, instead of merely saving it, you invest it in a taxable investment account with no tax advantages. Using annual compounding at 8 percent, you end up with $102,964 after twenty years. After applying taxes to your growth, you're left with $82,768 after twenty years.

THIRD EXAMPLE: This time, you're going to contribute to a 401(k), which means you get to contribute *pre-tax money* and pay taxes later. Now you'll see why a 401(k) is so powerful. Instead of contributing $2,250 in the above examples, you get to skip the taxes for now and contribute a full $3,000 to your 401(k). After investing there for twenty years, assuming no employer match, you'll end up with $137,286. When you withdraw the balance after age 59.5, assuming a 25 percent tax rate, you end up with $102,964. Not bad—you can see how those tax advantages start to add up.

FOURTH EXAMPLE: After paying taxes on your $3,000, you end up with $2,250 *post-tax* per year to invest in your Roth IRA. The special thing about a Roth IRA is that you're contributing post-tax money, but you pay no taxes on the investment gains. After twenty years, you'll have $102,964. Nice work. Notice this result is the same as above, but it can change dramatically if you have an employer match.

LAST EXAMPLE: You get savvy. You get serious. You decide to squeeze out every advantage you possibly can from your money. You invest $3,000 *pre-tax* in an HSA. Here's the beautiful part: You don't pay taxes on the money when you earn it—and you don't pay taxes on the investment earnings! After twenty years, you'll have $137,286. Incredible!

By the way, you can use the money for any qualified medical expense anytime, tax-free. And after the age of 65, you can spend that money on *anything*—say, a random trip to Santorini. Here are the things to be aware of: If you withdraw funds for non-qualified medical expenses before you're 65, you'll be charged a penalty. If you use your HSA funds for non-qualified medical expenses after age 65, it's taxable. Finally, some people see HSAs as such a good deal that they pay for as many medical expenses as possible out of pocket, since they prefer to let their HSA investments grow.

Do you see how powerful any one of these approaches can be? And do you see why an HSA can supercharge your investments? It's incredibly smart to "layer" these investing options on top of each other. Contributing to an HSA tax-free and investing the money you don't use eliminates the "drag" of taxes on your growth, which compounds faster than in almost any other investment account.

If you have the ability and the funds, you should absolutely use an HSA for investments. Just be sure the HSA you open offers solid funds. A good rule of thumb is they should offer low-cost funds, ideally a target date fund or a "total stock market" fund. More on this in Chapter 7.

Beyond Retirement Accounts

If you've taken full advantage of your 401(k) match, paid off all your credit card debt, topped out your Roth IRA, gone back to max out the remainder of your 401(k), optionally invested in an HSA, and you still have money to invest, there are even more choices to grow your money. I get lots of questions about alternative investments like cryptocurrencies. In Chapter 7, we'll get into the best strategies and options. But right now, I want you to buy a very nice gift for someone you love because you have a lot of money.

Congratulations!

Take a second to pat yourself on the back—you've started up the Ladder of Personal Finance. You now have a system set up to grow your money. This is so important. Having investment accounts means you're starting to think about rapid growth and distinguishing between short-term savings and long-term investing. And that $50 you sent may seem like a small step, but I believe it's the most significant $50 you'll ever invest.

ACTION STEPS

WEEK THREE

1 **Open your 401(k) (three hours).** Get the paperwork from your HR manager and fill it out. Check to see if your employer offers a match. If it does, contribute enough to get the full match. If not, leave your 401(k) account open but contribute nothing.

2 **Come up with a plan to pay off your debt (three hours).** Get serious about getting out of debt. Revisit page 62 in Chapter 1 and see page 284 in Chapter 9 for ideas on how to pay off your credit card debt and student loans. Run a calculation from bankrate.com to see how much you could save by paying an extra $100 or $200 per month.

3 **Open a Roth IRA and set up automatic payments (one hour).** Send as much as you can, but even $50/month is fine. We'll dive into the details a little later.

4 **Find out if you're eligible for an HSA and, if you are, open your account (three hours).**

Now that you've opened these accounts, let's figure out a way to get them as full as possible. In the next chapter, I'll show you how to take control of your spending to make your money go where you want it to go.

CHAPTER 4

CONSCIOUS SPENDING

How to save hundreds per month
(and still buy what you love)

I used to find it ridiculous when people said you could judge a person by their belt or shoes. Are you kidding me? Can I tell what kind of soup you like by the earrings you're wearing?

Get the hell out of here.

Recently, however, I discovered I was wrong. It turns out there *is* one universal shortcut to discovering someone's true character: if they eat chicken wings like an immigrant.

Because I don't understand or care about sports, last Super Bowl Sunday I decided to go on a wing crawl. It's like a pub crawl, but with wings. I quickly realized that the most interesting part of eating wings with friends is seeing how much meat they leave on the bone. Some people leave half the chicken and move on to the next wing. I never speak to these people again.

Then there are people who clean the bone so thoroughly, flawlessly ridding it of every last shred of meat and marrow, that you can conclude only two things: They will be stellar successes in all aspects of life, and they must be from another country. You see, immigrants (like my parents) never leave a shred of meat on a chicken wing—and we can all learn something from them.

That kind of dedication is rare these days. We spend more on our cell phones than most people in other countries do on their mortgages. We buy shoes that cost more than our grandparents paid for their *cars*. Yet we don't really know how much these individual costs add up to. How many times have you opened your bills, winced, then shrugged and said, "I guess I spent that much"? How often do you feel guilty about buying something—but then do it anyway? In this chapter, the antidote to unconscious spending, we're going to gently create a new, simple way of spending. It's time to stop wondering where all your money goes each month. I'm going to help you redirect it to the places you choose, like investing, saving, and even spending *more* on the things you love (but less on the things you don't).

Wait! Before you run away thinking this is a chapter on creating a budget, hang on a second. This isn't about creating a fancy budget that you'll have to maintain every day for the rest of your life. I hate budgeting. "Budgeting" is the worst word in the history of the world.

I have a hard time wrapping my brain around how to set a budget and then not actually spend more than the budget allows. I feel guilty that I'm a nerd in most other respects, but I just can't sit down and do the math about my spending.

—SARAH ROBESON, 28

"Create a budget!" is the sort of worthless advice that personal finance pundits feel good prescribing, yet when real people read about making a budget, their eyes glaze over. Who wants to track their spending? The few people who actually try it find that their budgets completely fail after two days because tracking every penny is overwhelming. Amusingly, in a 2015 survey by bankrate.com, 82 percent of Americans said they have a budget—which is complete nonsense. Just take a look at the people around you right now. Do you think eight out of every ten have a budget? I doubt eight out of ten could even name the planet we're on.

"There's probably a lot of wishful thinking in this response," says Jared Bernstein, director of the Living Standards Program of the Economic Policy Institute, referring to a 2007 study that found the same delusions about budgets. "It's probably more accurate to say that three-quarters think they should work on a monthly budget."

For the last fifty-plus years, budgeting has been the battleground for snobby personal finance writers who've tried to shove a daily tracking system down everyone's throats because it sounds logical. There's only one catch: NOBODY EVER DOES IT.

Most people wouldn't know where to start if I told them to stop spending and start saving. I might as well try to convince an ankylosaurus to dance a jig.

Many of my friends just throw up their hands when they have done something stupid with their money and don't learn from their mistakes. I see people get out of huge credit card debt and once their balances are wiped clean to zero, start the process of maxing out their cards again. **FRANK WILES, 29**

Because we know that budgets don't work, I'm going to show you a better way that's worked for tens of thousands of my readers.

Forget budgeting. Instead, let's create a Conscious Spending Plan. What if you could make sure you were saving and investing enough money each month, and then use the rest of your money guilt-free for whatever you want? Well, you can—with some work. The only catch is that you have to plan where you want your money to go *ahead of time* (even if it's on the back of a napkin). Would it be worth taking a couple of hours to get set up so you can spend on the things you love? It will automate your savings and investing and make your spending decisions crystal clear.

The Difference Between Cheap People and Conscious Spenders

A while back, a couple of friends and I were talking about where we want to travel this year, and one of them said something that surprised me: "You probably wouldn't approve, but I want to go to the Caribbean."

Huh? Why wouldn't I approve?

I get this sometimes. People find out I write about money and suddenly think I'm going to judge them for how they spend theirs.

I asked some personal trainer friends if they get the same comments when they eat out. "Do people apologize for what they order in front of you?"

One of them looked at me. "Every time. But I don't care what they order! I'm just trying to get lunch."

Apparently, my friend thought of me as a Finger-Wagging Money Judge, as if I silently disapproved of him for spending his money on something "frivolous." In other words, someone who writes about personal finance is automatically "the guy who tells me I can't do stuff because it costs too much money."

In reality, I love when people are unapologetic about spending on the things they love. You love fashion and want to buy $400 Brunello Cucinelli T-shirts? Awesome.

Now, I will call your ass out when you make mistakes. If you believe $400 seven-day juice cleanses are going to help you lose weight, you are a moron.

But I'm *not* the nagging parent who tells you to stop spending money on lattes. I spend lots of money on eating out and traveling, but I never feel guilty. Instead of taking a simplistic "Don't spend money on expensive things!!!" view, I believe there's a more nuanced approach.

Let's first dispense with the idea that saying no to spending on certain things means you're cheap. If you decide that spending $2.50 on Cokes when you eat out isn't worth it—and you'd rather save that $15 each week for a movie—that's not being cheap. That's consciously deciding what you value. Unfortunately, most Americans were never taught how to consciously spend, which means cutting costs mercilessly on the things you don't love, but spending extravagantly on the things you do.

Instead, we were taught to generically apply the principle of "Don't spend money on that!" to everything, meaning we try half-heartedly to cut back, fail, then guiltily berate ourselves—and continue overspending on things we don't even care about.

There is power in saying no to the things we don't care about. But there is even more power in saying a big YES to the things we love.

Ironically, the only thing we were really taught about money was to save it—usually with advice about cutting back on coffee and hoarding toilet paper. Everybody talks about how to save money, but nobody teaches you how to spend it.

As a country, we spend more than we make each year, and virtually nothing seems to change our behavior. Even though we may tighten our wallets during a downturn, we soon return to our usual spending behaviors. And frankly, nobody's interested in changing the status quo: Consumer spending accounts for about 70 percent of the American economy.

Conscious spending isn't just about our own choices. There's also the social influence to spend. Call it the *Sex and the City* effect, where your friends' spending directly affects yours. Next time you go shopping, check out any random group of friends. Chances are, they're dressed similarly—even though it's as likely as not that they have wildly different incomes. Keeping up with friends is a full-time job.

Too often, our friends invisibly push us away from being conscious spenders. For example, a while back I went to dinner with two friends. One of them was considering getting the new iPhone, and she pulled out her old phone. My other friend stared in disbelief: "You haven't gotten a new phone in four years? What's wrong with you?" she asked. "You need to get the iPhone." Even though it was only three sentences, the message was clear: There's something wrong with you for not getting a new phone (regardless of whether or not you need it).

Spend on What You Love

Conscious spending isn't about cutting your spending on everything. That approach wouldn't last two days. It is, quite simply, about choosing the things you love enough to spend extravagantly on—and then cutting costs mercilessly on the things you don't love.

The mindset of conscious spenders is the key to being rich. Indeed, as the researchers behind the landmark book *The Millionaire Next Door* discovered, 50 percent of the more than 1,000 millionaires surveyed have never paid more than $400 for a suit, $140 for a pair of shoes, or $235 for a wristwatch. Again, conscious spending is not about simply cutting your spending on various things. It's about making your own

CHEAP PEOPLE VS. CONSCIOUS SPENDERS

Cheap	Conscious
Cheap people care about the cost of something.	Conscious spenders care about the value of something.
Cheap people try to get the lowest price on everything.	Conscious spenders try to get the lowest price on most things but are willing to spend extravagantly on items they really care about.
Cheap people's cheapness affects those around them.	Conscious spenders' frugality affects only them.
Cheap people are inconsiderate. For example, when getting a meal with other people, if their food costs $7.95, they'll put in $8, knowing very well that tax and tip mean it's closer to $11.	Conscious spenders know they have to pick and choose where they spend their money. If they can spend only $10 on lunch, they'll order water instead of iced tea.
Cheap people make you uncomfortable because of the way they treat others.	Conscious spenders make you feel uncomfortable because you realize you could be doing better with your money.
Cheap people keep a running tally of how much their friends, family, and coworkers owe them.	Some conscious spenders do this too, but certainly not all.
Because of the fear of even one person suggesting they spent too much on something, cheap people are not always honest about what they spend.	Neither are conscious spenders. Everybody lies about their spending.
Cheap people are unreasonable and cannot understand why they can't get something for free. Sometimes this is an act, but sometimes it's not.	Conscious spenders will try as hard as cheap people to get a deal, but they understand that it's a dance, and in the end, they know they don't intrinsically *deserve* a special deal.
Cheap people think short-term.	Conscious spenders think long-term.

decisions about what's important enough to spend a lot on and what's not, rather than blindly spending on *everything*.

THE PROBLEM IS THAT HARDLY ANYONE IS DECIDING WHAT'S IMPORTANT AND WHAT'S NOT, DAMMIT! That's where the idea of conscious spending comes in.

How My Friend Spends $21,000 Per Year Going Out—Guilt-Free

I want you to consciously decide what you're going to spend on. No more "I guess I spent that much" when you see your credit card statements. No. Conscious spending means you decide exactly where you're going to spend your money—for going out, for saving, for investing, for rent—and you free yourself from feeling guilty about your spending. Along with making you feel comfortable with your spending, a plan keeps you moving toward your goals instead of just treading water.

The simple fact is that most young people are not spending consciously. We're spending on whatever, then reactively feeling good or bad about it. Every time I meet someone who has a Conscious Spending Plan ("I automatically send money to my investment and savings accounts, then spend extravagantly on the things I love"), I'm so enchanted that my love rivals Shah Jahan's for his wife, Mumtaz Mahal (look it up).

I'm going to tell you about three friends who are spending lots and lots of money on things you might consider frivolous—like shoes and going out—but whose actions are perfectly justified.

The Shoe Lover

My friend Lisa spends about $5,000/year on shoes. Because the kind of shoes she likes run more than $300, this translates to about fifteen pairs of shoes annually. "THAT'S RIDICULOUS!!!" you might be saying. And on the surface, that number is indeed large. But if you're reading this book, you can look a little deeper: This young woman makes a very healthy six-figure salary, has a roommate, eats for free at work, and doesn't spend much on fancy electronics, a gym membership, or fine dining.

Lisa loves shoes. A lot. She's funded her 401(k) and a taxable investment account (she makes too much for a Roth). She's putting away money each month for vacation and other savings goals, and giving some to charity. And she still has money left over. Now here's where it's interesting. "But, Ramit," you might say, "it doesn't matter. Three-hundred-dollar shoes are ridiculous. Nobody needs to spend that much on shoes!"

Before you chastise her for her extravagance, ask yourself these questions: Have you funded your 401(k) and Roth IRA, and opened additional investment accounts? Are you fully aware of where your spending money is going? And have you made a strategic decision to spend on what you love? Very few people decide how they want to spend their money up front. Instead they end up spending it on random things here and there, eventually watching their money trickle away. Just as important, have you decided what you don't love? For example, Lisa doesn't care about living in a fancy place, so she has a tiny room in a tiny apartment. Her decision to live in a small place means she spends $400 less every month than many of her coworkers.

After planning for her long-term and short-term goals, she has money left over to spend on the things she loves. I think she's right on.

The biggest shift for me was my mindset, specifically related to conscious spending (spending luxuriously on my priorities, scrimping on the rest) and automating my finances, which I have done. I transferred all my money into an interest-bearing account and automated all my bills. **—LISA JANTZEN, 45**

The Partier

My friend John spends more than $21,000 a year going out. "OMG, THAT'S SO MUCH *#%#%#% MONEY!" you might say. Well, let's break it down. Say he goes out four times a week—to dinners and bars—and spends an average of $100/night. I'm being conservative with the numbers here, because a dinner can run $60/person and drinks could be $15 each. I'm not including bottle service, which might cost $800 or $1,000. (He lives in a big city.)

Now, John also makes a healthy six-figure salary, so he's been able to make a Conscious Spending Plan without much difficulty. But even he has to decide what he doesn't want to spend on. For example, when his coworkers took a weekend trip to Europe (I am not kidding), he politely passed. In fact, because he works so hard, he almost never takes vacations. Similarly, because he's always at work, he doesn't care about decorating his apartment, so he's skipped virtually all decoration costs: He still has wire hangers holding up the few bargain suits that he wears, and he doesn't even own a spatula.

For John, the limiting factor is *time*. He knows he'd never send money regularly anywhere if he had to actively do it himself, so he set up his investment accounts to automatically withdraw money before he ever sees it. The key here is that John knows himself and has set up systems to support his weaknesses. In terms of spending, he works hard and plays hard, going out twice during the week and twice on the weekends. Yet, despite spending ungodly amounts at restaurants and bars, in just a couple of years John has saved more than almost any of my friends. And although $21,000 sounds outrageous on the surface, you have to take the context of his salary and priorities into consideration. Whereas other friends might spend thousands decorating their apartments or

Does Money Make Us Happy?

Yes!

I know, I know. You may have heard about a study that found money makes us happy up to $75,000, then it levels off. In reality, the 2010 study by Deaton and Kahneman found that "emotional well-being" peaks at $75,000. But if you take another measure, "life satisfaction," you find no plateau—not at $75,000, or $500,000, or even $1 million.

As Dylan Matthews notes in an excellent *Vox* article, there is strong data indicating that the more you earn, the more satisfied you are with your life. "For developing and developed countries alike, being richer is correlated with higher life satisfaction."

And if you want to know how to use money to live a happier life? Whillans et al. told the *New York Times* that "People who spent money to buy themselves time, such as by outsourcing disliked tasks, reported greater overall life satisfaction."

In short, don't believe the headlines. Money is a small, but important, part of a Rich Life. And you can strategically use it to live a more satisfied life.

taking vacations, John, after meeting his investment goals, chooses to spend that money going out.

The point here is that whether or not I agree with his choices, he's thought about it. He sat down, considered what he wanted to spend on, and is executing that plan. He's doing more than 99 percent of the young people I've talked to. If he had decided he wanted to spend $21,000/year on furry donkey costumes and Fabergé eggs, that would have been great too. At least he has a plan.

Over the last three years, I've become less guilty about buying lattes and buying lunch a few times a week because I am now conscious of where my money goes. I allocate up to $300 for eating out and coffee each month, and when I exhaust this, I turn to drinking instant coffee and packing my lunch.

—JAMES CAVALLO, 27

My Rich Life is guilt-free spending. I no longer say I can't afford X, Y, or Z. I say I choose not to spend on it. **—DONNA EADE, 36**

The Nonprofit Employee

You don't have to make a six-figure salary to be a conscious spender. My friend Julie works at a nonprofit firm in San Francisco, making about $40,000 per year, but she saves more than $6,000 per year—far more than most Americans.

She does this by being extremely disciplined: She cooks at home, shares rent in a small apartment, and uses all the benefits that her employer offers. When she's invited out to eat, she checks her envelope system (more on that on page 153) to see if she can afford it. If not, she politely declines. But when she *does* go out, she never feels guilty about spending, because she knows she can afford it. Yet it's not enough to save money on just rent and food. She also chooses to save aggressively, maxing out her Roth IRA and putting aside extra money for traveling. Each month, that money is the first to be automatically transferred out.

From talking to Julie at a party or over dinner, you would never know that she saves more than most Americans. We glibly make snap

Use Psychology Against Yourself to Save

One of my readers makes $50,000/year and, after working through some of my suggestions, realized 30 percent of her after-tax income goes to subscriptions. Subscriptions can be anything from Netflix to cell phone plans to your cable bill. They are a business's best friend: They let companies make a predictable income off you—automatically. When was the last time you scrutinized your monthly subscriptions and canceled one? Probably never. I offer you the À La Carte Method.

THE À LA CARTE METHOD takes advantage of psychology to cut our spending. Here's how it works: Cancel all the discretionary subscriptions you can: your magazines, cable—even your gym. Then, buy what you need à la carte: Instead of paying for a ton of channels you never watch on cable, buy only the episodes you watch for $2.99 each from iTunes. Buy a day pass for the gym each time you go (around $10 or $20).

The À La Carte Method works for three reasons:

1. YOU'RE PROBABLY OVERPAYING ALREADY. Most of us dramatically overestimate how much value we get from subscriptions. For example, if I asked you how many times a week you go to the gym, chances are you'd say, "Oh . . . two or three times a week." That's BS. In fact, one study showed gym members overestimate how much they'll use their membership by more than 70 percent. Members who chose a monthly fee of about $70 attended an average of 4.3 times per month. That comes out to more than $17 per gym visit—when in reality they'd have been better off buying pay-as-you-go passes for $10 each.

2. YOU'RE FORCED TO BE CONSCIOUS ABOUT YOUR SPENDING. It's one thing to passively look at your credit card bill and say, "Ah, yes, I remember that cable bill." It's quite another to spend $2.99 each time you want to buy a TV show—and when you actively think about each charge, your consumption *will* go down.

3. YOU VALUE WHAT YOU PAY FOR. You place a higher premium on the things you pay for out-of-pocket than things via subscription.

THE DOWNSIDE OF THE À LA CARTE METHOD. This method requires you to de-automate your life. This is the price you pay for saving money. Give it a shot for two months and see how it feels. If you don't like it, go back to your old subscriptions. Use this exercise to "wipe your spending slate clean"—then get creative when you rebuild it.

How to Implement the À La Carte Method:

1. Calculate how much you've spent over the last month on any discretionary subscriptions you have (for example, music subscriptions, Netflix, and the gym).

2. Cancel those subscriptions and begin buying these things à la carte.

3. In exactly one month, check and calculate how much you spent on these items over the last month. That's the descriptive part.

4. Now, get *prescriptive*. If you spent $100, try to cut it down to $90. Then $75. Not too low—you want your spending to be sustainable, and you don't want to totally lose touch with what's going on in the world. But you can control exactly how many movies you rent or how many magazines you buy, because each one comes out of your pocket.

Remember, this isn't about depriving yourself. The ideal situation is that you realize you were spending $50/month in subscriptions for stuff you didn't really want—now you can consciously reallocate that money to something you love.

Pre-IWT, my biggest mental barrier was negotiating prices. I just thought that the price of things was the price of things. The first step I took with IWT was to list my subscriptions/utilities and call and renegotiate each and every one. Looking back, this was the first time I really took the reins with my finances.

—MATT ABBOTT, 34

---

decisions about people's spending using the most cursory data: Their job and their clothes give us most of what we think we need to know to understand someone's financial situation. But Julie proves that the surface data isn't always enough. Regardless of her situation, she's chosen to put her investing and saving priorities first.

Materially, I am able to indulge my fashion habit without guilt and live in a safe, comfortable apartment. I can choose the healthiest foods and exercise routines. I've been able to quit my nine-to-five and try my hand at my own business. And my mental health (and marriage) is so much better since we are not constantly stressing about money. **—HILARY BUUCK, 34**

What They're Doing Right

The friends I wrote about above are exceptions to most people.

They have a plan. Instead of getting caught on a spending treadmill of new phones, new cars, new vacations, and new everything, they plan to spend on what's important to them and save on the rest. My shoe-loving friend lives in a microscopic room because she's hardly home, saving her hundreds per month. My partier friend uses public transportation and has exactly zero décor in his apartment. And my nonprofit friend is extraordinarily detailed about every aspect of her spending.

Each of them pays themselves first, whether it's $500/month or $2,000/month. They've built an infrastructure to do this automatically so that by the time money ends up in their checking account, they know they can spend it guilt-free. They spend less time worrying about money than most people! They already know about online savings accounts and credit cards and basic asset allocation. They're not experts—they've just got a head start.

To me, this is an enviable position to be in, and it's a big part of what *I Will Teach You to Be Rich* is about: automatically enabling yourself to save, invest, and spend—enjoying it, and not feeling guilty about those new jeans, because you're spending only what you have.

You can do it. All it takes is a plan. And it's really as simple as that.

So You Want to Judge Your Friends' Spending?

When it comes to judging our friends' spending, we look at surface characteristics and make snap judgments. "You spent $300 on jeans!" "Why do you shop at Whole Foods?" "Why did you decide to live in that expensive area?"

And, in fact, most of our judgments are right: Because young people are not carefully considering their financial choices in the context of their long-term goals—we're not paying ourselves first and we're not developing an investment/savings plan—you're probably correct when you think your friend can't afford those $300 jeans.

I've been trying to be less judgmental about this. I'm not always successful, but I now focus on the fact that the sticker price doesn't matter—it's the context around it. You want to splurge for a special tasting menu or expensive bottle of wine? And you already saved $20,000 this year at age twenty-five? Great! But if your friends are going out four times a week on a $25,000 salary, I bet they're not consciously spending.

So although it's fun to judge your friends, keep in mind that the context matters.

For more strategies on handling money and relationships, see page 292.

The *I Will Teach You to Be Rich* Conscious Spending Plan

Will you do an exercise with me? It will take about thirty seconds.

Imagine a pie chart that represents the money you earn every year. If you could wave a magic wand and divide that pie into the things you need and want to spend your money on, what would it look like? Don't worry about the exact percentages. Just think about the major categories: rent, food, transportation, maybe student loans.

What about savings and investing? Remember, for this exercise, you have a magic wand. And how about that once-in-a-lifetime trip you've always wanted to take? Put that in too.

Some readers told me this was the most challenging part of the book. But I believe it's also the most rewarding, because you get to consciously choose how you want to spend your money—and therefore, how you want to live your Rich Life.

So let's get on with the specifics of how you can make your own Conscious Spending Plan. Don't get overwhelmed by the idea that you need to create a massive budgeting system. All you need is to just get a simple version ready today and work to improve it over time.

Here's the idea: A Conscious Spending Plan involves four major buckets where your money will go: fixed costs, investments, savings, and guilt-free spending money.

CATEGORIES OF SPENDING

Fixed costs Rent, utilities, debt, etc.	50–60% of take-home pay
Investments 401(k), Roth IRA, etc.	10%
Savings goals Vacations, gifts, house down payment, emergency fund, etc.	5–10%
Guilt-free spending money Dining out, drinking, movies, clothes, shoes, etc.	20–35%

Monthly Fixed Costs

Fixed costs are the amounts you must pay, like your rent/mortgage, utilities, cell phone, and student loans. A good rule of thumb is that fixed costs should be 50 to 60 percent of your take-home pay. Before you can do anything else, you've got to figure out how much these add up to. You'd think it would be easy to figure this out, right?

Ha! It turns out this is one of the toughest questions in personal finance. To find the answer, let's walk through this step by step. Check out the chart on the next page with common basic expenses (the bare minimum that any ordinary person would use to live). If you see any glaring omissions of your major spending categories, add them. Notice that I didn't include "eating out" or "entertainment," as those come out of the guilt-free spending category. For simplicity, I also didn't include taxes (you can search for "IRS withholding calculator" to double-check the amount of taxes your employer "withholds" from each paycheck to pay your taxes). In these examples, we're just working with take-home pay.

Monthly Expense	Monthly Cost
Rent/mortgage	
Utilities	
Medical insurance and bills	
Car payment	
Public transportation	
Debt payments	
Groceries	
Clothes	
Internet/cable	

Fill in the dollar amounts you know offhand.

Now, to fill in the costs and categories you haven't yet accounted for, you're going to have to dive a little deeper. You'll need to look at your past spending to fill in all the dollar amounts and to make sure you've covered every category. Limit this to the past couple of months to keep things simple. The easiest way to get an idea of what you've spent where is to look at your credit card and banking statements. Sure, you may not capture every last expense doing it this way, but it's 85 percent of the way there, which is good enough for now.

Finally, once you've gotten all your expenses filled in, add 15 percent for expenditures you haven't counted yet. Yes, really. For example, you probably didn't capture "car repair," which can cost $400 each time (that's $33/month). Or dry cleaning or emergency medical care or charitable donations. A flat 15 percent will likely cover you for things you haven't figured in, and you can get more accurate as time goes on.

(I actually have a "stupid mistakes" category in my money system. When I first started this, I saved $20/month for unexpected expenses. Then, within two months, I had to go to the doctor for $600 and I got a traffic ticket for more than $100. That changed things quickly, and I currently save $200/month for unexpected expenses. At the end of the year, if I haven't spent it, I save half and I spend the other half.)

Once you've got a fairly accurate number here, subtract it from your take-home pay. Now you'll know how much you'll have left over to spend in the other categories—investing, saving, and guilt-free spending. Plus, you'll have an idea of a few targeted expense areas that you can cut down on to give yourself more money to save and invest.

Long-Term Investments

This bucket includes the amount you'll send to your 401(k) and Roth IRA each month. A good rule of thumb is to invest 10 percent of your take-home pay (after taxes, or the amount on your monthly paycheck) for the long term. Your 401(k) contributions count toward the 10 percent, so if you already participate in a 401(k), you'll need to add that amount to your take-home money to get a total monthly salary.

If you're not sure how much to allot to your investing bucket, open up an investment calculator from bankrate.com (try the "Investment Calculator") and enter some numbers. Experiment with contributing $100/month, $200/month, $500/month, or even $1,000/month. Assume an 8 percent return. You'll see dramatic differences over forty years.

Because most of your investments will be in tax-advantaged retirement accounts, which we'll cover in this chapter, remove the taxes to get a back-of-the-napkin calculation. Just understand that taxes ultimately will take a chunk out of your 401(k) returns. Remember, the more aggressively you save now, the more you'll have later.

Savings Goals

This bucket includes short-term savings goals (like holiday gifts and vacation), midterm savings goals (a wedding in a few years), and larger, longer-term goals (like a down payment on a house).

The 60 Percent Solution

You've heard me talk about the 85 Percent Solution, which focuses on getting most of the way there—until it's "good enough"—rather than obsessing about achieving 100 percent, getting overwhelmed, and ending up doing nothing at all. Well, Richard Jenkins, the former editor-in-chief of MSN Money, wrote an article called "The 60 Percent Solution," which suggested that you split your money into simple buckets, with the largest, basic expenses (food, bills, taxes), making up 60 percent of your gross income. The remaining 40 percent would be split four ways:

1. Retirement savings (10 percent)

2. Long-term savings (10 percent)

3. Short-term savings for irregular expenses (10 percent)

4. Fun money (10 percent)

The article has been widely distributed, although curiously, none of my friends had heard of it. My Conscious Spending Plan relates to Jenkins's 60 Percent Solution, but it's more focused toward young people. We spend a huge amount on eating out and going out, whereas our housing costs are lower because we can share apartments and rent more comfortably than older people with families.

To determine how much you should be putting away each month, check out these examples. They'll shock you:

Gifts for friends and family. Life used to be simple. The holidays meant presents for my parents and siblings. Then my family grew with nieces, nephews, and new in-laws. Suddenly I need to buy a lot more gifts every year.

Don't let things like gifts surprise you. You already know the common gifts you'll buy: holiday and birthday presents. What about anniversaries? Or special gifts like graduations?

For me, a Rich Life includes preparing for predictable expenses so they don't surprise me. Planning ahead isn't "weird," it's smart. You

How to Stop Feeling Guilty About Money

If there's one thing personal finance writers love to do, it's to make you feel guilty about spending money. I mean, have you ever read what they actually write?

"Buying a drink when you're out with friends? Why not water?"

"Going on a vacation? How about going for a walk in a public park?"

"Why would anyone need to get new jeans? Stains show character."

If they had it their way, we'd all be subsistence farmers growing grain in our backyards. Listen, I love *The Grapes of Wrath* as much as anyone, but that's not the kind of life I want.

Hilariously, the newest trend for personal finance writers is to take a single expense, extrapolate how much that would be worth if you invested that money for forty years, and then try to make you feel guilty.

For example, if you saved the money you were planning to spend on a $2,000 vacation and invested it for forty years, that would be worth over $40,000.

I mean, I guess that's true. Just like I guess the next time I go to the beach, I could collect the seawater in a thermos, walk it five hundred miles to a desalination plant, and beg the guy at the front desk to do me a favor and clean the water for me. Hey, why not?

You think I'm joking? One *USA Today* writer wrote an article called "How much for a sandwich? Try $90,000 in lost savings."

When it comes to your Rich Life, if you're counting pennies or calculating a sandwich as being worth $90,000, you've taken a very wrong turn somewhere.

There are real ramifications of reading these articles for decades and decades. You start to believe it. You start to think the only way to manage money is to hoard it and create an increasingly long list of noes. Soon, the guilt isn't just coming from money experts and the outside world. It's coming from you.

For example, I know TONS of IWT readers who earn over $200,000/

year and cannot bring themselves to spend money on themselves. They find it "wasteful" to eat out at a nice restaurant even once every six months.

THEY'VE CREATED THEIR OWN PRISON OF FRUGALITY. You don't want to end up like this person writing on the financial independence subreddit. *"Looking back at the past few years of my life and at my bank account, I would gladly give away a hefty chunk of it and work longer if it meant I could have experienced more of the world and found more passions. I built my savings, but I never built my life."*

Do you notice how so many money experts use words like "worry," "fear," and "guilt"? How they start their advice by telling you all the things you can't do with your money? They're all playing defense.

I have a different approach.

I believe that if you get the Big Wins in life right, you'll never have to worry about the price of lunch. Better yet, you won't even have to put "worry" and "guilt" in the same sentence as "money." You'll have guilt-free money that you can spend on anything you want. And not just a sandwich. Unforgettable vacations, amazing gifts for your friends, security for yourself and your family—you decide. *Guilt-free.*

already know you're going to buy Christmas gifts every December! Plan for it in January.

Now let me show you how to apply this principle to even bigger expenses.

Your wedding (whether you're engaged or not). The average wedding costs over $30,000—and in my experience, once you factor all expenses in, it's closer to $35,000. (To be more precise, Will Oremus writes in *Slate*, "In 2012, when the average wedding cost was $27,427, the median was $18,086. In Manhattan, where the widely reported average is $76,687, the median is $55,104." From a financial perspective, I always assume the worst, so I can plan conservatively. And as someone who planned a large wedding with my wife, I know how phantom expenses can easily push that number higher than you anticipate.)

So let's use $30,000 as an average number for easy math.

Because we know the average ages when people get married, you can figure out exactly how much you need to be saving, assuming you want to pay for it without help or debt: If you're twenty-five years old, you need to be saving more than $1,000/month for your wedding. If you're twenty-six, you should be saving more than $2,500/month. (I cover financing weddings, including my own, in detail on page 296.)

> *The biggest piece of advice I have used is to cut mercilessly on what is not important to me and to not feel guilty spending on what is since I have budgeted for it. I don't spend my money on cable or having a fancy new car and trendy clothes, but I do spend on traveling and have saved a good amount of money for a wedding and down payment on a house when I am ready for those steps.*
> **—JESSICA FITZER, 28**

Buying a house. If you're thinking about buying a house in a few years, log on to zillow.com and check home prices in your area. Let's just say the average house in your neighborhood costs $300,000 and you want to do a traditional 20 percent down payment. That's $60,000, so if you want to buy a house in five years, you should be saving $1,000/month.

Crazy, right? Nobody thinks like this, but it's truly eye-opening when you plot out your future spending for the next few years. It can almost seem overwhelming, but there's good news: First, the longer you have to save for these things, the less you have to save each month. If you instead decide to wait for ten years to buy a house, you'd only need to save $500/month for your down payment. But time can also work against you: If you started saving for an average wedding at age twenty, you would have to save about $333/month. By age twenty-six, however, you'd have to save $2,333/month. Second, we often get help: Our spouse or parents may be able to chip in—but you can't count on someone else coming to rescue you. Third, theoretically you could use some of your investment money to pay for these savings goals. It's not ideal, but you can do it.

Regardless of exactly what you're saving for, a good rule of thumb is to save 5 to 10 percent of your take-home pay to meet your goals.

Guilt-Free Spending Money

After all that spending, investing, and saving, this bucket contains the fun money—the stuff you can use for anything you want, guilt-free. Money here covers things like restaurants and bars, taxis, movies, and vacations.

Depending on how you've structured your other buckets, a good rule of thumb here is to use 20 percent to 35 percent of your take-home income for guilt-free spending money.

Optimizing Your Conscious Spending Plan

Now that you've worked out the basics of your Conscious Spending Plan, you can make some targeted improvements to tweak your spending and make your money go where you want it to go. Instead of having this dull, throbbing cloud of worry over your head—"I know I'm spending too much"—your plan will serve as a living, breathing system that signals you when something's broken. If the alarm bells aren't going off, you don't need to waste time worrying.

Go for Big Wins

Optimizing your spending can seem overwhelming, but it doesn't have to be. You can do an 80/20 analysis, which often reveals that 80 percent of what you overspend is used toward only 20 percent of your expenditures. That's why I prefer to focus on one or two big problem areas and solve those instead of trying to cut 5 percent out of a bunch of smaller areas.

Here's how I do this with my own spending. Over time, I've found that most of my expenses are predictable. I spend the same amount on rent every month, roughly the same on my subway pass, and even basically the same monthly amount on gifts (averaged out over a year).

Since I know the annual average, I don't need to waste time agonizing over a $12 movie ticket I buy here or there.

But I *do* want to zoom in on those two or three spending areas that vary wildly—and that I want to control.

For me, it's eating out, travel, and clothes. Depending on the time of year—or how nice a cashmere sweater I found—those numbers can vary by thousands of dollars a month.

My Tools of the Trade

'm often asked what tools I use to manage my finances.

The simplest way to start is to use Mint (mint.com), which will automatically sync with your credit card and banks to categorize your spending and show you trends. Mint is a great way to get a feel for your spending without much work, but you'll quickly see that Mint has its limitations.

To get more prescriptive about your spending, I recommend using a piece of software called You Need a Budget (youneedabudget.com) or YNAB (I know, the name is ironic in this chapter where I talk about how I hate budgets). YNAB lets you assign every dollar a "job," like "cell phone bill" or "guilt-free spending." Use it for two weeks—just two—and you'll get incredible insight into your spending.

Finally, at a certain point, you'll have investments in various accounts—a few thousand dollars in your last company's 401(k), a couple thousand bucks in an old Roth IRA, etc. You'll want to get a bird's-eye view of all your investments and see your overall asset allocation.

Some people use Personal Capital (personalcapital.com) but I just use my Vanguard account. Every major brokerage account lets you add outside investments for a unified view.

My system has changed since the first edition of this book. I used to use Mint, but then Intuit bought it and let it deteriorate, so now I don't use it (and after you use it for a few weeks and get familiar with your spending, neither should you). My next step was to use YNAB, which is much better.

I also used to track my cash spending by hand. Because I rarely spend cash anymore—it's pretty much only for tips—I don't do that. Instead, I looked at how much cash I spent over six months, averaged it, and set it as a line item in my Conscious Spending Plan, and now I don't need to track it. I know that over a month or two, I'll be within a few dollars of my average cash spend.

Finally, as I've gotten more experienced, I now know that there are only a few areas of significant fluctuation in my spending—eating out, travel, and clothes. Those are "key areas" that I keep an eye on, which I'll show you how to in the next few pages.

For investing—specifically, for my asset allocation—I use Vanguard. As my net worth has increased, I enlisted the help of a "Personal CFO" who can report my key numbers once a month. (More on this in my course, Advanced Personal Finances, on my website.)

I use myfico.com to get my credit score and report each year. Yes, I could get it for free, but this is more convenient for me.

To run calculations on investment scenarios, I use the calculators at bankrate.com.

Finally, I don't know about you, but I have a true hatred of paper catalogs and bills. To cut back on mail, I've opted out of credit card offers at optoutprescreen.com, and I use a service called Catalog Choice (catalogchoice.org) to keep from getting unwanted catalogs in the mail.

So that's where I focus.

To run an 80/20 analysis yourself, do a Google search for "conducting a Pareto analysis."

Let's take an example: Brian takes home $48,000 per year after taxes, or $4,000/month. According to his Conscious Spending Plan, here's how his spending should look:

- Monthly fixed costs (60 percent): $2,400

- Long-term investments (10 percent): $400/month

- Savings goals (10 percent): $400/month

- Guilt-free spending money (20 percent): $800/month

Brian's problem is that $800 isn't enough for his spending money. When he looks at what he spent for the last couple of months, he finds that he actually needs $1,050 every month for spending money. What should he do?

Bad answer: Most people just shrug and say, "I dunno," while stuffing their face with an English muffin and then logging onto reddit to complain about the economy. They've never thought about getting ahead of their money, so this is totally foreign to them.

Slightly better, but still a bad answer: Brian can decrease his contributions to his long-term investments and savings goals. Sure, he could do that, but it will cost him down the line.

A better way is to tackle the two most problematic areas in his monthly spending: monthly fixed costs and guilt-free spending money.

Good answer: Brian decides to pick his three biggest expenses and optimize them. First, he looks at his monthly fixed costs and realizes that because he's been consistently paying the minimum monthly payment on his credit card debt at 18 percent, he has $3,000 of debt left. Under his current plan, it will take him about twenty-two years and cost him $4,115 in interest to pay off his debt. But he can call his credit card company to request a lower interest rate (see page 40 for details). With his new lower credit card APR of 15 percent, it will take him eighteen years and he'll pay $2,758 in interest. He saves fifty-three months and $1,357 of payments. That's only $6/month, but over eighteen years it adds up to a lot.

Next, he checks his subscriptions and realizes he's been paying for a Netflix account and a Star Wars membership site, both of which he rarely uses. He cancels them, saving $60/month and increasing his chances of getting a girlfriend.

Finally, he logs in to his money management account at YNAB and realizes that he's spending $350 eating out each month, plus $250 at bars—$600 in total. He decides that over the next three months, he'll ratchet that amount down to $400/month, saving him $200/month.

Total amount saved: $260/month. By adjusting his spending, Brian was able to create a Conscious Spending Plan that works for him.

Brian was smart to focus on changing the things that mattered. Instead of promising that he'd stop spending money on Cokes every time he ate out, he picked the Big Wins that would really make an impact on his total dollar amount. You'll see this a lot: People will get really inspired to budget and decide to stop spending on things like appetizers with dinner. Or they'll buy generic cookies. That's nice—and I definitely encourage you to do that—but those small changes will have very little effect on your total spending. They serve more to make people feel good about themselves, which lasts only a few weeks once they realize they still don't have any more money.

Try focusing on Big Wins that will make a large, measurable change.

I focus on my critical two or three Big Wins each month: eating out, clothes, and travel. You probably know what your Big Wins are. They're the expenses you cringe at, the ones you shrug and roll your eyes at, and say, "Yeah, I probably spend too much on _____."

Set Realistic Goals

In my business, we create video courses on self-development in areas like personal finance, starting a business, and psychology. A while back, we were testing a fitness program. We enrolled dozens of beta students and worked to help them lose weight.

Here was a common situation: John was forty-five pounds overweight, he ate poorly and hadn't worked out in years, and he was ready to make a change. So ready, in fact, that he told us he wanted to cut his calories by 50 percent and start working out five times a week.

"Whoa, whoa," we told him. "Let's take it slow." But he insisted on going from zero to five workouts overnight.

Predictably, he dropped out within three weeks.

Do you know people who get so obsessed with something new that they go completely overboard and burn out? I would rather do less but make it sustainable.

I once had a woman who emailed me saying, "I always tell myself I want to run three times a week, but I never go." I wrote back and said,

Big Win: No More Fees

I recently had breakfast with someone who told me the most interesting story. He'd been dating his girlfriend for two years before they talked about finances. "It took me that long to gain her trust," he said. She was a schoolteacher with a modest salary. When he looked at her finances, he noticed that she had a lot of overdraft fees. He asked her to estimate how much she had spent on these fees. "About $100 or $200?" she guessed.

It turns out that her overdraft fees had totaled $1,300 in the last year.

Did he freak out or start yelling about how to negotiate out of bank fees? No, he simply pointed out something very gently: "What if you focused on your overdrafts? If you eliminated just those fees, you'd be so much better off." Simply avoiding overdraft fees was a Big Win for her.

"What about going for a run once a week?" She replied, "Once a week? What's the point?"

She would rather *dream* about running three times a week than *actually* run once a week.

This idea of sustainable change is central to personal finance. Sometimes I get emails from people who say things like, "Ramit! I started managing my money! Before, I was spending $500 a week! Now I only spend $5 and I save the rest!" I read this and just sigh. Although you might expect me to get really excited about someone contributing $495/month to their savings, I've come to realize that when a person goes from one extreme to another, the behavioral change rarely lasts.

This is why I just shake my head when I see personal finance pundits giving families advice to go from a zero percent savings rate to a 25 percent savings rate ("You can do it!!!"). Giving that kind of advice is not useful. Habits don't change overnight, and if they do, chances are they won't be sustainable.

When I make a change, I almost always make it a bite-sized one in an area that matters (see my discussion of Big Wins on page 147) and work in increments from there. For example, if I started keeping track of my expenses and discovered I was short $1,000/month (this happens more than you'd think), I'd pick the two Big Wins—two items that I spend a lot on but know I could cut down with some effort—and focus my efforts on them. Say I was spending about $500/month eating out, here's how it would look:

Month 1: .... $475 on eating out
Month 2: .... $450 on eating out
Month 3: .... $400 on eating out
Month 4: .... $350 on eating out
Month 5: .... $300 on eating out
Month 6: .... $250 on eating out

It's not a race, but within six months, I'd have cut my eating out spending *in half*. Apply that same spending to a second Big Win and we're talking about hundreds of dollars of savings per month. And it'd be much more likely to be sustainable.

The other way to do it is to look at your current spending, freak out, and cut half your total spending. Then you're suddenly forced to spend in a completely different way, without the means to cope. How long do you think your ambitious spending goal will last?

How many times have you heard friends say something like, "I'm not going to drink for a month"? I don't understand the point of short-term whims like that. A month from now, okay, you spent only 50 percent of what you normally do. And . . . then what? If you can't keep it up and you bounce right back to your normal spending habits, what did you really accomplish? I'd rather have people cut their spending by 10 percent and sustain it for thirty years than cut 50 percent for just a month.

Whether you're implementing a change in your personal finances, eating habits, exercise plan, or whatever . . . try making the smallest change today. Something you'll hardly notice. And follow your own plan for gradually increasing it. In this way, time is your friend, because each month gets better than the one before it, and it adds up to a lot in the end.

Use the Envelope System to Target Your Big Wins

All this conscious spending and optimizing sounds nice in theory, but how do you do it? I recommend the envelope system, in which you allocate money for certain categories like eating out, shopping, rent, and so on. Once you spend the money for that month, that's it: You can't spend more. If it's really an emergency, you can dip into other envelopes— like your "eating out" envelope—but you'll have to cut back until you replenish that envelope. These "envelopes" can be figurative (like in YNAB or even Excel) or literally envelopes that you put cash in. This is the best system I've found for keeping spending simple and sustainable.

One of my friends, for example, has been carefully watching her spending for the last few months. When she started tracking it, she noticed that she was spending an unbelievable amount going out every week. So she came up with a clever solution to control her discretionary spending. She set up a separate bank account with a debit card. At the beginning of each month, she transfers, let's say, $200 into it. When she goes out, she spends that money. And when it's gone, it's gone.

These are training wheels. Build the habit first. Systematize it later.

Tip: If you set up a debit account like this, tell your bank that you don't want them to allow you to spend more than you have in your

The Envelope System

1. Decide how much you want to spend in major categories each month. (Not sure? Start with one: Eating out.)

2. Put money in each envelope (category).

$200	$150	$60
Groceries	Eating out	Entertainment

3. You can transfer from one envelope to another . . .

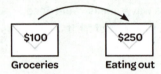

$100	$250
Groceries	Eating out

. . . but when the envelopes are empty, that's it for the month.

account. Say, "If I have only thirty dollars in my account and I try to charge thirty-five dollars on my debit card, I don't want your system to let me." Some banks can handle this request. If you don't do this, you'll likely run up tons of overdraft fees.

Whatever system you want to use to divvy up the money is fine. Just decide how much you want to spend in major categories each month. (Pick your Big Wins to start.) Put the allotted money in each "envelope." When the envelopes are empty, that's it for the month. You can transfer from one envelope to another . . . but that money is coming out of another category, so your total spending doesn't actually increase.

Some of my nerdier friends even get more detailed with their systems. One of my readers created this table:

	Eating out	Taxis	Books
Times per month	12	8	5
Amount per event	$23	$9	$17

"Each month, I try to cut the quantity and amount I spend on something," he told me. In less than eight months, he cut his spending by 43 percent (he knew the exact figure, of course). In my opinion, that level of analysis is overkill for most people, but it shows how detailed you can get once you set up a Conscious Spending Plan.

What If You Don't Make Enough Money?

D epending on your financial situation, setting up a workable Conscious Spending Plan may seem out of reach for you. Some people have already cut their spending to the bone and still don't have any extra money. For me to suggest that they put away 10 percent for retirement is, frankly, insulting. How can they be expected to contribute 10 percent toward long-term savings when they don't have enough to fill the car with gas?

Sometimes this is reality, and sometimes it's perception. Many of the people who've written me saying they live paycheck to paycheck actually have more wiggle room in their budgets than they think (cooking instead of eating out, for example, or not buying a new cell phone every year). They just don't *want* to change their spending.

However, it's true that many people really cannot afford to cut more spending and really are living check to check. If you simply can't cut more out of your budget, this spending plan may be a useful theoretical guide, but you have more important concerns: making more money. There's a limit to how much you can cut, but no limit to how much you can earn. Once you increase your earnings, you can use the Conscious Spending Plan as your guide. Until then, here are three strategies you can use to earn more.

Negotiate a Raise

If you already have a job, it's a no-brainer to negotiate for a raise.

The Society for Human Resource Management (SHRM) notes that the average cost per hire is $4,425. If they've already spent nearly $5,000 recruiting you, and thousands more training you, would they really want to lose you?

Asking for a raise takes careful planning. Don't do what my friend Jamie did. When he realized he was being drastically underpaid for his contributions, he seethed without taking any action for more than two months. When he finally got up the courage to ask his boss for a raise, he said it in the most timid way: "Do you think I might possibly ask you about a raise?" If you're a manager, the first thing you'd think is, "Oh God, not another thing in my day." Jamie's boss brushed him off, leaving Jamie frustrated and underpaid.

Remember that getting a raise is not about you. It's about you demonstrating your value to your employer. You can't tell them you need more money because your expenses are higher. Nobody cares. You *can*, however, show how your work has been contributing to the company's success and ask to be compensated fairly. Here's what you need to do:

Three to six months before your review: Become a top performer by collaboratively setting expectations with your boss, then exceeding those expectations in every way possible.

One to two months before your review: Prepare a "briefcase" of evidence to support the exact reasons why you should be given a raise.

One to two weeks before your review: Extensively practice the conversation you'll have with your boss, experimenting with the right tactics and scripts.

Three to six months before you ask for a raise, sit down with your boss and ask what it would take to be a top performer at your company. Get crystal clear about what you'd need to deliver. And ask how being a top performer would affect your compensation.

Set up the meeting:

Hi Boss,

How are you? Hope you had a great New Year's! I'm really excited to kick things off this year, especially with our new X and Y projects coming up.

I really want to do an exceptional job, and I'd like to chat with you for a few minutes about how I can be a top performer. I have some ideas of my own, but I'd love to get your guidance as well. Would a 15-minute chat next week be okay? If so, how about I swing by your desk Monday morning at 10 a.m.?

Thanks,

Your Name

Notice how gradual this process is. You're not coming straight out and asking for a raise. You're not even asking what it takes to be a top performer. You're simply asking for the meeting.

In the meeting:

YOU: Hi Boss, thanks for taking the time to meet with me. As I mentioned, I've been doing a lot of thinking about the position and what I can do to really be a top performer this year, and I'd like to discuss that with you if that's okay.

BOSS: *Sure.*

YOU: So the way I see it, my role in the position can be broken down into three main areas: A, B, and C. I think I'm doing pretty well with A, and I'm picking up B pretty rapidly. And I need a little help with C, as we've discussed before. Does that sound about right to you?

BOSS: *Yes, that sounds right.*

YOU: I've been thinking a lot about these three areas and how I can really take them to the next level. I have some initial thoughts of my own, and I'd be happy to talk about those, but I'd actually like to get your thoughts first. In your eyes, what would be the most meaningful things I can do in these three areas to really be considered a top performer?

BOSS: *Hm . . . I'm not really sure. Maybe blah, blah, and blah.*

YOU: Yeah, I agree—we're on the same page here. So here's what I was thinking: Specifically, I'd like to achieve goals A, B, and C, and I'd like to do all this in six months. That's pretty aggressive, but I think it's doable. Would you agree that's something that you'd like to see from me, and that it would also help peg me as a top performer?

BOSS: *Yes, it would. That sounds perfect.*

YOU: Okay, great. I really appreciate it, Boss. So I'll get to work on this and keep you in the loop with a status update every four weeks as usual. The last thing I'd like to talk about is: If I do an extraordinary job, then at the end of the six months all I ask is that we sit down to discuss a possible compensation adjustment. But let's cross that bridge when we get to it, OK?

BOSS: *Sounds fine. Looking forward to seeing what you can do.*

YOU: Great. I'll type up these notes and send them to you. Thanks again!

You've made it clear what you want: to be a top performer. You've enlisted your boss's help on getting specific about what that means. You've also taken the initiative to follow up—in writing—to clarify those goals.

Now it's time to deliver. Start tracking everything you do at work and the results you get. If you were on a team that sold 25,000 widgets, figure out what you did to help make that happen and, as much as possible, quantify it. If you can't figure out the exact results you're driving, ask someone at work who's more experienced and knows how to tie your work to company results.

Be sure to keep your boss in the loop so he or she knows how you're progressing. Managers don't love surprises; they love brief status updates roughly every week or two.

Approximately two months before you ask for a raise, meet with your boss again and demonstrate your tracking from the previous month. Ask what you could do better. You want to know if you're on the right track with your work, and it's important that you regularly communicate your progress.

One month before the big event, mention to your boss that because you've been doing so well, you'd like to discuss compensation at a meeting the next month. Ask what you'll need to bring to make it a fruitful discussion. Listen very carefully to what he or she says.

Around this time, it wouldn't hurt to ask your fellow coworkers to put in a good word with the boss. This assumes, of course, that you've been exceeding expectations and driving concrete results. I learned this technique from a Stanford professor of mine, who put in a good word to an admissions committee for me. Here's what a sample coworker email could look like:

Hi Boss,

I wanted you to know how much of an impact [Your Name] is having on the Acme project. She managed to convince our vendor to cut their fees by 15 percent, which saved us $8,000. And she's running two weeks ahead of schedule, which speaks to her ability to stay organized and keep us on track.

Thanks,

Awesome Coworker

Now you've set the stage.

Two weeks before you ask for a raise, ask a couple of friends to role-play your job negotiation. This seems really weird, but negotiating is *not* a natural behavior. It will feel extremely odd and uncomfortable the first couple of times you do it. Better to do it for the first time with friends since you'll eventually be negotiating with your boss. And pick good friends—people who have business experience and will give you feedback on how you performed.

Specifically, while I'm hoping your boss immediately recognizes your work and agrees to a raise, sometimes it isn't that easy. Prepare for the following scenarios:

- **"You didn't hit those goals."** If you genuinely didn't hit your goals, you should have communicated that earlier and decided on a

Cool Trick: Quickly Discover How Much You Make

To find your annual salary, just take your hourly rate, double it, and add three zeros to the end. If you make $20/hour, you make approximately $40,000/year. If you make $30/hour, you make approximately $60,000/year.

This also works in reverse. To find your hourly rate, divide your salary by two and drop the three zeros. So $50,000/year becomes approximately $25/hour.

This is based on a general forty-hour workweek and doesn't include taxes or benefits, but it's a good general back-of-the-napkin trick. And it's very useful when you're deciding whether to buy something or not. If that pair of pants is going to cost you eight hours of work, is it worth it?

plan of action with your boss. But if your boss is simply using this as an excuse—to obfuscate what the goals were, or to move the goalposts—here's your response: "If there are areas for me to grow, I'd love to discuss them. But on [date], you and I agreed to these goals. And I've sent you a weekly update since then. I'm all for exceeding goals—which I've done, as you can see from [Specific Project]—but I want to be compensated in good faith."

- **"I didn't agree to a raise."** Your response: "That is true. But as we discussed on [date], we both agreed that if I hit these goals, I'd be considered a top performer—and that we'd discuss a compensation adjustment in the future." (Pull out a printout of the email chain.)

- **"We can discuss this another time."** Your response: "I understand if there's a timeline for raises and we're off cycle. But I've put six months of work in to hit these goals and I've updated you along the way. I plan to continue exceeding my goals, but I'd like to get clear that I'm on track for a raise on our next cycle—in writing."

On the day you negotiate, come in with your salary, a couple of competitive salaries from salary.com and payscale.com, and your list of accomplishments, and be ready to discuss fair compensation. Remember, you're not asking your mommy for lemonade; you're a professional who's asking to be compensated fairly. You want to proceed as partners, as in "How do we make this work?"

This is the culmination of all your preparation and hard work. You can do this!

If you get the raise you were looking for, congratulations! That was a huge first step toward increasing your income. If you don't, ask your boss what you can do to excel in your career, or consider leaving to find another company that will give you greater room to grow.

Get a Higher-Paying Job

This takes us to the second way to increase your income. If you find that your existing company doesn't offer you growth potential, or you're in the process of getting a new job, negotiating your salary will never be easier. During the job hiring process, you have more leverage than you'll ever have.

I cover negotiating a new salary in detail on page 307.

Do Freelance Work

One of the best ways to earn more is to start freelancing. A simple example is becoming an Uber driver, but go deeper. Think about what skills or interests you have that others could use. You don't necessarily have to have a technical skill. Babysitting is an example of freelancing (and it pays very well). If you have free time at home, you can sign up to be a virtual assistant on sites like upwork.com.

When you embrace the idea that you can earn more, one of the biggest surprises you'll discover is that you already possess skills others would pay for—and you've never even realized it. In my business, we built an entire course around this, called Earn1K, and I absolutely love highlighting the different ideas that my students turned into profitable businesses.

For example, one of my readers, Ben, loves to dance. Through our Earn1K course, he learned how to turn that skill into a business of teaching men how to dance. Soon after he launched his business, *Good Morning America* called to feature him.

And then there's Julia, a caricature artist who was charging $8 per hour to draw faces. We showed her how to turn that into a six-figure business.

There are thousands of other possibilities, even ones as simple as tutoring and dog walking. Remember, busy people want others to help them with their lives. A great place to start is the jobs section on craigslist.

If you have expertise in something, reach out to companies who might need someone like you. For example, when I was in high school, I emailed fifty websites from different industries that looked interesting but had poor marketing and copywriting. I offered to help them rewrite their websites. About fifteen responded, and I ended up editing copy for one company that eventually promoted me to run their sales department.

Later, during college, I consulted for venture capitalists, teaching them about marketing with email and social media. This is stuff you and I know like the backs of our hands, but it was new to these VCs—and valuable enough that they paid a great consulting fee.

Maintaining Your Spending Plan

Once you've done what you can to design and implement a Conscious Spending Plan that you're comfortable with, give yourself some time to settle into a rhythm with it. Sure, eventually you can spend your time on strategic money decisions— "Should I be contributing 10 percent or 12 percent to my monthly savings goals?"—but first, you've got to get the basics down. As you go along from month to month with this new system, you'll discover some surprises you hadn't anticipated.

You'll always have unexpected cash expenses, like having to take a cab or needing an umbrella when you forgot yours. And don't flip out if you miss tracking a few dollars here or there—the minute your system becomes too oppressive for you to use is the minute you stop using it. I try to make as many purchases on my credit card as possible so the spending is automatically recorded in my software (whether you're using YNAB, Mint, or another tool). I try to minimize cash spending altogether. After years of tracking my spending, I know how much I spend in cash every month, on average. I record the average monthly amount in my Conscious Spending Plan and move on.

Like anything, this takes time in the beginning, but it gets much easier. Make tracking your spending a weekly priority. For example, set aside thirty minutes for it every Sunday afternoon.

How to Handle Unexpected and Irregular Expenses

It can be frustrating to have a spending plan that keeps getting disrupted by surprise expenses like wedding gifts, car repairs, and late fees. So another key to having a plan you'll use is to account for the unexpected and build in a bit of flexibility.

Known irregular events (vehicle registration fees, Christmas gifts, vacations). There's an easy way to account for this type of irregular event. In fact, this is already built into your spending plan: Under savings goals, allocate money toward goals where you have a general idea of how much it will cost. It doesn't have to be exact, but try to get a ballpark figure and then save every month toward that goal. For example, if you know you'll have to spend about $500 on Christmas gifts, start saving $42/month (that's $500 divided by twelve months) in January. By the time December rolls around, you won't have to take a huge hit on your spending.

Unknown irregular events (surprise medical expenses or traffic tickets). These types of surprises fall under your monthly fixed expenses, because no matter how hard you try to avoid them, there will always be unexpected expenses. Earlier, I suggested that you add about 15 percent to your estimate of your fixed costs to accommodate these surprises. In addition, I recommend starting by allocating $50/month for unexpected expenses. You'll soon realize that this cartoonishly low figure is not enough. But with some time, you'll have a better idea of what the figure should actually be and can change the amount accordingly. As a fun incentive to myself, if I still had money left over in the account by the end of the year, I'd save half of it—and spend half on something fun.

	Regular	Irregular
Known	• Rent • Loan payments • Utilities	• Christmas gifts • Vehicle registration
Unknown	• I guess if you're a gambling addict, you could classify your losses here.	• Wedding gifts • Medical expenses • Traffic tickets

Fortunately, with each month that goes by, you'll get a more accurate picture of your spending. After about a year or two (remember, think long term), you'll have a very accurate understanding of how to project. The beginning is hard, but it only gets easier.

The "Problem" of Extra Income

Just as there are surprise expenses, there is also surprise income. It's tempting to take a windfall and blow it all on something fun, but I urge you not to follow that instinct. Instead, work within your Conscious Spending Plan.

Unexpected one-time income. Sometimes money falls in your lap, like a birthday gift, a tax return, or an unexpected freelance contract. Believe it or not, I don't encourage you to save all of this money. Instead, whenever I receive money I didn't expect, I use 50 percent of it for fun—usually buying something I've been eyeing for a long time. Always! This way, I keep motivating myself to pursue weird, offbeat ideas that may result in some kind of reward. The other half goes to my investing account. Compare this with not having a plan and letting your money "just sort of" get spent. Handling unexpected one-time income like this—consciously—is so much more meaningful in the short term and long term.

Raises. A raise is different from one-time income because you'll get it consistently, and it's therefore much more important to do the right thing financially. There's one key thing to remember when you get a raise: It's okay to increase your standard of living a little—but bank the rest. For example, if you get a $4,000 raise, take $1,000 and spend it! But save or invest the remaining $3,000. It's too easy to think a single raise lets you move up to a totally different financial level in a single step.

If you get a raise, be realistic: You earned it, and you should enjoy the results of your hard work. Treat yourself to something nice that you've been wanting for a long time, and make it something you'll remember. After that, however, I strongly encourage you to save and invest as much of it as possible, because once you start getting accustomed to a certain lifestyle, you can never go back. After buying a Mercedes, can you ever drive a Toyota Corolla again?

Working retail for five years I made a goal of saving up $10,000 to be able to invest in the stock market. I decided everything I saved before the age of twenty-eight was available for me to fiddle with stocks; everything after twenty-eight was to be put in a blend of investment funds safe from my amateur investing styles. I was able to accomplish saving up $10,000 on a meager retail wage by putting half of every raise into my 401(k) plan. Every 4 percent raise was a 2 percent raise to my retirement plan.

—JASON HENRY, 33

The Beauty of a Conscious Spending Plan

The best part about setting up a strategic Conscious Spending Plan is that *it* guides your decisions, letting you say no much more easily— "Sorry, it's not in my plan this month"—and freeing you up to enjoy what you do spend on. This is guilt-free spending at its best. Sure, there will be tough decisions. Deciding to change the way you spend is the most difficult part of this book. It involves making choices and saying no to certain things. Your system, however, makes this much less painful. If a friend asks you out to dinner and you don't have enough spending money left, it will be easier to politely pass. After all, it's not personal— it's just your *system*. Remember that most people are, by definition, ordinary. They go through their lives feeling a gnawing sense that they "should" do something about their money—tomorrow. Most don't think about saving until their mid-forties. And yet, you are now extraordinary, because you see that setting up a simple system will let you make the tough decisions up front and spend your money guilt-free.

ACTION STEPS

WEEK FOUR

1 Get your paycheck, determine what you've been spending, and figure out what your Conscious Spending Plan should look like (thirty minutes). Do this now and don't overthink it. Just break your take-home income into chunks of fixed costs (50–60 percent), long-term investments (10 percent), savings goals (5–10 percent), and guilt-free spending money (20–35 percent). How does it fit?

2 Optimize your spending (two hours). Dig deeper into your savings goals and monthly fixed costs. Try the À La Carte Method. How much does your insurance actually cost—can you improve on that? How much will you spend for Christmas gifts and vacation this year? Break these expenses down into monthly chunks, then recalculate your plan.

3 **Pick your Big Wins (five hours).** Open an account at You Need a Budget or Personal Capital. Assuming you want to cut your spending by $200/month, what one or two Big Wins will you target? Start using the envelope system.

4 **Maintain your Conscious Spending Plan (one hour per week).** Enter any cash receipts into your system each week. Tweak the percentages you send to each part of your spending plan (we'll cover this in detail in the next chapter). And most important, make sure your system is realistic enough that you'll stick with it for the long term.

All right, deep breath. You did it. You made it through the most difficult part of the book! Now you've got a strategic spending plan. You no longer have to constantly worry about how much money you're spending. Phrases like "Can I afford this?" and "I know I'm going to worry about this later, but for now . . ." will be erased from your vocabulary. Now we're going to automate this system so each new dollar that comes into it gets instantly sent to the right area, whether it's fixed costs, investments, savings, or guilt-free spending.

CHAPTER 5

SAVE WHILE SLEEPING

Making your accounts work together—automatically

Y ou know the way you look at cute newborn babies, with their tiny little hands and big eyes? The cute little sneezes, the pure, innocent smiles?

That's how I look at systems. I see beauty in systems, like the one I lovingly built to apply to sixty-five scholarships and pay my way through undergrad and grad school at Stanford. Or the system I built to read two thousand emails a day, or to make sure my plants get watered when I go on vacation.

You might not relate to an intimate love of systems—yet. But by the end of this chapter, you're going to.

That's because automating your money will be the single most profitable system you ever build. I built my own automated personal finance system over fifteen years ago, and since then, it's run in the background every single day, generating more and more money and requiring almost no time to maintain.

You can do this too and completely change the way you think about saving, investing, and even spending. Other people sigh and say, "I need to buckle down and save more" (though they almost never do). That's playing defense.

Instead, we're going to play offense by building a system that acknowledges our normal human behavior—we get bored, distracted, and unmotivated—and uses technology to ensure we're still growing our money.

In other words, do the work now and benefit forever—automatically! You're in control.

You might say, "That's all well and good if you have a consistent income." But what if your income is irregular? I know freelancers who earn $12,000 in a single month . . . then don't have another client for three months. How are you supposed to automate your finances when your income is so spiky? (I've got you covered on page 181.)

In the last chapter, you set up a Conscious Spending Plan to determine how much you want to spend in each category (fixed costs, investments, savings goals, and guilt-free spending money). You didn't think you'd have to manually transfer money each month, did you? Not a chance. In this chapter, we'll create an Automatic Money Flow to manage your money for you. It will take the accounts you've set up—your credit cards and your checking, savings, and investment accounts—and create automatic transfers so your money goes where it needs to go.

I automated most of my finances so that I didn't really need to worry about budgeting each month. The biggest accomplishment for me is not having to think about finances each week. I probably review my investments and think about my spending habits a few times a year. **—JENNA CHRISTENSEN, 26**

Do More Before Doing Less

I don't know about you, but I plan to do less and less work as I go through my life. When I meet people on a career path that will have them working more, not less, I'm always puzzled. That's like being a real-life Mario Brother, where every level you beat means your life gets progressively more difficult. Why would you want that?

That's why I love systems: You front-load the work now, then you get to benefit for years and years. By investing a little now, we don't have to invest a lot later. Of course, that's easier said than done. Somehow we just never get around to consistently managing our money—and let's be honest: That will never change. Because who really cares about managing money? It's about as appealing as cleaning the garage . . . every week for the rest of your life. We dream of having an automated system that handles most of our to-dos for us; something that just works.

You can make this dream come true if you follow my advice about automating. This is all driven by a principle I'll call the Curve of Doing More Before Doing Less:

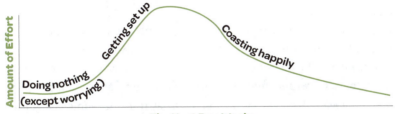

The Next Few Weeks

This is as much about where to invest your time as it is about where to put your money. Sure, setting up an Automatic Money Flow will take you a few hours. It would be easier to do nothing—but that would mean you'd have to manage your money constantly for the rest of your life. By spending a few hours up front, you'll end up saving huge amounts of time over the long term. Your money flow will be automatic, and each dollar that comes in will be routed to the right account in your Conscious Spending Plan from Chapter 4 without you really having to think about it.

The payoff for these few hours is huge, because this automatic system will let you focus on the fun parts of life. No more worrying about whether you paid that bill or if you're going to be overdrawn again. You'll start to see money as a tool for getting what you want without the manual drudgery of tracking categories and transferring money from one account to another each week.

I read the book at 23, when I had $17,000 in savings. I set up a robust system of automated savings for long-term goals (retirement, emergency savings) and short- to medium-term goals (car repairs, vacations, even Christmas gifts); ten years later, I have $170,000 saved. I've also used the book to get the best deal when buying a car and negotiating cell phone bills, saving hundreds of dollars. —**LISA LUNSFORD, 33**

The Power of Defaults

We know people are incredibly lazy and will do whatever requires no work—often at their own financial expense. Think about how many people lose thousands of dollars per year by not taking advantage of 401(k) matches alone. How much more money do we lose from inaction overall?

The key to taking action is, quite simply, making your decisions automatic. You think you'll actually do the work each week? No, you won't. You don't care. Sure, you might care right now, but in two weeks it'll be back to Twitter and Netflix. Nobody really cares about managing their money. Hell, I don't even care. Get away from me, endless mailings from banks and investment accounts.

Your money management must happen by default. We've already talked about this in reference to 401(k)s, but now we're going to apply it to every dollar you make. You'll be making your contributions to your savings and investing accounts grow passively—with no action required. In fact, by setting up an automatic payment plan, you actually make it difficult to stop the contributions to your retirement account! Not because you can't—you can adjust your system anytime—but because you're lazy and you won't. Hey, I'm lazy too. You just have to know how to take advantage of it. Once it's set up, this system is so hands-off that if you got eaten alive by a Komodo dragon, your money system would continue transferring money from account to account by default, a ghostlike reminder of your financial prescience. Haunting, but cool.

If you want to build wealth over your lifetime, the only sure way to do it is to get your plan on autopilot and make everything that's financially important in your life automatic. . . . I recommend that people automate a handful of things in their financial lives. You can set it up once in less than an hour and then go back to your life.

—DAVID BACH, AUTHOR OF *THE AUTOMATIC MILLIONAIRE*

How to Spend Only 90 Minutes a Month Managing Your Money

I hope I've convinced you by now that automation is the way to go. In Chapter 4, you set up a basic system—the Conscious Spending Plan—that gave you an idea of where you're going to distribute your money. As a refresher, check out the rough percentages assigned to the four categories (or buckets) in the table below.

CATEGORIES OF SPENDING

Use these as guidelines for your spending and tweak as necessary.

Fixed costs Rent, utilities, debt, etc.	50–60% of take-home pay
Investments 401(k), Roth IRA, etc.	10%
Savings goals Vacations, gifts, house down payment, cash for unexpected expenses, etc.	5–10%
Guilt-free spending money Dining out, drinking, movies, clothes, shoes, etc.	20–35%

Now let's take your Conscious Spending Plan and make it automatic. To do this, I use a concept called the Next $100. This means, simply, where will the next $100 you make go? Will it all go to your investment account? Will you allocate 10 percent to your savings account? Most people just shrug and don't take any time to think about how their money will be allocated—

which means it gets thoughtlessly spent and I sob uncontrollably.

But there's a better way! It involves actually using the guidelines you established in your Conscious Spending Plan. If you did things right in Chapter 4, you already know how much money you have to contribute to your fixed costs and how much is left over for investments, savings, and spending money. So, if you made $100 and your plan resembled the example above, you might put $60 toward your fixed costs, $10 into your investment account, and $10 into savings, and then you'd spend the remaining $20 on whatever you felt like. Pretty cool, right? Well, it gets even better, because once everything is automated, that money will be shunted from your checking account right into the appropriate accounts without you even thinking about it.

To see how it works, let's use my friend Michelle as an example:

Michelle gets paid once a month. Her employer automatically deducts 5 percent of her pay—an amount she set up by talking to her HR department—and puts it in her 401(k). The rest of Michelle's paycheck goes to her checking account by direct deposit. (For simplicity, I'm not including taxes here, but you can control how much your employer withholds from each paycheck to pay taxes by speaking to your HR department.)

About a day later, her Automatic Money Flow begins transferring money out of her checking account. Her Roth IRA retirement account will pull 5 percent of her salary for itself. (That combines with the 401(k) contribution to complete the 10 percent of take-home pay for investing.) One percent will go to a wedding sub-savings account, 2 percent to a house down-payment sub-savings account, and 2 percent is earmarked for her emergency fund. (That takes care of her monthly savings goals, with a total of 5 percent of take-home pay going into savings.)

I spend about an hour per month managing my money—paying bills, checking the balance on my credit card and my bank accounts, and watching a few holdings in my portfolio (but I'm not an active trader—just maintaining situational awareness). Once a month, I might evaluate my savings plan to see if I can plan a vacation or make a larger purchase.

—**JENNIFER CHANG, 32**

Her system also automatically pays her fixed costs. She's set it up so that most of her subscriptions and bills are automatically paid by her credit card. Some of her bills can't be put on credit cards—for example, utilities and loans—so they're automatically paid out of her checking account. Finally, her credit card company automatically emails her a copy of her bill for a 5-minute review. After she's reviewed it, the bill is also automatically paid in full from her checking account.

The money that remains in her account is used for guilt-free spending money. She knows that no matter what, she's already hit her savings and investing goals before she spends a cent of her guilt-free money—so she can truly enjoy buying what she wants.

To make sure she doesn't overspend, she's focused on two Big Wins: eating out and new clothes. She sets alerts in You Need a Budget (YNAB) to notify her if she goes over her spending goals, and she keeps a reserve of $500 in her checking account just in case. (The couple of times she went over her spending, she paid herself back using her "unexpected expenses" money from her savings account.) To track spending more easily, she uses her credit card to pay for all of her fun stuff as often as possible. She knows from her spending trend that she tends to spend $100 a month in cash on coffee and tips, so she includes that in her guilt-free spending. No tracking receipts or manually entering data.

In the middle of the month, Michelle's calendar reminds her to check her financial software to make sure she's within her limits for her spending money. If she's doing fine, she gets on with her life. If she's over her limit, she decides what she needs to cut back on to stay on track for the month. Luckily, she has fifteen days to get it right, and by politely passing on an invitation to eat out she gets back on track.

Using a tool like You Need a Budget gives me a more detailed view of my finances. In YNAB, it's super easy to mark money that's available for discretionary spending vs. needed for bills, and that really appeals to my analytical side.

—KYLE SLATTERY, 30

By the end of the month, she's spent less than two hours monitoring her finances, yet she's invested 10 percent, saved 5 percent (in sub-buckets for her wedding, house down payment, and emergency fund),

COMMON INVISIBLE SCRIPTS ON AUTOMATION

When it comes to automation, it "sounds" really good—yet almost none of us do it. Here's why.

Invisible script	What it means
"It feels like I have more control when I know I can invest when the market is down."	I can understand being nervous about automating your finances. The good news is you're in control. You can always check on it and stop or change any setting you want. More important, be honest: Have you actually invested consistently every month? Does all your money go where it should? Do you automatically rebalance? If the answer is no, you've lost money. Let's fix that.
"I only have a little money to start with. It doesn't seem worth it."	Start now and build the habit. As your income increases, your habits will be aligned and your system will automatically grow with you.
"I manually invest based on my variable income. It's hard to automate when my income can vary widely."	Irregular income is handled in this automation system. See page 181.
"The honest answer is because I don't know how."	Thank god, finally someone answers with a real answer, not some concocted bullshit about how they want "control" of their investments. We're talking about investment returns, people! Nothing wrong with not knowing this stuff. Read on.
"The fees are lower when I do it myself. I have more control of where my money is going (or, at least, it feels like it). It's also a forced check-in on my goals and progress."	Sigh. Feelings. Sometimes your feelings are finely tuned instincts that you should listen to. But other times, your feelings are capricious and misguided and lead you astray—and you should really follow the evidence. This is one of those cases. Bottom line: Automating your finances will give you more time, more money, and higher investment returns.

paid all of her bills on time, paid off her credit card in full, and spent exactly what she wanted to spend. She had to say "no" only once, and it was no big deal. In fact, none of it was.

Create Your Automatic Money Flow

Now that you see how it works, it's time to implement your Automatic Money Flow. You'll start by linking all your accounts together. Then, you'll set up automatic transfers to happen on various days. Below, I'll assume that you're paid once per month, but I'll also cover slight tweaks to implement if you're paid biweekly or if you're a freelancer who's paid irregularly.

To get set up, you'll need a complete list of all your accounts, their URLs, and your logins and passwords. As I mentioned, I use a LastPass account to securely store all of this information. However you choose to store it, it's well worth taking a half hour to get all these handy account numbers in one place so you never have to do this again.

Tip: If you don't already have direct deposit, talk to your HR rep and set it up with your checking account. (This is easy. It basically entails giving your checking account number to your employer.) In addition, you need to get everything squared away with your 401(k) contribution. Ideally you already set up your 401(k) way back in Chapter 3, but if not, DO IT NOW! Even if you already have a 401(k) going, you may have to adjust the amount you contribute every month based on your shiny new Conscious Spending Plan.

I automated my finances and am saving for retirement, wedding, and emergencies with no extra thought. That has been revolutionary—I feel free to spend on different things each month, not concerning myself with low-level budgeting. When I read the book, I didn't think saving for a wedding was important, but now that I'm close to getting engaged and I see how expensive weddings are, I understand! My boyfriend only just came to this realization, while I've been saving for years. The book definitely gave me a leg up.

—JULIA WAGNER, 28

Link Your Accounts

Now it's time to link your accounts together so you can set up automatic transfers from one account to another. When you log in to any of your accounts, you'll usually find an option called something like "Link Accounts," "Transfer," or "Set Up Payments."

These are all the links you need to make:

- If you haven't already done this, connect your paycheck to your 401(k), so it's automatically funded each month. (I cover this on page 110.)

- Connect your checking account to your savings account.

- Connect your checking account to your investment account/ Roth IRA. (Do this from your investment account, rather than from your bank account.)

- Connect your credit card to any bills you've been paying via your checking account. (And if you've actually been paying bills by writing checks with a pen, please understand that man has discovered fire and combustible engines and join our modern times.) For example, if you've been paying your cable bill by check each month, log in and switch it so that the bill is paid by your credit card instead.

- Some bills, like rent and loans, can't be paid using a credit card. Link these regular bills to your checking account. (Do this by logging in to the company's website and initiating the transfer from your checking account to the company.)

- Set it up so that all your credit card accounts are paid from your checking account. (This is set up from your credit card's "Transfer" or "Link Accounts" page.)

You likely have a few payments that simply can't be automatically drawn from your checking account. For example, if you're renting from a little old lady, she may not have a sophisticated financial infrastructure including a website where you can enter your checking account information and automatically transfer money each month. Sigh. Get it together, Mildred.

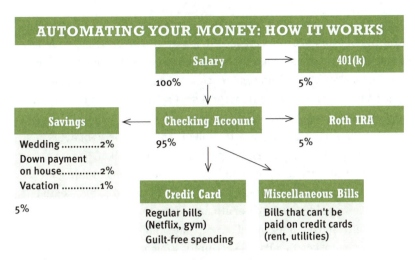

Note: For simplicity, this diagram does not include taxes.

Anyway, you can still automate payment using your checking account's bill-pay feature, which is free with nearly every account. Example: If you pay rent by writing a check and sticking it in an envelope each month, log in to your checking account and set up automatic bill pay for your rent. Your bank will then write a check for you each month and mail it to your landlord. Just make sure you schedule it so that it has enough time to reach your landlord via the postal service by the due date.

HOW TO CONNECT YOUR ACCOUNTS

This account . . .	. . . should fund this account
Paycheck	■ 401(k) ■ Checking account (direct deposit)
Checking account	■ Roth IRA ■ Savings account (which is subdivided into savings goals) ■ Credit card ■ Fixed costs that don't allow credit card payment (like rent) ■ Occasional-spending cash
Credit card	■ Fixed costs ■ Guilt-free spending

Set Up Your Automatic Transfers

Now that all your accounts are linked, it's time to go back into your accounts and automate all transfers and payments. This is really simple: It is just a matter of working with each individual account's website to make sure your payment or transfer is set up for the amount you want and on the date you want.

One thing you want to pay attention to is picking the right dates for your transfers. This is key, but people often overlook it. If you set automatic transfers at weird times, it will inevitably necessitate more work. For example, if your credit card is due on the first of the month but you don't get paid until the fifteenth, how does that work? If you don't synchronize all your bills, you'll have to pay things at different times and that will require you to reconcile accounts. Which you won't do.

The easiest way to avoid this is to get all your bills on the same schedule. To accomplish this, gather all your bills together, call the companies, and ask them to switch your billing dates. Most of these will take five minutes each to do. There may be a couple of months of odd billing as your accounts adjust, but it will smooth itself out after that. If you're paid on the first of the month, I suggest switching all your bills to arrive on or around that time too. Call and say this: "Hi, I'm currently being billed on the seventeenth of each month, and I'd like to change that to the first of the month. Do I need to do anything besides ask right here on the phone?" (Of course, depending on your situation, you can request any billing date that will be easy for you.)

Now that you've got everything coming at the beginning of the month, it's time to actually go in and set up your transfers. Here's how to arrange your Automatic Money Flow, assuming you get paid on the first of the month.

2nd of the month: *Part of your paycheck is automatically sent to your 401(k). The remainder (your "take-home pay") is direct-deposited into your checking account. Even though you're paid on the first, the money may not show up in your account until the 2nd, so be sure to account for that. Remember, you're treating your checking account like your email inbox—first, everything goes there, then it's filtered away to the appropriate place. Note: The first time you set this up, leave a buffer amount of money—I recommend $500—in your checking account just in case a transfer doesn't go right. You can "cash out" that buffer after a* couple of months. And don't worry: If something does go wrong, use the negotiation tips on page 89 to get any overdraft fees waived.

5th of the month: *Automatic transfer to your savings account.* Log in to your savings account and set up an automatic transfer from your checking account to your savings account on the 5th of every month. Waiting until the fifth of the month gives you some leeway. If, for some reason, your paycheck doesn't show up on the first of the month, you'll have four days to correct things or cancel that month's automatic transfer.

Don't just set up the transfer. Remember to set the amount too. (To calculate the amount, use the percentage of your monthly income that you established for savings in your Conscious Spending Plan—typically 5 to 10 percent.) But if you can't afford that much right now, don't worry—just set up an automatic transfer for $5 to prove to yourself that it works. The amount isn't important: $5 won't be missed, but once you see how it's all working together, it's much easier to add to that amount.

5th of the month: *Automatic transfer to your Roth IRA.* To set this up, log in to your investment account and create an automatic transfer from your checking account to your investment account. Refer to your Conscious Spending Plan to calculate the amount of the transfer. Ideally, it should be about 10 percent of your take-home pay, minus the amount you send to your 401(k).

7th of the month: *Auto-pay for any monthly bills you have.* Log in to any regular payments you have, like cable, utilities, car payments, or student loans, and set up automatic payments to occur on the seventh of each month. I prefer to pay my bills using my credit card, because I earn points, I get automatic consumer protection, and I can easily track my spending using tools like You Need a Budget. But if your merchant doesn't accept credit cards, they should let you pay the bill directly from your checking account, so set up an automatic payment from there if need be.

7th of the month: *Automatic transfer to pay off your credit card.* Log in to your credit card account and instruct it to draw money from your checking account and pay the credit card bill on the seventh of every month—in full. (Because your bill arrived on the first of the month, you'll never incur late fees using this system.) If you have credit card debt and you can't pay the bill in full, don't worry. You can still set up an automatic payment; just make it for the monthly minimum or any other amount of your choice. (See page 38 to learn why this is a very good idea.)

WHEN THE MONEY FLOWS

On this date . . .	. . . these actions happen
1st of the month	■ Your salary is direct-deposited into your checking account
2nd of the month	■ Part of your salary goes into your 401(k)
5th of the month	■ Automatic transfer from checking account to savings account ■ Automatic transfer from checking account to Roth IRA
7th of the month	■ Automatic payment of bills from checking account and credit card ■ Automatic transfer from checking account to pay off credit card bill

By the way, while you're logged in to your credit card account, also set up an email notification (this is typically under "Notifications" or "Bills") to send you a monthly link to your bill, so you can review it before the money is automatically transferred out of your checking account. This is helpful in case your bill unexpectedly exceeds the amount available in your checking account—that way you can adjust the amount you pay that month.

The automated investing principles have made saving so much easier. I used to debate which stock to buy, how much, limit prices, etc. I was spending a lot of mental energy on these tasks, and probably still being beaten regularly by the market or those who had significantly more time than me. I have a managed investment account as well, and the automation has beat the managed account for the last eight years running. **—RYAN LETT, 38**

Tweaking the System for You

That's the basic Automatic Money Flow schedule. "Great, if you have a regular income," you may be thinking, "but I'm not paid on a straight once-a-month schedule." That's not a problem. You can just adjust the above system to match your payment schedule.

If you're paid twice a month: Replicate the above system on the first and the fifteenth—with half the money each time. The key is to make sure you pay your bills on time, which is why it's important to move your bills' due dates to the first of the month. Now—to oversimplify it for explanation's sake—you'll pay your bills with your first paycheck of the month, and you'll fund your savings and investing accounts with your second paycheck of the month.

I've also got two other options for you to use this system if you're paid twice a month:

- Another way to work your system is to do half the payments with one paycheck (retirement, fixed costs) and half the payments with the second paycheck (savings, guilt-free spending), but that can get clunky.

- Save a "buffer" of money, which you can use to simulate getting paid once a month. You're essentially using a pool of money to pay your bills and contribute to your savings and checking account, then getting "paid back" by your paycheck each month. For example, if your take-home pay is $4,000/month (or $2,000 bimonthly), you could keep $6,000 in your checking account and follow my automation system as outlined in this chapter. Why $6,000? Because each month, your automation system will begin transferring money for bills and savings and checking, and you want to build in a little extra in case something goes wrong (such as your paycheck arriving late). If you can afford to do this, this is a great way to simplify your system and simulate getting paid once a month—even if you get paid bimonthly.

If you have irregular income: I know lots of freelancers and others who earn $12,000 one month, then nothing for the next two months. How can you deal with spikes in income?

Good news: This system will accommodate irregular income with no problem—you just need to take an extra step. Here's the quick summary of what you're going to do: In months where you make a lot, you're going to save and build a buffer for the slow months. Over time, you'll build enough of a buffer that you can simulate a stable income, letting you use this system as designed. Even in slow months, you can pay yourself from your buffer.

Here's how you do it.

First—and this is different from the Conscious Spending Plan—you'll have to figure out how much you need to survive on each month. This is the bare minimum: rent, utilities, food, loan payments—just the basics. Those are your bare-bones monthly necessities. Take a second to write it down.

Now, back to the Conscious Spending Plan. Add a savings goal of three months of bare-bones income before you do any investing. For example, if you need at least $3,500/month to live on, you'll need to have $10,500 in a savings buffer, which you can use to smooth out months where you don't generate much income. The buffer should exist as a sub-account in your savings account. To fund it, use money from two places: First, forget about investing while you're setting up the buffer, and instead take any money you would have invested and send it to your savings account. Second, in good months, any extra dollar you make should go into your buffer savings.

Once you've saved up three months of money as a cushion, congratulations! (To go the extra mile, work toward a six-month emergency fund.) You've built a stable buffer and you can simulate a stable income.

Think about it: If you have a bad month—even a really bad month, where you make $0—you can easily cover your expenses. And when you have a really good month, you can simply rebuild toward your three- or six-month goal. Through automated savings, you've bought yourself time and stability.

Now go back to a normal Conscious Spending Plan where you send money to investing accounts. Because you're self-employed, you probably don't have access to a traditional 401(k), but you should look into a Solo 401(k) and SEP-IRA, which are great alternatives. Just keep in mind that it's probably wise to sock away a little more into your savings account in good months to make up for the less profitable ones.

Review Your Credit Card Bill

I pay with my credit card as much as possible because it lets me automatically download my transactions and categorize my spending. Plus, I get travel points and extra consumer protection, like a free additional warranty for any electronic device (for more on this, see page 45).

HOW I CHECKED MY SYSTEM IN THE EARLY DAYS: I used to do a weekly five-minute review of all the charges on my card. If I took no action, my credit card reached into my checking account once a month and paid the full amount automatically. No late fees, no worries. If I did see an error, I just called my credit card company and got it fixed.

Let's talk about those weekly reviews for a second. I liked to keep an eye on my credit card charges whenever there was tipping involved, so I would keep my receipts whenever I went to restaurants and store them in a paper folder on my desk. Every Sunday night, I'd check the folder and spend about five minutes comparing my receipts with what my credit card's website says. I'd just do a "Ctrl + F" for the amount (for example, $43.35) and confirm that it's correct. If I wrote $43.35 as the full amount after tip, but saw that the restaurant had charged me $50, I knew someone was trying to make a quick buck off me. And in that case, you need to ask yourself one question: **WWAID?** (What would an Indian do?)

Answer: A quick call to the credit card company will resolve this.

HOW I CHECK MY SYSTEM NOW: I don't do those weekly reviews to catch a $6 added tip anymore. The more experienced you get, the more you can spot unusual deviations to your own spending—and even if someone adds $6 to a tip, it doesn't matter.

Believe me, I know how weird that sounds. I built this system by being ultra-aware of every transaction that ran through it. But eventually you realize the system exists to help you focus on the big picture. In any meaningful system, there's always a certain amount of waste. If someone adds $5 to my tip (and my credit card company doesn't catch it), that's life.

I've set up a system with the appropriate safeguards and reviews, but I know that there will inevitably be certain things that slip through the cracks. That's okay as long as I'm keeping my eye on the big picture.

When Do I Get to Spend My Money?

Okay. You've got your automatic infrastructure set up. Each month, you've got money flowing automatically to your investing accounts and savings accounts. You've even cut your spending by focusing on a couple of Big Wins. So when do you get to spend all this money?

What a great question. The only people who've ever asked me this are actually concerned about saving too much.

The answer is simple: Once you've gotten your money under control and you're hitting your targets, you absolutely should spend your leftover money. Look to your savings goals. If you don't have something in there for "vacation" or "new snowboard," maybe you should. Otherwise, what is all this money for?

Money exists for a reason—to let you do what you want to do. Yes, it's true, every dollar you spend now would be worth more later. But living only for tomorrow is no way to live. Consider one investment that most people overlook: yourself. Think about traveling—how much will that be worth to you later? Or attending that conference that will expose you to the top people in your field? My friend Paul has a specific "networking budget" that he uses to travel to meet interesting people each year. If you invest in yourself, the potential return is limitless.

If you're meeting your goals, another route you could take is to start saving less and increase the amount you allocate to your guilt-free spending money.

One final thing: I hope this doesn't sound too cheesy, but one of the best returns I've ever gotten has been with philanthropy. Whether it's your time or your money, I can't emphasize enough how important it is to give back, be it to your own community or to the global community. Volunteer your time at a local school or youth organization (in NYC, I volunteer through New York Cares) or donate to a charity that supports a cause you care about (I've donated to Pencils of Promise [pencilsofpromise.org]). For more on giving back, see page 331.

Saving too much is a good problem to have. Fortunately, there are great solutions too.

I automated my finances, and over seven years I have saved around $400,000. I also earned enough to max out my retirement accounts. **—DAN SHULTZ, 35**

One final note on taxes: As a freelancer, you're responsible for your self-employment tax, which your employer would normally handle if you were a traditional employee. Self-employed taxes can get very tricky very quickly, so I'm going to give you my rule of thumb, then encourage you to talk to a professional.

Since many freelancers don't know the rules around self-employed taxes, they can get surprised when tax time comes around. I've known a lot of freelancers who were stunned to owe unexpectedly large amounts for taxes. As a rule of thumb, you should set aside 40 percent of your income for taxes. Some people save 30 percent, but I prefer to be conservative: It's better to end up oversaving than owing money at the end of the year.

Your bookkeeper can advise you on exactly how much to set aside, and how to automate your quarterly payments, so see a professional. It's worth it. I also recommend using You Need a Budget as a planning tool if you have an irregular income.

Your Money Is Now Automatic

Congratulations! Your money management is now on autopilot. Not only are your bills paid automatically and on time, but you're actually saving and investing money each month. The beauty of this system is that it works without your involvement and it's flexible enough to add or remove accounts anytime. You're accumulating money by default.

I love this system for three reasons:

Your automated money flow takes advantage of human psychology. Right now, you're motivated to manage your money. Imagine life in three months—or three years. You'll get busy, distracted, and focused on other things. That's normal. But your system will continue growing your money for you. This system has worked for hundreds of thousands of people, and it will work for you too.

Your system will grow with you. You can contribute $100/month and
your system will just work. Now imagine getting a series of raises, and
consistent returns from your investments, and other unexpected income
(such as a tax refund). In fact, imagine you're contributing $10,000 per
month—or even $50,000 per month! Your system will still work beautifully.

Your system lets you go from "hot" to "cool." One thing I love about
this system is it takes you out of the day-to-day, emotionally "hot"
decisions and lets you focus on longer-term, "cool" ones. For example,
think about the way most people describe their daily purchases: They
"struggle" to "resist" dessert, or they feel "guilty" about buying coffee,
or they admit to being "bad" if they splurge for a nice handbag.

I hate those words. Money should be about all the good things it can
do, not the bad. To do that, you can't agonize over thousands of micro-
decisions per month—you have to focus on the bigger picture.

This system means you get to bring your vision of a Rich Life alive.
I believe that you can tell a lot about your own values by where your
money goes. As I always say, "Show me someone's calendar and their
spending, and I'll show you their priorities." Now you have an answer to
the question: What does your spending say about you?

For example, I spend a lot on clothes—guilt-free! I have a pair of
cashmere sweatpants that are insanely expensive. They also feel like
you're wearing a cloud. When one of my friends found out how much they
cost, he was aghast. And taken out of context, as a singular purchase,
it's true: They are "ridiculously" expensive. But taken in the context
of a full automation system, which includes saving and investing and
contributing to charity, the pants are simply a guilt-free purchase that
I love. No more words like "crazy" and "ridiculous." These are just
something I wanted and I could afford, so I bought them.

There's more to money than just extravagance. You can also use it to
create memories and experience true joy. When I got married, I sat down
with my wife and we decided on the key things that were important
to us. We're fortunate that both sets of our parents are together and
healthy. One of our dreams was to invite our parents to join us on our
honeymoon—part of it!—and create amazing memories together. We
invited them to Italy and took them on food tours, cooking classes, and
wine tastings and basically treated them like royalty.

We knew we wanted to create the memories. To make it happen, we made a few changes to our Automatic Money Flow, and the money was redirected automatically.

We will never forget seeing the four of them together with us, tasting new cheeses for the first time in their lives. This is what I mean when I say that money is a small, but important, part of living a Rich Life.

You might be wondering what's going to happen with your investment money. Right now, it's growing each month as you contribute to your 401(k) and Roth IRA, but it's just sitting there. You need to put it to work by investing it in something. In the next chapter, we'll talk about how you can become your own investment expert and how to go about getting the best return on your investment money.

ACTION STEPS

WEEK FIVE

1 **List all your accounts in one place (one hour).** As you start linking accounts to one another, you'll need to log in to all of them. Make your life easier by getting all the login information in one place that you can access from home and work.

2 **Link your accounts together (three to five days).** To set up your Automatic Money Flow, link your accounts together. Connecting them is free and quick, but allow three to five days for the accounts to verify the links.

3 **Set up your Automatic Money Flow (five hours).** Once your accounts are linked together, set up the core of your Automatic Money Flow: automatic payments. Your system will automatically send money to your investing accounts, your savings account, and your fixed costs, and leave you money for guilt-free spending. Remember, you'll want to reset your billing cycles so you can create a well-timed Automatic Money Flow.

CHAPTER 6

THE MYTH OF FINANCIAL EXPERTISE

Why professional wine tasters and stock pickers are clueless—and how you can beat them

I f I invited you to a blind taste test of a $12 wine versus a $1,200 wine, could you tell the difference?

In 2001, Frederic Brochet, a researcher at the University of Bordeaux, ran a study that sent shock waves through the wine industry. Determined to understand how wine drinkers decided which wines they liked, he invited 57 recognized experts to evaluate two wines: one red, one white.

After tasting the two wines, the experts described the red wine as "intense," "deep," and "spicy"—words commonly used to describe red wines. The white was described in equally standard terms: "lively," "fresh," and "floral." But what none of these experts picked up on was that the two wines were *exactly the same wine*. Even more damning, the wines were actually *both* white wine—the "red wine" had been tinted with food coloring.

THE MYTH OF FINANCIAL EXPERTISE

Think about that for a second. Fifty-seven wine experts couldn't even tell they were drinking two identical wines.

There's something we need to talk about when it comes to experts.

Americans love experts. We feel comforted when we see a tall, uniformed pilot behind the controls of a plane. We trust our doctors to prescribe the right medications, we're confident that our lawyers will steer us right through legal tangles, and we devour the words of the talking heads in the media. We're taught that experts deserve to be compensated for their training and experience. After all, we wouldn't hire someone off the street to build a house or remove our wisdom teeth, would we?

All our lives, we've been taught to defer to experts: teachers, doctors, investment "professionals." But ultimately, expertise is about results. You can have the fanciest degrees from the fanciest schools, but if you can't perform what you were hired to do, your expertise is meaningless. In our culture of worshipping experts, what have the results been? When it comes to finances in America, they're pretty dismal. We've earned failing grades in financial literacy—recent results show that high school students answered only 61 percent of questions correctly on the National Financial Literacy test, while college students answered 69 percent right. Keep in mind this is *basic financial literacy*.

We think "investing" is about guessing the next best stock. (It's not.) Instead of enriching ourselves by saving and investing, most American households are in debt. Something's not right here.

When it comes to investing, it's easy to get overwhelmed by all the options: small-, mid-, and large-cap stocks; REITS; bonds; growth, value, or blend funds—not to mention factoring in expense ratios, interest rates, allocation goals, and diversification. That's why so many people say, "Can't I just hire someone to do this for me?" This is a maddening question because, in fact, financial experts—in particular, fund managers and anyone who attempts to predict the market—are often no better at the job than amateurs. In fact, they're often *worse*. The vast majority of people can earn more than the so-called "experts" by investing on their own. No financial adviser. No fund manager. Just automatic investments in low-cost funds (which I'll get to in the next chapter). So, for the average investor, the value of financial expertise is a myth. There are several reasons for this that I'll detail below, but I urge you to think about how you treat the experts in your life. Do they deserve to be put on a pedestal? Do they deserve tens of thousands of your dollars in fees? If so, what kind of performance do you demand of them?

In truth, being rich is within *your* control, not some expert's. How rich you are depends on the amount you're able to save and on your investment plan. Acknowledging this fact takes guts, because it means admitting that there's no one else to blame if you're not rich—no advisers, no complicated investment strategy, no "market conditions." But it also means that you control exactly what happens to you and your money over the long term.

You know what the most fun part of this book is for me? No, it's not the personal finance chants that I constantly wish I got when walking outside ("Let's hear it for A-S-S-E-T A-L-L-O-C-A-T-I-O-N"). It's the disbelieving emails I've gotten after people have read this chapter. Whenever I point out how people waste their money by investing in expensive mutual funds or by relying on a financial adviser who generates below-market returns, I get emails that say, "You're full of it." Or they say, "There's no way that's true—just look at my investment returns," not really understanding how much they've made after factoring in taxes and fees. But surely they must be making great returns, because they wouldn't continue investing if they weren't making lots of money . . . right?

In this chapter, I'm going to show you how you can outperform the financial pundits by sidestepping their "expertise" (and fees) and taking the simplest approach to investing. It's not easy to learn that reliance on so-called "experts" is largely ineffective, but stick with me. I've got the data to back it up, and I'll show you how to invest on your own.

Experts Can't Guess Where the Market Is Going

Before we move on to discuss how you can beat the experts, let's look a little more deeply into how they operate and why their advice so often misses the mark.

The most visible financial "experts" are the pundits and portfolio managers (the people who choose the specific stocks in mutual funds). They love to regale us with their predictions about where the market is going: Up! Down! They go on and on about how interest rates and oil production and a butterfly flapping its wings in China will affect the stock market. This forecasting is called "timing the market." But the truth is they simply cannot predict how high, how low, or even in which direction the market will go. I get emails from people wondering what I think about the energy sector, currency markets, or Google every single day. Who knows about those things? I certainly don't, especially in the short term. Unfortunately, the fact is that nobody can predict where the market is going. Still, the talking heads on TV make grandiose predictions every day, and whether they're right or wrong, they're never held accountable for them.

The media feeds off every little market fluctuation. One day, the pundits spread gloom and doom about a multi-hundred-point loss in the market. Then, three days later, the front page is filled with images of hope and unicorns as the market climbs 500 points. It's riveting to watch, but step back and ask yourself, "Am I learning anything from this? Or am I just being overwhelmed by information about the market going up one day and down another?" More information is not always good, especially when it's not actionable and causes you to make errors in your investing. The key takeaway here is to completely ignore any predictions that pundits make. They simply do not know what will happen in the future.

Even though you'd think they'd know better, fund managers also fall prey to financial hype. You can see this in the trading patterns of funds themselves: Mutual funds "turn over" stocks frequently, meaning they buy and sell stocks a lot (incurring trading fees and, if held outside a tax-advantaged account, taxes for you). The managers chase the latest hot stock, confident of their abilities to spot something that millions of others have not. What's more, they also demand extraordinary compensation. And despite that, fund managers across the board still fail to beat the market 75 percent of the time.

"But, Ramit," you might say, "my fund is different. The manager returned 80 percent over the last two years!" That's great, but just because someone beat the market for a few years doesn't mean they'll beat the market the next year. Starting in 2000, S&P Dow Jones Indices did a sixteen-year study and found that the fund managers who beat their benchmarks one year had an extremely difficult time getting similar returns the next year. "If you have an active manager who beats the index one year, the chance is less than a coin flip that the manager

A Startling Example of How "Experts" Can't Time the Market

Pundits and the media know exactly how to get our attention: flashy graphics, loud talking heads, and bold predictions about the market that almost never come true. These may be entertaining, but let's look at actual data that will shock you.

Putnam Investments studied the performance of the S&P 500 over fifteen years, during which time the annualized return was 7.7 percent. They noted something amazing: During that fifteen-year period, if you missed the ten best days of investing (the days where the stock market gained the most points), your return would have dropped from 7.7 percent to 2.96 percent. And if you missed the thirty best days, your returns would have dropped to -2.47 percent—*negative returns*!

In actual dollar values, if you'd invested $10,000 and kept your money in the market over those fifteen years, you'd end up with $30,711. If you missed the ten best investing days, you'd end up with $15,481. And if you missed the thirty best investing days, you'd end up with $6,873—less than you began with.

This math is startling. It makes you wonder about the certainty of friends and pundits, who say it's "obvious" that the market is going down. Ignore them. It may feel good to try to predict where the market is going to go. But candidly, when it comes to investing and compound interest, your feelings will lead you astray.

The only long-term solution is to invest regularly, putting as much money as possible into low-cost, diversified funds, even in an economic downturn. This is why long-term investors have a phrase they use: Focus on *time* in the market, not *timing* the market.

will beat the index again next year," said Ryan Poirier, senior analyst at S&P Dow Jones Indices.

If I asked you to name the best stock from 2008 to 2018, you might guess Google, but would you have guessed Domino's Pizza? Back in January 2008, if you invested $1,000 in Google stock, ten years later it would be worth a little over $3,000. Tripling your money in ten years is fantastic. But if you'd taken that same $1,000 and purchased Domino's stock, your investment would have gone almost up to *$18,000*.

The problem is that nobody can consistently guess which funds or stocks will outperform, or even match, the market over time. Anyone who claims they can is lying.

So ignore the pundits' predictions. Ignore once-in-a-lifetime freakish results. And ignore the last year or two of a fund's performance—a fund manager may be able to perform very well over the short term. But over the long term that manager will almost never beat the market because of expenses, fees, and the growing mathematical difficulty of picking outperforming stocks (more on that later in this chapter). When you're evaluating a fund, the only way to really gauge it is by looking at its track record for the last ten years or more.

How Financial Experts Hide Poor Performance

As I've shown, the "experts" are often wrong, but even more irritatingly, they know how to cover their tracks so we don't catch on to their failures. In fact, the financial industry—including both companies that administer mutual funds and so-called experts—are sneakier than you'd imagine.

One of the biggest tricks they use is to never admit they were wrong. Daniel Solin, author of *The Smartest Investment Book You'll Ever Read*, describes a study that illustrates how financial ratings companies like Morningstar—which provides stock ratings that investors can use to get a quick take on many stocks' performance—continue to give thumbs-up ratings even as the companies they purport to be evaluating crater and lose billions of dollars of shareholder value. The study found the following:

> Forty-seven of the fifty [advisory] firms continued to advise investors to buy or hold shares in the companies up to the date the companies filed for bankruptcy.
> Twelve of the nineteen companies continued to receive "buy" or "hold" ratings on the actual date they filed for bankruptcy.

Companies like Morningstar offer ratings of funds that are supposedly simple reflections of their value, but the idea of Morningstar's five-star ratings is actually complete nonsense. Why? For two reasons:

First, receiving five golden stars doesn't actually predict success. A study by researchers Christopher Blake and Matthew Morey showed that although the low-star ratings were on target in predicting poor-performing stocks, the high-star ratings were not accurate. They wrote: "[F]or the most part, there is little statistical evidence that Morningstar's highest-rated funds outperform the next-to-highest and median-rated fund." Just because a company assigns five shiny stars to a fund does not mean it will perform well in the future.

Second, when it comes to fund ratings, companies rely on something called *survivorship bias* to obscure the picture of how well a company is doing. Survivorship bias exists because funds that fail are not included in any future studies of fund performance for the simple reason that they don't exist anymore. For example, a company may start a hundred funds but have only fifty left a couple of years later. The company can trumpet how effective their fifty funds are but ignore the fifty funds that failed and have been erased from history. In other words, when you see "Best 10 Funds!" pages on mutual-fund websites and in magazines, it's just as important to think about what you *aren't* seeing: The funds on that page are the ones that didn't close down. Out of that pool of already successful funds, *of course* there will be some five-star funds.

A number of mutual-fund management complexes employ the practice of starting "incubator" funds. A complex may start ten small new equity funds with different in-house managers and wait to see which ones are successful. Suppose after a few years only three funds produce total returns better than the broad-market averages. The complex begins to market those successful funds aggressively, dropping the other seven and burying their records.
—BURTON G. MALKIEL, *A RANDOM WALK DOWN WALL STREET*

Three Legendary Investors Who Did Beat the Market

Now, there are indeed investors who have beaten the market consistently for years. Warren Buffett, for example, has produced a 20.9 percent annualized return over fifty-three years. Peter Lynch of Fidelity returned 29 percent over thirteen years. And Yale's David Swensen has returned 13.5 percent over thirty-three years. They have phenomenal investing skills and have earned their titles as some of the best investors in the world. But just because these guys can consistently beat the market doesn't mean you or I can.

Yes, theoretically, it is possible to consistently beat the market (which typically returns around 8 percent after you account for inflation), in the same way it is *possible* for me to become a heavyweight boxing champion. With millions of people around the globe trying to beat the market, statistically there are bound to be a few extreme outliers. Who knows whether their success is due to statistics or skill? But even the experts themselves agree that individual investors shouldn't expect to equal their returns. Swensen, for example, has explained that he achieves outsize returns because of top-notch professional resources, but more important, access to investments that you and I will never have—such as the very best venture capital and hedge funds, which he uses to bolster his asset allocation. These professionals spend every waking hour studying investments and they have access to proprietary information and deals. Mom and pop investors have no chance of competing with them.

Financial companies know very well about survivorship bias, but they care more about having a page full of funds with great performance numbers than revealing the whole truth. As a result, they've consciously created several ways to test funds quickly and market only the best-performing ones, thus ensuring their reputation as the brand with the "best" funds.

These tricks are especially insidious because you'd never know to look out for them. When you see a page full of funds with 15 percent returns, you naturally assume they'll keep giving you 15 percent returns in the future. And it's even better if they have five-star ratings from a trusted company like Morningstar. But now that we know about survivorship bias and the fact that most ratings are meaningless, it's easy to see that financial "experts" and companies are just looking to fatten their wallets, not ensure that you get the best return for your money.

How to Engineer a Perfect Stock-Picking Record

Since we know it's almost impossible to beat the market over the long term, let's turn to probability and luck to explain why some funds seem irresistibly compelling. Although a fund manager might be lucky for one, two, or even three years, it's mathematically unlikely he'll continue beating the market. To examine probability theory, let's take a simple example of an unscrupulous scammer who wants to sell his financial services to some naive investors.

He emails ten thousand people, telling half that Stock A will go up and telling the other half Stock B will go up. "This is just a freebie email to demonstrate my insider knowledge," he might say. After a couple of weeks, he notices that Stock A has indeed gone up by chance.

He eliminates the Stock B group and focuses on the Stock A group, emailing them an "I told you so" note. This time, he splits the mailing in half again. Twenty-five hundred people are told about Stock C and twenty-five hundred are told about Stock D. If either C or D goes up, on the next cycle, at least 1,250 people will have seen him pick two stocks successfully. And each cycle will make the recipients increasingly awed by his "ability."

Because we like to create order where there is none, we will ascribe magical stock-picking abilities to the scammer—even though it was literally by chance—and buy whatever "investment success kit" he's selling. The same is true of the pages of "five-star funds" you see. Moral of the story: Don't trust purported financial expertise just because of a few impressive stats.

I Bet You Don't Need a Financial Adviser

Y ou've heard my rants against the media hype surrounding investment and the poor performance of most professional investors. Now there's one more category of financial professionals that I want to warn you about: financial advisers.

Some of you might say, "But, Ramit, I don't have time to invest! Why can't I just use a financial adviser?" Ah, yes, the old outsourcing argument. We outsource our car cleaning, laundry, and housekeeping. So why not the management of our money?

Most young people don't need a financial adviser. We have such simple needs that with a little bit of time (a few hours a week over the course of, say, six weeks) we can get an automatic personal finance infrastructure working for us.

Plus, financial advisers don't always look out for your interests. They're supposed to help you make the right decisions about your money, but keep in mind that they're actually not obligated to do what's best for you. Some of them will give you very good advice, but many of them are pretty useless. If they're paid on commission, they usually will direct you to expensive, bloated funds to earn their commissions.

At my first job, my company offered seminars hosted by a former employee who was now doing investments. He gave pretty standard advice (e.g., save in your 401(k), use a Roth IRA, etc.). I went for a consult and set up a Roth IRA with him. He also sold me on the investment advantages of whole life insurance policies. Then my wife looked at the details and said, "Ummm . . . nope." She called them up to cancel everything and get our money back. We got everything back, which was good, because initial outlays were almost five figures. Around that time, I got your book and moved my Roth from him to Vanguard . . . Haven't looked back since. —**TOM T., 35**

My Friend Realizes His Financial Adviser Has Been Taking Him for a Ride

Years ago, my friend Joe emailed me asking me to take a look at his investments. He suspected he was being taken for a ride by his financial adviser. Within five minutes of talking to him, I knew he was in a bad situation. Joe is a young entrepreneur with high earnings, so this adviser figured he was a meal ticket for the next four decades.

I told him the following:

- There are certain keywords that are major red flags when it comes to investing, including "whole life insurance," "annuities," and "primerica." Any one of those words means, at best, you're almost certainly overpaying and at worst, you're being scammed.

- You're being overcharged, and with your income, the fees you pay will be in the hundreds of thousands of dollars (or even $1,000,000+ over your lifetime).

- You should move everything to a low-cost broker. You'll pay lower fees and get better performance. When you do this, your adviser will freak out and use every emotional tool in his arsenal to prevent you from doing this. Therefore, communicate in writing.

The show was about to begin. I sat back in my chair and rubbed my hands. I live for this shit.

Over the course of the next week, he and his adviser emailed back and forth. Predictably, the adviser was absolutely shocked—shocked, I tell you!—that his client wanted out. Here are some of the words he used:

"[I am shocked] Especially since we have spoken several times in the last few months and I have not heard any complaints or concerns . . ."

". . . taking on a large task of doing all your own planning and investing doesn't seem like a good idea . . ."

My favorite was this: "However, if you still feel that you would like to fire me, I can list out instructions to close your accounts."

The most hilarious part was that my friend refused to be baited by the emotional manipulation. He replied and said,

"I'm not confident that some of the decisions we made together were truly in my best interest. Whether the loss of confidence is justified or not, it'll be hard to have a professional relationship going forward with how I currently feel."

I give Joe an A+. Not only will he keep hundreds of thousands of dollars in fees, he's shown us what having a backbone with your own money looks like.

If you're currently working with a financial adviser, I encourage you to ask them if they are a fiduciary (i.e., if they're required to put your financial interests first). Joe's adviser was not a fiduciary; he was a salesman. That was instantly obvious by his recommendation that Joe (a single man in his twenties) "invest" in life insurance. The only reason for someone like Joe to have life insurance is if he has a dependent—not to fatten his adviser's wallet.

If you discover that your adviser is not a fiduciary, you should switch. Don't be worried about the variety of emotional tactics they'll use to get you to stay. Keep your eye on the prize and put your financial returns first.

By contrast, fee-only financial advisers simply charge a flat fee and are much more reputable. (Neither is necessarily better at providing good investment returns, or your top line; they simply charge differently, affecting your bottom line.)

The key takeaway is that most people don't actually need a financial adviser—you can do it all on your own and come out ahead. But if your choice is between hiring a financial adviser or not investing at all, then sure, hire one. People with really complex financial situations, those who have inherited or accumulated substantial amounts of money (i.e., over $2 million), and those who are *truly* too busy to learn about investing for themselves also should consider seeking an adviser's help. It's better to pay a little and get started investing than to not start at all. If you're determined to get professional help, begin your search at the National Association of Personal Financial Advisors (napfa.org). These advisers are fee-based (they usually have an hourly rate), not commission-based, which means that they want to help you, not profit off their recommendations.

But remember, many people use financial advisers as a crutch and end up paying tens of thousands of dollars over their lifetime simply because they didn't spend a few hours learning about investing. If you don't learn to manage your money when you're young, you'll cost yourself a ton one way or another—whether you do nothing or pay someone exorbitant fees to "manage" your money.

Oh jeez. I lucked into a one-time windfall and tried to do the "smart thing" by using a financial planner recommended by my bank (at that time Comerica—may they die a painful death). He put me in terrible funds that both underperformed the S&P 500 *AND* had insane fees. Lost about 30 percent of my money. Eventually moved everything to Vanguard Index Funds (in a brokerage account I set up myself with Vanguard). No regrets about the move. Nothing but regrets about the wasted time and money "trusting a professional." —**DAVE NELSON, 40**

When Two Wealth Managers Tried to Recruit Me

A few years ago, a friend suggested I talk to a "wealth manager." I declined, but he was insistent. "Why not?" my friend asked.

I said, I dunno, maybe BECAUSE I WROTE A *NEW YORK TIMES* BESTSELLING BOOK ON INVESTING AND PERSONAL FINANCE? But I took a deep breath and reminded myself, "Be humble, Ramit." I decided to take the call.

The friend told me that these advisers worked for a wealth management firm that I won't name.

LOL, who am I kidding? They worked for Wells Fargo Private Wealth Management. Let me digress for a moment and remind you why I hate Wells Fargo and Bank of America.

These big banks are pieces of shit. They rip you off, charge near-extortionate fees, and use deceptive practices to beat down the average

So You Really Think You Need a Financial Adviser?

f you really want to look into hiring a financial adviser, here's an introductory email you can adapt and send:

Hi Mike,

I'm looking for a fee-only financial planner, and I found you on napfa.org. A little bit about me: I have about $10,000 in total assets—$3,000 in a Roth IRA (uninvested), $3,000 in a 401(k), and $4,000 in cash. I'm looking for investments that will maximize long-term returns while minimizing costs.

If you think you can help me, I'd like to meet for half an hour and ask you some specific questions. I'd also like to hear how you've worked with similar people with similar goals. Would next Friday, 2/6, at 2 p.m. work? Alternatively, Monday, 2/9, is wide open for me.

Thanks, Ramit

For your thirty-minute meeting—which shouldn't cost you anything—you'll want to come prepared with questions. There are hundreds of sample questions available online (search for "financial adviser questions"), but at the very least, ask these three:

- Are you a fiduciary? How do you make your money? Is it through commission or strictly fee-only? Are there any other fees? (You want a fee-only adviser who is a fiduciary, meaning they put your financial interests first. Any response to this question other than a clear "yes" is an instant no-hire.)

- Have you worked with people in similar situations? What general solutions did you recommend? (Get references and call them.)

- What's your working style? Do we talk regularly, or do I work with an assistant? (You want to know what to expect in the first thirty, sixty, and ninety days.)

consumer. Nobody will speak up against them because everyone in the financial world wants to strike a deal with them. I have zero interest in deals with these banks. If you use them, don't. You're asking to be mistreated if you do. Google "Ramit best accounts" for the best checking and savings accounts and credit cards. I make no money from these recommendations. I just want you to avoid getting ripped off.

Anyway, back to the story: When I heard these guys worked for Wells Fargo, I knew I had to take the call. Mostly because I hate almost all wealth managers (and I love role-playing).

A quick background on what "wealth managers" do. They find a person with money, ask them a bunch of questions, and help them plan their finances and investments. Sounds good, right? They also give you "prestige services," like portfolio analysis, international mortgage assistance, tax planning services, etc. In exchange for this, they charge you a fee based on percentage of assets. A small number, like 1 percent or 2 percent. Oh my god, the fees. We'll get to that in a minute.

So I get on the phone with these two advisers. They work in Beverly Hills and have amazing, buttery British accents. I love British accents.

THEY KNOW NOTHING ABOUT ME. They didn't do two seconds of research. "This is going to be fun," I think to myself.

They ask me what I do for a living. I tell them "Internet entrepreneur." They work with entrepreneurs and celebrities, they tell me. Celebrities are targets for wealth managers because (1) celebs make a lot of money for (2) a short period of time, and (3) they just want to delegate it. They start telling me about their services. How they help their clients focus on their work and handle all the financial "stuff." (The implication being that I'm too busy buying Lamborghinis and bottle service to pay attention to my investments. Little do they know I love asset allocation and actively study it for fun.) They tell me how they keep my money safe. How they know that I need the money to be here for me tomorrow (playing on my fear of loss).

I play dumb and ask a lot of basic questions. "How does it work? What do you do with my money?" I'm careful not to use phrases like "tax-loss harvesting," "dollar-cost averaging," or even "compound interest." Instead, I ask things like, "Can you guys help with taxes?" We were on a phone call, but I could almost feel their eyes lighting up as

Pundits Worth Reading

Here are three money columnists and one forum that I love.

MORGAN HOUSEL writes one of the most interesting blogs on psychology and money out there. Read his posts to understand why you do what you do (and why the herd does what it does). collaborativefund.com/blog

DAN SOLIN, author of a number of great investing books, writes a terrific newsletter where he names names and calls out the BS of the investing industry. Here are a few topics he's tackled: "Cracks in the Robo-Advisor Facade," "Active Fund Managers Are Losers," and "Find the Courage to Be 'Different.'" danielsolin.com

RON LIEBER writes the Your Money column for the *New York Times*. I love the variety of topics he tackles, and he's always pro-consumer. ronlieber.com

Finally, I love the **BOGLEHEADS FORUM**, where you can find good investing advice. They'll steer you clear of scams and fads and refocus you on low-cost, long-term investing. bogleheads.org/forum

they eagerly told me the complicated ways they can save me money on taxes (in reality, there are relatively few tax loopholes for the wealthy).

Then, in their beautiful accents, they say something that sounds innocuous but is actually extremely revealing: "We don't try to match the market. We focus on asset preservation."

Did you catch that?

What they mean is: "Our investment returns will be below what you could get from a cheap Vanguard fund." In plain English: "You can buy salt for $1. We will give you worse salt and charge you $2. But we'll deliver it on a beautiful leather tray every six months." NOW I'M LAUGHING OUT LOUD. I hit mute on the phone so I can keep up the charade.

They never ask about my goals. Such as . . . why would a guy in his early thirties, early in his career, be focused on wealth preservation instead of growth?

More important, how much do their services cost? I innocently ask about fees. At this point, I can't stop smiling because I know what's about to happen. I literally can't wait. This is the best part. Oh my god, the fees. When I ask how much it costs, their tone changes to dismissive—if you've ever been around rich people talking about how much something costs, you know what I mean. They say, "The investment fee is a really nominal 1 percent, but we're here to focus on the long-term relationship of getting your finances . . ."

Did you catch *that*?

First, they glossed over the fee. "The fee is a nominal 1 percent." One percent? Who cares about that? Second, notice that they quickly redirected the conversation back to comfortable words like "long-term relationship" that their target client would want to hear. Why? Well, here's why. (BTW, if I recall, the fee was actually somewhere between 1 and 2 percent. Let's just call it 1 percent to be conservative.) One percent for all of this? Not bad, right?

DID YOU KNOW THAT OVER TIME A 1 PERCENT FEE CAN REDUCE YOUR RETURNS BY AROUND 30 PERCENT? No, you didn't. Nobody does. That means if I invested $100,000 with them, their fees would reduce my $2.1 million to $1.5 million—which they would pocket! THAT 1 PERCENT FEE IS MASSIVE!

No thanks—I prefer to keep my money for myself. The average person doesn't understand how crushing these fees really are because the math is extremely counterintuitive. Wall Street has engineered this to be opaque. One percent doesn't seem like a lot, but it is gargantuan.

Investing on my own, I could get better returns *and* pay less.

Want to play a fun game? Ask your parents what their investment fees are. They don't know, and if they found out what it actually cost them, they would be depressed. On second thought, don't do this.

One percent can cost you 28 percent of your returns. A 2 percent fee can cost you 63 percent of your returns. This is unreal stuff. It's why Wall Street is so rich. It's also why I insist you learn this for yourself and why I get so mad when Wall Street rips off individual investors.

IF YOU ARE READING THIS AND YOU'RE PAYING OVER 1 PERCENT IN FEES, I'M GOING TO KILL YOU. Get smart. You should ideally be paying 0.1 to 0.3 percent. Think about that. Think about the hundreds of thousands of dollars—even millions—that you can keep instead of paying some wealth manager. You might pay someone to mow your lawn or clean your apartment. But your money is different. Fees compound. The good news is, you're reading this book right now. If you can breathe oxygen and read English, this book will make you a lot of money—more than you could possibly imagine, compared to leaving it sitting in a savings account.

So, back to the advisers. In retrospect, it would have been awesome if I had just dropped a super-technical question on them, something about Black-Scholes or foreign currency exchange, then said, "Well, TTYL!" Unfortunately I suck at coming up with really good comebacks on the spot.

Here are the takeaways from this story:

1. I love pretending I know nothing about money with so-called professional advisers. This was one of the best days of my life.

2. The vast majority of you do not need a wealth manager or even a financial adviser. You've already got this book. Read it and use it. Living a Rich Life is not that hard if you follow advice that works for everyone.

3. Wealth managers know they cannot beat the market, so they try to focus on other ways they can "add value," such as: "Anyone can make money in a bull market. We'll help you when the market shifts." And "We can advise on taxes, wills, and trusts, and insurance." All of these are legit—but none of them requires a commission-based adviser. If you get skittish when the market goes down, I think the better answer is to develop the skills to stay resilient and focused during a market downturn yourself. Don't make decisions out of fear. Trust in yourself and your financial system.

4. Once you have seven figures in assets, or complex transactions involving kids or retirement or taxes, you've earned the right to consider advanced advice. Hire a fee-only financial adviser for a few hours or see my website for my advanced course on personal finance.

Active vs. Passive Management

Please know that even with all of this doom and gloom about professional investor performance, I'm not in any way saying that investing is a waste of money. You just have to know where to invest.

Mutual funds—which are simply collections of different investments like stocks or bonds—are often considered the simplest and best way for most people to invest. But, as we've seen, fund managers fail to beat the market 75 percent of the time, and it can be hard to tell which funds will actually perform well over the long term. And no matter how good a mutual fund is, the returns are hampered by the large fees they charge. (Sure, there are some low-cost mutual funds, but because of the way they compensate their own portfolio managers and other employees, it's virtually impossible for them to compete with the low costs of passively managed index funds, which I'll talk more about in a minute.)

When it comes to investing, as discussed, fees are a huge drag on your returns. This is a little counterintuitive, since we're used to paying for service, like our gym membership or admission to Disneyland. If we're getting something out of it, we should pay a fair price, right? The key is "fair," and many of the financial "experts" we turn to for guidance make an effort to squeeze every last cent out of us.

> *I signed up for this retirement fund that charged a lot for management and now I have to put in money every month for five years to get it out. At the time, I was convinced by the financial adviser's demeanor and fancy words. I am debating whether I should get the money out with a $1,000 loss for the cancellation fees. I feel like such an idiot for signing up for a dumb fund with a crazy fee like this.* —**SUNG WOO KIM, 28**

You see, mutual funds use something called "active management." This means a portfolio manager actively tries to pick the best stocks and give you the best return. Sounds good, right? But even with all the fancy analysts and technology they employ, portfolio managers still make fundamentally human mistakes, like selling too quickly, trading too much, and making rash guesses. These fund managers trade frequently so they can show short-term results to their shareholders and prove they're doing something—anything!—to earn your money. Not only do they usually fail to beat the market, but they charge a fee to do this. Mutual funds typically charge 1 to 2 percent of assets managed each year. (This percentage is known as a fund's expense ratio.) In other words, with a 2 percent expense ratio and a $10,000 portfolio, you'd pay $200 per year in fees. Some funds even tack on additional sales charges, or "loads," to the purchase price (a front-end load) or sales price (back-end load) of the fund. These are just some of the tricky ways mutual fund managers make money whether they perform or not.

Two percent doesn't sound like much until you compare it with the alternative: "passive management." This is how index funds (a cousin of mutual funds) are run. These funds work by replacing portfolio managers with computers. The computers don't attempt to find the hottest stock. They simply and methodically pick the same stocks that an index holds—for example, the five hundred stocks in the S&P 500—in an attempt to match the market. (An index is a way to measure part of the stock market. For example, the NASDAQ index represents certain technology stocks, while the S&P 500 represents five hundred large US stocks. There are international indexes and even retail indexes.)

Most index funds stay close to the market (or to the segment of the market they represent). Just as the stock market may fall 10 percent one year and gain 18 percent the next year, index funds will rise and fall with the indexes they track. The big difference is in fees: Index funds have lower fees than mutual funds, because there's no expensive staff to pay. Vanguard's S&P 500 index fund, for example, has an expense ratio of 0.14 percent.

Remember, there are all kinds of index funds. International funds, healthcare funds, small-cap funds. There are even funds that match the overall US stock market, which means if the market goes down, these index funds will also go down. But over the long term, the overall stock market has consistently returned about 8 percent after inflation.

Let's look at the performance from two sides: the downside (fees) and the upside (returns). First, let's compare the fees for a passively managed fund with those for an actively managed fund.

WHAT'S A BETTER DEAL?

Assuming an 8 percent return on an investment of $100/month	Passively managed index fund (0.14% expense ratio)	Actively managed mutual fund (1% expense ratio)	Investors pay how much more in fees with an actively managed fund?
After 5 years, you have . . .	$7,320.93	$7,159.29	$161.64
After 10 years, you have . . .	$18,152.41	$17,308.48	$843.93
After 25 years, you have . . .	$92,967.06	$81,007.17	$11,959.89

Now let me show you how these numbers change at higher levels. Remember: What seems like a small fee actually turns into a huge drag on your performance. This time, assume you put $5,000 into an account and you add $1,000 a month, with the same 8 percent return.

After 5 years, you have . . .	$80,606.95	$78,681.03	$1,925.92
After 10 years, you have . . .	$192,469.03	$183,133.11	$9,335.92
After 25 years, you have . . .	$965,117.31	$838,698.78	$126,418.53

John Bogle, the Vanguard founder, once shared a shocking example with PBS documentary series *Frontline*. Let's assume you and your friend Michelle each invested in funds with identical performance over fifty years. The only difference is that you paid 2 percent lower fees than she did. So your investment returned 7 percent annually, while hers returned 5 percent. What would the difference be?

On the surface, 2 percent in fees doesn't seem like much. It's natural to guess that your returns might differ by 2 percent or even 5 percent. But the math of compounding will shock you.

"Assuming a fifty-year horizon, the second portfolio would have lost 63 percent of its potential returns to fees," Mr. Bogle said.

Think about that. A simple 2 percent in fees can cost you over *half* of your investment returns.

Or that 1 percent fee. One percent can't be that much, right? For the same fifty-year time period, that fee will cost you 39 percent of your returns. I know, I know. Maybe fifty years is too long to think about. Let's try a thirty five-year outlook. What would a 1 percent fee cost you? Try a 28 percent reduction in your retirement returns, according to the Department of Labor.

This is why I'm so fanatical about reducing fees. In investing, fees are your enemy.

If your decision was determined by fees alone, index funds would be the clear choice. But let's also consider another important factor: returns.

Just before I got married I decided to speak to a financial adviser. I wanted to get a good picture of my position before I merged my financial life with my husband's. His fee wasn't ridiculous compared to the top of the market, but the advice certainly was, scaring me into buying managed products (with ongoing fees) I didn't need. It made my financial position seem more complex than it actually was, and I still had no idea of what to do. While on honeymoon I read I Will Teach You to Be Rich *for the first time, and when I got back, I reversed most of the decisions the financial adviser had made.* **—LUCINDA B., 33**

Despite my hammering home the fact that mutual funds fail to beat the market 75 percent of the time, I will say that they do occasionally provide great returns. In some years, some mutual funds do extraordinarily well and far outperform index funds. In a good year, for example, a fund focused on Indian stocks might return 70 percent— but one or two years of great performance only gets you so far. What you really want is solid, long-term returns. So, if you're thinking about using a broker or actively managed fund, call them and ask them a simple, point-blank question: "What were your after-tax, after-fee returns for the last ten, fifteen, and twenty years?" Yes, their response must include all fees and taxes. Yes, the return period must be at least ten years, because the last five years of any time period are too volatile to matter. And yes, I promise they won't give you a straight answer,

INVISIBLE SCRIPTS ABOUT FINANCIAL ADVISERS

Invisible script	What it means
"I don't know, I just want to pay someone to take it off my hands."	It's natural to be intimidated by all the jargon and confusing advice. But this is *your* money. Learning the fundamentals will be the most profitable decision you ever make. There's a famous quote from self-development legend Jim Rohn, who says, "Don't wish it was easier, wish you were better. Don't wish for less problems, wish for more skills." Don't wish for someone to hold your hand like you're a four-year-old skipping rope and chewing bubblegum. Wish to build discipline of long-term investing, like an adult. Others have done it and you can too.
"I like him. He's really trustworthy. Also, my dad used him."	I like my local bagel guy. Does that mean I should invest with him? Our tendency to conflate "likable" with "trustworthy" is amazing. One great study at the University of Chicago demonstrated this. The title of the study: "US doctors are judged more on bedside manner than effectiveness of care." Your adviser might be likable. He might be funny and thoughtful. But when it comes to your money, focus on results.
"I'm afraid of losing money."	Good. Then you should know that every dollar you're paying to an adviser via fees is a dollar you could have invested. For example, a 1 percent fee can reduce your returns by around 30 percent.
"My guy has beaten the market the last four years."	Maybe he has. More likely he hasn't, once you factor in all fees and taxes, which he'll naturally obscure. As research shows, just because someone is hot now doesn't mean they will be in the future.

because that would be admitting that they didn't beat the market consistently. It's *that* hard to do.

So, the safe assumption is that actively managed funds will too often fail to beat or match the market. In other words, if the market returns 8 percent, actively managed funds won't return at least 8 percent more than three-fourths of the time. In addition, when combined with their high expense ratios, actively managed funds have to outperform cheaper, passively managed funds by at least 1 to 2 percent just to break even with them—and that simply doesn't happen.

In *The Smartest Investment Book You'll Ever Read*, Daniel Solin cites a study conducted by Professor Edward S. O'Neal from the Babcock Graduate School of Management (now the Wake Forest School of Business). O'Neal tracked funds whose sole purpose was to beat the market. What he discovered was that from 1993 through 1998, less than half of these actively managed funds beat the market. And from 1998 through 2003, only 8 percent beat the market. But there's more. When he looked at the number of funds that beat the market in both time periods, the results were "sad indeed. The number of funds that beat the market in *both* periods was a whopping ten—or only 2 percent of all large-cap funds . . . Investors, both individual and institutional, and particularly 401(k) plans, would be far better served by investing in passive or passively managed funds than in trying to pick more expensive active managers who purport to be able to beat the markets."

Bottom line: There's no reason to pay exorbitant fees for active management when you could do better, for cheaper, on your own. Yet you and I know that money isn't purely rational—even seeing the clear math here. It's emotional. So once and for all, let's tackle the invisible money scripts on the facing page that keep people believing that active investment is worth it—then we can start investing.

Now that you've read about the myth of expertise, it's time to see exactly how you can invest your own money to get better returns for lower cost. In the next chapter, I'll teach you everything you need to know about investing, and we'll cover all the technical aspects of selecting and automating your investments. Let's do this.

P.S.—If you're looking for Action Steps, keep reading. This chapter is strictly informational, but in the next section you'll make some major decisions.

CHAPTER 7

INVESTING ISN'T ONLY FOR RICH PEOPLE

*Spend the afternoon picking a simple portfolio
that will make you rich*

In the previous chapter, you read about how useless investing "experts" are—and how we can do better on our own. Now we've arrived at the promised land, the chapter where you'll learn how to choose your own investments, pay less in fees, and get superior performance. You're going to determine your investing style by asking yourself some key questions: Do you need your money next year, or can you let it grow for a while? Are you saving up for a house? Can you withstand big day-to-day changes in the stock market, or do they make you queasy? Then you're going to research funds and pick exactly the right investments to meet your goals. This includes all your investment accounts, like your 401(k) and Roth IRA. (When people talk about their "investment portfolio," they're referring to money in their 401(k), Roth IRA, and perhaps even other investment accounts.) By the end of this chapter, you'll know exactly what to invest in—and why. And you'll do it with minimal human involvement, incurring minimal expense.

My goal is to help you pick the simplest investment to get started—and to make your portfolio easy to maintain. By doing just those two things, you'll be on the way to getting rich. You'll realize that lots of people with high salaries have no savings or investments. You'll start noticing the excuses people make to justify not investing, including "I don't have time" and "Stocks can go down, and I don't want to lose my money."

Most people don't know the first thing about how to pick investments—but now you will! Ah, the promised land is sweet.

I used the advice from IWT to set up my Schwab IRA, personal investment account, and checking account prior to starting my first job when I was twenty-four. I'm now thirty and have over $300,000 saved between my personal investment account, 401(k), and IRA. **—SMIT SHAH, 30**

A Better Way to Invest: Automatic Investing

L et's be honest. Nobody really loves managing their money. I'd rather be *using* my money, like by taking a food tour in Tokyo or a weekend ski trip with friends. Basically, I'm always on the lookout for ways to spend less time and get better results. When I was applying to colleges, for example, I created a system to write three scholarship applications per day and ended up winning more than $200,000 in six months to pay for school. These days, I manage more than fifteen hundred emails per day about my blog and this book. This isn't to brag about how busy I am, but to show that when it comes to money, I'm very, very interested in paying less attention while getting better returns. I've taken pains to research investments that don't take lots of time to maintain and also pay off. That's why I urge you to combine a classic low-cost investing strategy with automation.

Automatic investing is not some revolutionary technique that I just invented. It's a simple way of investing in low-cost funds that is recommended by Nobel Laureates, billionaire investors such as Warren Buffett, and most academics. It involves spending most of your time choosing how your money will be distributed in your portfolio, then picking the investments (this actually takes the least amount of time), and finally automating your regular investments so you can sit and watch TV while growing your money. Hey, we're lazy. We might as well embrace it and use it to our advantage.

Automatic investing works for two reasons:

Lower expenses. As I discussed in Chapter 6, nothing kills your investment performance more than expensive funds that invisibly drain your returns. Investing in them is especially crazy when you can earn better returns with lower fees. Why would you pay for the privilege of losing your money? With automatic investing, you invest in low-cost funds—which replace worthless, expensive portfolio managers—and you save tens of thousands of dollars in trading fees, taxes incurred by frenetic trading, and overall investment expenses, thereby outperforming most investors.

It's automatic. Automatic investing frees you from having to pay attention to the latest "hot stock" or micro-change in the market. You pick a simple investment plan that doesn't involve any sexy stocks or guessing whether the market is going up or down, and then you set up automatic contributions to your investment accounts. In this way, you effectively trick yourself into investing because it requires no work from you. This means you can focus on living your life—doing your job well, spending time with friends, traveling to different countries, eating at great restaurants—instead of worrying about your money. I might well call this Zen Investing for People Who Have Real Lives. (And that is why I'll never be a naming consultant.)

Too Good to Be True?

The way I described automatic investing was basically the same as saying "Puppies are cute." Nobody would ever disagree with it. Automatic investing sounds perfect, but what happens when the market goes down? It's not as easy to go along for the ride then. For example, I know several people who had automatic investment plans, and when

Do You Believe Everything Your Friends Tell You?

Q: *MY FRIENDS TELL ME THAT INVESTING IS TOO RISKY AND THAT I COULD LOSE ALL MY MONEY. IS THAT TRUE?*

A: That's an instinctive, emotional reaction, not a well-reasoned, logical response. I can understand being nervous about investing, especially when you read press articles that use phrases like "Market Correction" and "Stock Drops 10% Overnight." With headlines like that, it's easy to practice the "DNA" style of investing—the Do Nothing Approach. It's very unfortunate that the people who are afraid of investing in the market right now are usually the very same people who buy when prices are soaring. As Warren Buffett has said, investors should "be fearful when others are greedy and greedy when others are fearful."

For you, it's different. You understand how investing works, so you can put a long-term perspective into practice. Yes, in theory it's possible for you to lose all your money, but if you've bought different investments to create a balanced (or "diversified") portfolio, you won't.

You'll notice that your friends are concerned with the downside: "You could lose everything! How will you have time to learn to invest? There are so many sharks out there to take your money."

What about the downside of the money they're losing every day by not investing?

Ask your friends what the average return of the S&P 500 has been for the past seventy years. How much money would they have if they invested $10,000 today and didn't touch it for ten years—or fifty years? They won't know, because they don't even know the basic return rate to assume (try 8 percent). When people say investing is too risky, it's because they don't know what they don't know.

the stock market incurred huge losses in late 2008, they immediately canceled their investments and took their money out of the market. Big mistake. The test of a real automatic investor is not when things are going up, but when they are going down. For example, in October 2018, the stock market dropped and one of my investment accounts decreased by more than $100,000. I did what I always do—kept investing, automatically, every single month.

It takes strength to know that you're basically getting shares on sale—and, if you're investing for the long term, the best time to make money is when everyone else is getting out of the market.

I started investing about three years ago, after reading a bunch of finance books, including yours. I started pretty late, was almost thirty-one, but I feel pretty good about my progress. I'm maxing out my Roth, where I'm investing more aggressively, and also putting 15 percent in my 401(k) with Vanguard, all index funds. I'm the first in my family to do this, so it took a while to figure out, but now it's on autopilot, so it feels great. **—JOE FRUH, 34**

Bottom line: Automatic investing may not seem as sexy as trading in hedge funds and biotech stocks, but it works a lot better. Again, would you rather be sexy or rich?

The Magic of Financial Independence

I remember going on TV to talk about *I Will Teach You to Be Rich*. Before the camera started, the anchor leaned over to me and congratulated me on my book. "Great job," he said. "So do you have to work anymore?"

I sat back and realized I'd never thought about that. "No," I told him. "I don't have to work anymore."

That was a powerful moment. And it's an example of the crossover point, where your investments earn enough to fund your expenses—automatically.

Imagine one day you woke up and you had enough money in your accounts to never work again. In other words, your investments were generating so much money that *your money was actually producing more money than your salary*. That's the Crossover Point, first described by Vicki Robin and Joe Dominguez in their book, *Your Money or Your Life*.

It's an incredibly influential idea in personal finance: Money makes money, and at a certain point, your money is generating so much new money that all of your expenses are covered. This is also known as being "financially independent" (FI).

What can you do once you hit the Crossover Point? At a minimum, you can do nothing. Wake up, spend three hours at brunch, go work out, see friends, and practice your hobby. You can choose to work, or not—after all, you could spend the rest of your life spending down your investments.

Many call this "retiring early" (RE); together, they're Financial Independence + Retiring Early = FIRE. There's "LeanFire," which is people who've decided they can live on a "lean" amount of money— often $30,000 to $50,000 a year in perpetuity. They reject materialism and embrace simplicity, often in an extreme way.

"FatFire" is for people who want to live an extravagant life at the highest levels of spending. Ever wonder how celebrities can spend $250,000 on a single party? That's because their money is earning so much money that they actually have to *work* to spend it all. For example, in 2018, Oprah Winfrey bought a house for $8 million. That seems outrageously expensive, right? Here's the twist: Because her net worth at the time was over $4 billion, if that money was even conservatively invested and returned 4 percent, her investments alone—not even counting her salary—would generate $160 million that year, effectively making the house "free" to her.

Now apply that to your life. Most people won't get to $125 million in net worth—but what if you had $1 million? $2 million? $5 million? Run the numbers (assuming an 8 percent return) to see how much that would generate for you. It's eye-opening.

When you hit the point of financial independence, you're being paid to live because of decisions you made years ago. It's like an Indian kid studying ten hours a day to nail the SATs, then getting amazing jobs and opportunities decades later. Little Raj doesn't remember the hours he spent studying—he just loves the results of that hard work, even twenty-five years later.

Again, a summary of the terms:

- FI: Financial Independence. Where you've earned enough that your investments will pay for your life in perpetuity

- RE: Retiring Early, often in your thirties or forties

- FIRE: Financial Independence + Retiring Early. Think of someone who retires in their thirties and will technically never have to work again because their investments cover their annual living expenses, every year, forever.

- LeanFire: People who want to live a "lean" life, often on around $30,000 per year. They are likely doing fun things like going for walks in the park and bird-watching.

- FatFire: People who want to be financially independent and retire early, but live an extravagant lifestyle. Think of flying first class and staying at the Four Seasons, or putting three kids through private school.

Achieving FIRE isn't easy. And typically, most people dismiss it out of hand. "I'm too young to think about that," they say. Then, just a few years later, "It's too late for me to start." (Funny how that excuse changes so fast.) Or the final flourish of rationalization: "I'd rather spend my money now than nickel-and-dime myself for the next thirty years."

The real answer, of course, is that you can choose whether the Crossover Point is part of your Rich Life—and if you want to reach it, you can choose how to achieve it.

Many people in the financial independence community focus on saving a huge portion of their salary. Forget about the usual 10 percent or 20 percent savings rates, they say—how about 70 percent?

For example, if your household income is $80,000 and your monthly expenses are $6,000, you could reach your crossover point in thirty-eight years by following the usual advice of saving and investing 10 percent . . . or you could reach it a lot faster.

How?

I'll show you with some real numbers.

Option 1: You could cut your monthly expenses down to $3,000. Many people find it difficult to imagine living on $36,000 (or, put another way, to imagine cutting their spending in half). But there are countless online examples of LeanFire followers actually doing it. Following this strategy, you could reach your crossover point in just over twelve years. (Keep in mind the tradeoff here: Twelve years is extremely fast for a crossover point, but you've targeted ongoing spending of $36,000 per year.)

Option 2: You could raise your income. Let's say you follow the advice on my website to negotiate your salary and you receive a 30 percent raise. If you take all that extra money and invest it, you'd hit your crossover point in twenty-two years. Again, notice that this takes longer than the above—a lot longer—but in this example, you've targeted spending $72,000 per year.

Option 3: You could do a combination of both. If you increased your income by 30 percent and cut your spending by 30 percent, you'd hit your crossover point in nine years. Here, you see an extremely short time to your crossover point, combined with relatively high spending. This shows the power of targeting your income and expenses.

Most people never think about their earnings and spending in this way. As a result, they do the same thing as most other people: save a tiny amount every year, end up working for decades, and find themselves ranting about taxes on Twitter without knowing what the hell they're talking about. With this chapter alone, you'll realize that if you wanted to, you could dramatically change the way you approach your working years. Earn more. Spend less. Or earn more and spend more! *You* decide on your Rich Life.

By the way, I have mixed feelings about FIRE. On one hand, I love any strategy that helps people get more conscious about spending and saving. FIRE is an antidote to Americans' tepid savings rate: It absolutely obliterates the usual 10 percent standard by showing that saving 25 percent, 40 percent, even 70 percent of your income is possible—if you get crystal clear about your goals.

On the other hand, many FIRE adherents exhibit classic signs of stress, anxiety, and even depression, and think that hitting some mythical number in their spreadsheet will solve their unhappiness. It won't.

You can see this by going to the "financial independence" subreddit, where you'll find thousands of people who are obsessed with quitting their job as quickly as possible so they can retire.

As one redditor wrote:

"I look back at the past few years of my life and at my bank account and I would gladly give away a hefty chunk of it and work longer if it meant I could have experienced more of the world and found more passions I could have for the rest of my life, especially with someone I had loved so much. I built my savings, but I never built my life."

I have no problem with setting an aggressive financial goal (in fact, I love it). I have no problem with people who have different financial goals than mine. But when people use words like "miserable," "rat race," and "anxiety," that's a red flag.

My suggestion: Remember that life is lived outside the spreadsheet. Be as aggressive as you want with your goals—dream bigger than you ever thought!—but remember that money is just a small part of a Rich Life.

I was afraid to get started with investing before reading the IWT book. I had a 401(k), but wasn't maxing it out, didn't have an IRA, and had no investments. My parents drilled scarcity mindsets into me growing up and were extremely risk averse. I finally set up a Roth IRA and have maxed it out every year. Last year I maxed out my 401(k) for the first time and am on track to do it again this year. I set up a personal investment account and automatically add to it every month. I did all of those things without affecting my current lifestyle, and actually living a little more extravagantly. Through the investment accounts, I've got over $100,000 growing for retirement, and $8,000 in the personal investment account.

—DAVID CHAMBERS, 35

More Convenience or More Control: You Choose

I want investing to be as painless as possible for you, so here's what I'm going to do: I'll give you an easy version and a more advanced version. If you're the kind of person who wants your money to grow with the least possible effort on your part and you don't care about all the theory, turn to page 238. There you'll find a step-by-step guide for picking a single investment—a target date fund—and you'll get started investing in just a few hours.

But if you're a type A nerd like me who wants to learn how it works—and maybe even customize your own portfolio for more control—read on. I'll walk you through the building blocks of a portfolio, and I'll help you construct one that's both aggressive and balanced.

Investing Is Not About Picking Stocks

Really, it's not. Ask your friends what they think investing means, and I bet they'll say, "Picking stocks." Guys, you cannot reliably pick stocks that will outperform the market over the long term. It's way too easy to make mistakes, such as being overconfident about choices or panicking when your investments drop even a little. As we saw in Chapter 6, even experts can't guess what will happen to the stock market. But because they've heard it repeatedly from the many investment blogs and YouTube videos, people think that investing is about picking winning stocks and that anyone can be successful. They can't. I hate to say it, but not everyone is a winner. In fact, most of these so-called financial "experts" are failures.

Anyway, the little-known fact is that the major predictor of your portfolio's volatility doesn't stem from the individual stocks you pick, as most people think, but instead from your mix of stocks and bonds. In 1986, researchers Gary Brinson, Randolph Hood, and Gilbert Beebower published a study in *Financial Analysts Journal* that rocked the financial world. They demonstrated that more than 90 percent of your portfolio's volatility is a result of your asset allocation. I know "asset allocation" sounds like a BS phrase—like "mission statement" or "strategic alliance." But it's not. Asset allocation is your plan for investing, the way you distribute the investments in your portfolio between stocks, bonds, and cash. In other words, by diversifying your investments across different asset classes (like stocks and bonds or, better yet, stock funds and bond funds), you can control the risk in your portfolio—and therefore control how much money, on average, you'll lose due to volatility. It turns out that the way you allocate your portfolio—whether it's 100 percent stocks or 90 percent stocks and 10 percent bonds—makes a profound difference on your returns. (Later, other researchers tried to measure how closely volatility and returns were correlated, but the answer ends up being pretty complicated.) Suffice it to say that asset allocation is the most significant part of your portfolio that you can control.

Think about that remarkable fact: *Your investment plan is more important than your actual investments*.

Take, for example, this book. If we apply the same principle here, it means that the way I organized this book—my table of contents—is more important than any given word in it. That makes sense, right? Well, the same is true of investing. If you allocate your money properly—for example, not all in one stock, but spread out across different kinds of funds—you won't have to worry about a single stock possibly cutting your portfolio's value in half. Indeed, by diversifying your investments, you'll make more money as an individual investor. To know how to allocate your assets, you have to know the basic options you have for investing, which is where we're headed next.

Since you cannot successfully time the market or select individual stocks, asset allocation should be the major focus of your investment strategy, because it is the only factor affecting your investment risk and return that you can control.

—WILLIAM BERNSTEIN, *THE FOUR PILLARS OF INVESTING: LESSONS FOR BUILDING A WINNING PORTFOLIO*

The Building Blocks of Investing

I f you're not interested in the mechanics of investing and want to skip ahead to see what the simplest investment choice is, turn to page 238. But if you want to know more about what's going on under the hood, stay with me.

The Pyramid of Investing Options on the next page represents your possible choices for different investments. At the bottom is the most basic level, where you can invest in stocks or bonds or just hold your money in cash. I'm oversimplifying, because there are tons of different kinds of stocks and bonds, but you get the idea. Above them are index and mutual funds. And finally, at the top of the pyramid, are target date funds.

THE PYRAMID OF INVESTING OPTIONS

TARGET DATE FUNDS

More convenience

Less control

More predictable returns over the long term

INDEX FUNDS/MUTUAL FUNDS

Somewhat convenient

Can have low fees (index funds) or high fees (many mutual funds)

More control than target date funds, less control than stocks/bonds

Returns are fairly predictable over the long term

STOCKS / BONDS / CASH

Individual stocks and bonds are very inconvenient to choose and maintain

High control

Individual stocks offer extremely unpredictable returns that often fail to beat the market (but sometimes trounce it)

Bonds offer extremely predictable returns, but on average return less than stocks

Let's look at each category of investment (also known as "asset classes") to see what lies beneath.

Stocks

When you buy stock, you buy shares of a company. If the company does well, you expect your stock in it to do well. When people talk about "the market," they're usually referring to an index of stocks like the Dow Jones (thirty large-cap stocks) or the S&P 500 (500 companies with large market capitalization). Investment nerds may be wondering: What's the difference between the indexes? There are many differences, but in general, they're not really important to your personal finances. Each index is like a college: There are committees that determine the criteria for allowing companies on their index, and they may change those criteria over time.

Overall, stocks as a category provide excellent returns. As we know, on average the stock market returns about 8 percent per year. In fact, you can do significantly better than the market if you pick a winning stock—or significantly worse if you pick a loser. Although stocks as a whole provide generally excellent returns over time, individual stocks are less clear. If you invest all your money in one stock, for example, you might make a huge return, but it's also possible the company could tank and you could lose it all.

Stocks have been a good way to earn significant returns over the long term, but I discourage you from picking individual stocks, because it's extremely difficult to choose winning ones on your own. The tricky thing about stocks is you never know what will happen. For example, in 2018 Snapchat announced a redesign of their app interface. The stock plunged 9.5 percent in one day. The opposite can happen if a company announces good news.

In Chapter 6, I demonstrated that even professionals whose livelihoods depend on it can't predict stock returns. And remember, these are highly trained analysts who can read stock prospectuses like I can read an Indian restaurant menu—flawlessly. If these experts who devour annual reports and understand complicated balance sheets can't beat the market, what chance do you have of picking stocks that will go up?

You have very little chance. That's why individual investors like you and me should not invest in individual stocks. Instead, we'll choose funds, which are collections of stocks (and sometimes, for diversification, bonds). They let you reduce your risk and create a well-balanced portfolio that will let you sleep at night . . . but more on that later.

Bonds

Bonds are essentially IOUs from companies or the government. (Technically, bonds are longer-term investments of ten-plus years, whereas certificates of deposits, or CDs, involve lending money to a bank. Because they're very similar, let's just call them both bonds to simplify things.) If you buy a one-year bond, it's the same as if the bank says, "Hey, if you lend us $100, we'll give you $103 back a year from now."

The advantages of bonds are that you can choose the term, or length of time, you want the loan to last (two years, five years, ten years, and so on), and you know exactly how much you'll get when they "mature" or pay out. Also, bonds, especially government bonds, are generally stable and let you decrease the risk in your portfolio. See, the only way you'd lose money on a government bond is if the government defaulted on its loans—and it doesn't do that. If it runs low on money, it just prints more of it. Now that's gangsta.

But because bonds are such a safe, low-risk investment, the return—even on a highly rated bond—is much lower than it would be on an excellent stock. Investing in bonds also renders your money illiquid, meaning it's locked away and inaccessible for a set period of time. Technically, you can withdraw early, but you'll face severe penalties, so it's a bad idea.

With these qualities, what kind of person would invest in bonds? Let's see: extremely stable, essentially guaranteed rate of return, but relatively small returns . . . Who would it be?

In general, rich people and old people like bonds. Old people like them because they want to know exactly how much money they're getting next month for their medication or whatever it is they need. Also, some of these grannies and grampies can't withstand the volatility of the stock market because they don't have much other income to support themselves and/or they have very little time left on this earth to recover from any downturn.

Rich people, on the other hand, tend to become more conservative because they have so much money. Put it this way: When you have $10,000, you want to invest aggressively to grow it because you want to make more money. But when you have $10 million, your goals switch from aggressive growth to preservation of capital. Chuck Jaffe once wrote a CBS Marketwatch column where he shared this old story about Groucho Marx, the famous comedian and avid investor.

One trader asked, "Hey Groucho, where do you invest your money?"

"I keep my money in treasury bonds," he replied.

"They don't make you much money," a trader shouted back.

"They do," Groucho said drolly, "if you have enough of them."

If you have a lot of money, you'll accept lower investment returns in exchange for security and safety. So a guaranteed bond at 3 percent or 4 percent is attractive to a wealthy person—after all, 3 percent of $10 million is still a lot.

Cash

In investing terms, cash is money that's sitting on the sidelines, uninvested and earning only a little money in interest from money market accounts, which are basically high-interest savings accounts. Traditionally, cash has been the third part of a portfolio, alongside stocks and bonds. You want to have totally liquid cash on hand for emergencies, and as a hedge if the market tanks. Of course, you pay a price for this security: Cash is the safest part of your portfolio, but it offers the lowest reward. In fact, you actually lose money by holding cash once you factor inflation in.

That's why I say it's traditionally been part of a portfolio. As long as you're contributing toward your savings goals as I described in Chapter 5 and have enough to cover emergencies and ideally more, you're fine. Don't worry about having cash in your investment account. Let's keep this simple.

Asset Allocation: The Critical Factor That Most Investors Miss

If you bought all different kinds of stocks or stock funds, you'd be diversified—but still only within stocks. That's like being the hottest person in Friendship, Wisconsin—it's nice, but we're talking about modest competition. (Friendship is actually a real place. My friend grew up there, and he told me what he and his buddies used to use as a gang sign: two hands clasping in friendship.)

It is important to diversify within stocks, but it's even more important to allocate across the different asset classes—like stocks and bonds. Investing in only one category is dangerous over the long term. This is where the all-important concept of asset allocation comes into play. Remember it like this: Diversification is D for going deep into a category (for example, buying different types of stocks: large-cap, small-cap, international, and so on), and asset allocation is A for going across all categories (for example, stocks *and* bonds).

90 YEARS OF AVERAGE ANNUAL RETURNS FOR STOCKS AND BONDS

NYU corporate finance professor Aswath Damodaran analyzed ninety years of investment returns. These numbers show us the returns of the S&P 500 over a very long period of time.

Stocks	Bonds	Cash
Higher risk	Lower risk	Ultra-low risk. Stored in an interest-generating money-market account, not under your mattress.
11.5%	5.2%	3.4%

You should note that the past is no predictor of future results. For the more technical, you should also note that those returns are an arithmetic mean (Compound Interest Growth Rate is 9.5%) and do not include inflation.

In determining where to allocate your assets, one of the most important considerations is what returns each category offers. Of course, based on the different types of investments you make, you can expect different returns. Higher risk generally equals higher potential for reward. Take a look at the chart above. At first glance, it seems clear that stocks return the most. So let's all invest there!!

Not so fast. Remember, higher rewards entail higher risk, so if you're loaded up on stocks and your portfolio dips 35 percent next year, all of a sudden you're financially immobile, eating only Triscuits, waiting to see whether your money climbs back up or you die first.

Your asset allocation is actually one of the most important decisions you'll make in life—it's a decision that could be worth hundreds of thousands of dollars to you and for some, millions. But in a peculiar quirk of human nature, we're more likely to talk about a new restaurant or TV show instead of our asset allocation.

In fact, how many of us have never even heard the phrase "asset allocation" before now?

That's because the financial media thinks it's too complicated for us to understand, so they resort to words like "safety" and "growth." In reality, asset allocation is one of the *only* things that matters, and I think you're smart enough to learn it.

Asset allocation has real-world consequences. For example, many of us have heard of fifty- and sixty-year-olds who saw catastrophic drops in their portfolios during the last recession. Their assets were not properly allocated: They should never have invested in all equities. (Nor should they have sold during the downturn—had they stayed in the market, they would have been rewarded handsomely over time.)

Age and risk tolerance matter. If you're twenty-five years old and have dozens of years to grow your money, a portfolio made up of mostly stock-based funds probably makes sense. But if you're older, retirement is coming up within a few decades and you'll want to tamp down your risk. Even if the market tanks, you have control over your asset allocation. If you're older—especially if you're in your sixties or older, for god's sake—a sizable portion of your portfolio should be in stable bonds.

Bonds act as a counterweight to stocks, generally rising when stocks fall and reducing the overall risk of your portfolio. By investing part of your money in bonds, you reduce some of your overall risk. Sure, if that biotech stock went up 200 percent, you'd wish your bond money was all in the stock—but if the stock went down, you'd be glad your bonds were there as a buffer against losing everything. Although it may seem counterintuitive, your portfolio will actually have better overall performance if you add bonds to the mix. Because bonds will generally perform better when stocks fall, bonds lower your risk a lot while limiting your returns only a little.

"But Ramit," you might say, "I'm young and I want to invest aggressively. I don't need bonds." I agree. Bonds aren't really for young people in their twenties. If you're in your twenties or early thirties and you don't necessarily need to reduce your risk, you can simply invest in all-stock funds and let time mitigate any risk.

STOCKS AND BONDS HAVE MANY FLAVORS

Stocks	Bonds
Large-Cap Big companies with a market capitalization ("market cap," which is defined as outstanding shares times the stock price) over $10 billion	**Government** An ultra-safe investment that's backed by the government. In exchange for their low risk, government bonds tend to return less than stocks.
Mid-Cap Midsized companies with a market cap between $1 billion and $5 billion	**Corporate** A bond issued by a corporation. These tend to be riskier than government bonds but safer than stocks.
Small-Cap Smaller companies with a market cap less than $1 billion	**Short-Term** Bonds with terms of usually less than three years
International investments Stocks from companies in other countries, including emerging markets (like China and India) and developed markets (like the United Kingdom and Germany). Americans may sometimes buy these directly, but may have to buy them through funds.	**Long-Term** These bonds tend to mature in ten or more years and, accordingly, offer higher yields than shorter-term bonds.
Growth Stocks whose value may grow higher than other stocks, or even the market as a whole	**Municipal** Also known as "munis," these are bonds issued by local governments
Value Stocks that seem bargain priced (i.e., cheaper than they should be)	**Inflation-Protected** Treasury inflation-protected securities, or TIPS, are ultra-safe investments that protect against inflation.

Note that because of their complicated structure, REITs, "real estate investment trusts"—which are types of investments that let you invest in real estate through a single ticker symbol, just like a stock—don't neatly fall into any of these categories.

But in your thirties and older, you'll want to begin balancing your portfolio with bonds to reduce risk. And what if stocks as a whole don't perform well for a long time? That's when you need to own bonds to offset the bad times.

Another interesting scenario that calls for lower risk via more bonds: If you've accumulated a very large portfolio, you have a different risk profile. In one famous example, personal finance expert Suze Orman was asked about her net worth in an interview. She replied, "One journalist estimated my liquid net worth at $25 million. That's pretty close. My houses are worth another $7 million."

The journalist asked where she puts her money. With the exception of $1 million in the stock market, she said, the rest was in bonds.

The personal finance world was horrified. All that money in bonds?

But she has approximately 25 million good reasons that most don't. As a financial adviser once told me, "Once you've won the game, there's no reason to take unnecessary risk."

The Importance of Being Diversified

Now that we know the basics of the asset classes (stocks, bonds, and cash) at the bottom of the pyramid, let's explore the different choices within each asset class. Basically, there are many types of stocks, and we need to own a little of all of them. Same with bonds. This is called "diversifying," and it essentially means digging in to each asset class—stocks and bonds—and investing in all their subcategories.

As the table on the previous page shows, the broad category of "stocks" actually includes many different kinds of stocks, including large-company stocks ("large-cap"), mid-cap stocks, small-cap stocks, and international stocks. To add yet another wrinkle, none of them performs consistently. In the same year, small-cap stocks might gain huge percentages but international stocks might tank—and this performance can vary from year to year. Similarly, different types of bonds offer different benefits, including different rates of return and tax advantages. In his 2012 book *Skating Where the Puck Was*, William Bernstein says to "resign yourself to the fact that diversifying yourself

WHAT A GRANNY NEEDS: TYPICAL ASSET ALLOCATIONS BY AGE

Here's what typical investors' asset allocations—remember, that's the mix of different investments—might look like as they get older. These figures are taken from Vanguard's target date funds.

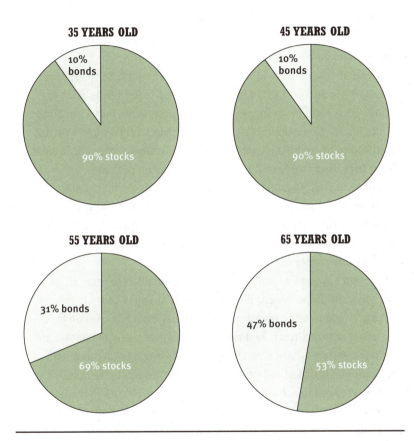

among risky assets provide[s] scant shelter from bad days or bad years, but that it does help protect against bad decades and generations, which can be far more destructive to wealth." Diversification is about safety in the long term.

The fact that performance varies so much in each asset class means two things: First, if you're trying to make a quick buck off investing, you'll usually lose money, because you have no idea what will happen in the near future. Anyone who tells you they do is a fool or a commission-based salesman. Second, you should own different categories of stocks (and maybe bonds) to balance out your portfolio. You don't want to own only US small-cap stocks, for example, or funds that own only small-cap stocks. If they didn't perform well for ten years, that would really suck. If, however, you own small-cap stocks, plus large-cap stocks, plus international stocks, and more, you're effectively insured against any one area dragging you down. So if you were to invest in stocks, you'd want to diversify, buying all different types of stocks or stock funds to have a balanced portfolio.

These allocations are just general rules of thumb. Some people prefer to have 100 percent in stocks until they're in their thirties or forties. Others are more conservative and want some money in bonds. But the big takeaway here is that if we're in our twenties and thirties, we can afford to be aggressive about investing in stocks and stock funds—even if they drop temporarily—because time is on our side.

And honestly, if you're nervous about investing and just starting out, your biggest danger isn't having a portfolio that's too risky. It's being lazy and overwhelmed and not doing any investing at all. That's why it's important to understand the basics but not get too wrapped up in all the variables and choices.

Over time, you can manage your asset allocation to reduce risk and get a fairly predictable return on investments. Thirty years from now, you're going to need to invest very differently from how you do today. That's just natural: You invest much more aggressively in your thirties than in your sixties, when you find yourself growing older and telling long-winded stories about how you trudged through three miles of snow (each way) to get to school every morning. The real work in investing comes with creating an investment plan that's appropriate for your age and comfort level with risk.

All of this sounds completely reasonable: "I invest aggressively when I'm younger, and as I get older, I get more conservative."

There's just one problem.

How the hell are you actually supposed to do it? What specific investments should you choose? Should you invest in individual stocks? (No.) Most people stop here, thinking that investing is only about stocks. Not surprisingly, when they try to think more deeply about this, they get confused and delay the decision to invest until someday in the future.

Don't let this happen to you! Let's go further up the Pyramid of Investing Options to cover another key to investing: funds.

Mutual Funds: Not Bad, Pretty Convenient, but Often Expensive and Unreliable

The financial industry isn't stupid. Those people are ingenious at creating products to meet investor needs (or what the industry wants people to need). In 1924, mutual funds, which are just baskets filled with different types of investments (usually stocks), were invented. Instead of requiring investors to perform the Herculean task of picking individual stocks themselves, mutual funds allowed average investors to simply choose types of funds that would suit them. For example, there are large-cap, mid-cap, and small-cap stock mutual funds, but also mutual funds that focus on biotechnology, communication, and even European or Asian stocks. Mutual funds are extremely popular because they allow you to pick one fund that contains different stocks and not worry about putting too many eggs in one basket (as you likely would if you bought individual stocks), monitoring prospectuses, or keeping up with industry news. The funds provide instant diversification because they hold many different stocks.

Most people's first encounter with mutual funds is through their 401(k), where they choose from a bewildering array of options. You buy shares of the fund, and the fund's manager picks the stocks he or she thinks will yield the best return.

Mutual funds are incredibly useful financial tools—over the past eighty-five years, they have proven to be very popular and extremely profitable. Compared with other investments, they've been a cash cow for Wall Street. That's because in exchange for "active management" (having an expert choose a fund's stocks), the financial companies charge big fat fees (also known as expense ratios). These fees eat a hole in your returns. For what? For nothing! You don't need to pay that! Sure, there are some low-fee funds out there, but most mutual funds have high expense ratios.

Now, I don't fault the financial companies for selling mutual funds. They got average Americans to invest, and, even after fees, mutual funds are an excellent investment choice compared with doing nothing. But things have changed. As we saw in Chapter 6, there are now better choices for investing: lower-cost, better-performing index funds.

Advantages of a mutual fund: Hands-off approach means an expert money manager makes investment decisions for you. Mutual funds hold many varied stocks, so if one company tanks, your fund doesn't go down with it.

Disadvantages: Annual fees can equal tens of thousands of dollars or more over the lifetime of an investment by using expense ratios, front-end loads, and back-end loads (worthless sales charges that add nothing to your returns)—all tricky ways to make mutual funds more money. Also, if you invest in two mutual funds, they may overlap in investments, meaning you may not really be as diversified as you think. Worst of all, you're paying an "expert" to manage your money, and 75 percent of them do not beat the market.

In short, mutual funds are prevalent because of their convenience, but because actively managed mutual funds are, by definition, expensive, they're not the best investment anymore. Active management can't compete with passive management, which takes us to index funds, the more attractive cousin of mutual funds.

I put my first chunk of money in an actively managed fund about a year before I read your book and really began to understand mutual funds. It was a long-term investment, so it certainly made money, but when compared to a benchmark index fund, I missed out on some growth. I finally found myself at a point where paying capital gains tax made sense, so I've now been able to roll it into lower-cost investments. Thanks, Ramit, for showing us the light.

—ANAND TRIVEDI, 35

Index Funds:
The Attractive Cousin in an
Otherwise Unattractive Family

In 1975, John Bogle, the founder of Vanguard, introduced the world's first index fund. These simple funds buy stocks and match the market (more precisely, to match an "index" of the market, such as the S&P 500), versus the traditional mutual fund, which employs an expensive staff of "experts" who try to predict which stocks will perform well, trade frequently, incur taxes in the process, and charge you fees. In short, they charge you to lose.

Index funds set a lower bar: No experts. No attempts to beat the market. Just a computer that automatically attempts to match the index and keep costs low for you. Index funds are the financial equivalent of "If you can't beat 'em, join 'em." And they do so while also being low cost and tax efficient and requiring hardly any maintenance at all. In other words, index funds are simply collections of stocks that computers manage in an effort to match the index of the market. There are index funds for the S&P 500, for Asia-Pacific funds, for real estate funds, and for anything else you can imagine. Just like mutual funds, they have ticker symbols (such as VFINX).

Bogle argued that index funds would offer better performance to individual investors. Active mutual fund managers could not typically beat the market, yet they charged investors unnecessary fees.

There's a funny effect called illusory superiority, which refers to how we all think we're better than other people (especially Americans). For example, in one study, 93 percent of respondents rated themselves in the top 50 percent of driver skills—an obviously impossible number. We believe we have a better memory, and that we're kinder and more popular and more unbiased than others. It feels good to believe it! Yet psychology has shown us that we are flawed.

Once you understand this, Wall Street makes a lot more sense: Every mutual fund manager believes he can beat the market. To accomplish this, managers use fancy analysis and data, and they trade frequently. Ironically, this results in lots of taxes and trading fees, which, when combined with the expense ratio, makes it virtually impossible for the average fund investor to beat—or even match—the market over time. Bogle opted to discard the old model of mutual funds and introduce index funds.

Today, index funds are an easy, efficient way to make a significant amount of money. Note, however, that index funds simply match the market. If you own all equities in your twenties and thirties and the stock market drops (like it has from time to time), your investments will drop. Expect it! It's normal for your investments to go up and down.

Professionals Agree— Index Funds Are Great Investments

You don't have to take my word for it. Here, a few experts on the benefits of index funds:

"I believe that 98 or 99 percent—maybe more than 99 percent— of people who invest should extensively diversify and not trade. That leads them to an index fund with very low costs."

—WARREN BUFFETT, ONE OF AMERICA'S GREATEST INVESTORS

"When you realize how few advisers have beaten the market over the last several decades, you may acquire the discipline to do something even better: become a long-term index fund investor."

—MARK HULBERT, FORMER EDITOR OF HULBERT FINANCIAL DIGEST

"The media focuses on the temporarily winning active funds that score the more spectacular bull's eyes, not index funds that score every year and accumulate less flashy, but ultimately winning, scores."

—W. SCOTT SIMON, AUTHOR OF INDEX MUTUAL FUNDS: PROFITING FROM AN INVESTMENT REVOLUTION

Over the long term, the stock market has always gone up. As a bonus for using index funds, you'll anger your friends in finance because you'll be throwing up your middle finger to their entire industry—and you'll keep their fees for yourself. Wall Street is terrified of index funds and tries to keep them under wraps with increased marketing of mutual funds and nonsense like "5-star funds."

HIGH EXPENSE RATIOS COST MORE THAN YOU THINK		
Amount in your portfolio	Annual expenses of a low-cost index fund (.14%)	Annual expenses of an actively managed mutual fund (1%)
$5,000	$7	$50
$25,000	$35	$250
$100,000	$140	$1,000
$500,000	$700	$5,000
$1,000,000	$1,400	$10,000

Advantages: Extremely low cost, easy to maintain, and tax efficient.

Disadvantages: When you're investing in index funds, you typically have to invest in multiple funds to create a comprehensive asset allocation (although owning just one is better than doing nothing). If you do purchase multiple index funds, you'll have to rebalance (or adjust your investments to maintain your target asset allocation) regularly, usually every twelve to eighteen months. Each fund typically requires a minimum investment, although this is often waived with automatic monthly investments.

Okay, so index funds are clearly far superior to buying either individual stocks and bonds or mutual funds. With their low fees, they are a great choice if you want to create and control the exact makeup of your portfolio.

But what if you're one of those people who knows you'll just never get around to doing the necessary research to figure out an appropriate asset allocation and which index funds to buy? Let's be honest: Most people don't want to construct a diversified portfolio, and they certainly don't want to rebalance and monitor their funds, even if it's just once a year.

If you fall into this group, there is the option at the very top of the investment pyramid. It's an investment option that's drop-dead easy: target date funds.

Target Date Funds: Investing the Easy Way

Whether you're just arriving here direct from page 222 or you've read through the basics of investing and decided you want to take the easy way after all, no problem—target date funds are the easiest investment choice you'll ever need to make.

Target date funds are my favorite investment of all because they embody the 85 Percent Solution: not exactly perfect, but easy enough for anyone to get started—and they work just fine.

The most beneficial part of the book for me was the section that explained the basics of what you really need in a retirement account and the 85 Percent Solution that helps you get your investments "good enough," so you're not stressing about which type of fund to choose. I like the idea that taking action and picking some type of basic lifecycle [target date] fund is better than getting stuck in analysis-paralysis and not saving.

—KAREN DUDEK-BRANNAN, 37

Target date funds are simple funds that automatically diversify your investments for you based on when you plan to retire. (Let's assume you'll retire at age 65 throughout this book.) Instead of you having to rebalance stocks and bonds, target date funds do it for you. If more Americans owned target date funds, for example, during the last recession far fewer retirees would have seen precipitous drops in their retirement accounts, because the target date funds would have automatically changed to a more conservative asset allocation as they approached their golden years. Target date funds are actually "funds of funds," or collections made up of other funds, which offer automatic diversification. For example, a target date fund might include large-cap, mid-cap, small-cap, and international funds. (And those funds, in turn, will hold stocks from each of those areas.) In other words, your target date fund will own many funds, all of which own stocks and bonds. It sounds complicated, but believe it or not, this actually makes things simple for you, because you'll have to own only one fund, and all the rest will be taken care of for you.

Target date funds are different from index funds, which are also low cost but require you to own multiple funds if you want a comprehensive asset allocation. Multiple funds mean you have to rebalance your funds regularly, usually every year, which is a laborious process of redistributing your money to different investments so you get back to your target asset allocation (or your "pie chart" of stocks vs. bonds vs. cash). What a pain.

Luckily, target date funds automatically pick a blend of investments for you based on your approximate age. They start you off with aggressive investments in your twenties and then shift investments to become more conservative as you get older. You do no work except continuing to send money into your target date fund.

Target date funds aren't perfect for everyone, because they work on one variable alone: when you plan to retire. If you had unlimited resources—more time, more money, and more discipline—you could conceivably squeeze out slightly better returns by building a custom portfolio based on your exact needs. But while we all grew up with our parents telling us we were special and different, the truth is that most of us are mostly the same. And very few of us have the resources or desire to constantly monitor our portfolios. That's why target date funds are great: They're designed to appeal to people who are lazy. In other words, for many people, the ease of use of these funds far outweighs any minor loss of returns that might occur from taking the one-size-fits-all approach. In my opinion, if it means it will get you investing, the benefits of having one fund that handles all of your investments make up for any shortcomings.

Target date funds aren't all created equal—some of them are more expensive than others—but as a general rule, they're low cost and tax efficient. Best of all, they take no work beyond automatically contributing money once a month, quarter, or year. You won't have to actively invest and monitor and rebalance on your own, because target date funds handle the messy work for you. Cool, right?

One thing to note is that you'll need between $100 and $1,000 as a minimum to buy into a fund. If you don't have it, make it a savings goal. Once you save the minimum needed to invest, you can open your fund and set up an automatic transfer each month. I cannot recommend target funds enough. They're easy, low cost, and they simply work.

Choosing and Actually Buying Your Investments

By now, you should know what you want to invest in: a target date fund or index funds. If you're even considering buying individual stocks because you think you can beat the market or it's sexier, I want you to take all your money, put it in a big Ziploc bag and light it on fire. At least you'll be skipping the middleman.

If you don't want to spend a billion years managing your money and you're satisfied with the 85 Percent Solution of investing in a convenient fund that's good enough and will free you up to live your life and do what you love, then go for a target date fund. If you're more of a personal finance geek, are willing to spend some time on your investments, and want more control, then choose index funds. Whichever category you fall into, you'll want to figure out exactly what to invest in. Let's get started.

A Common Investment Option: Your 401(k)

As we discussed in Chapter 3, if you get a 401(k) match from your employer, you need to pay into your 401(k) before you do any other investing. If your employer doesn't offer a 401(k) match, skip to the Roth IRA section on the next page. You should have already set up your 401(k), but now it's time to focus on how you allocate the money you're investing in it. (If you had to pick funds when you opened your account, you can always go back in and change your allocation.

Just ask your human resources person for the proper form or, better yet, change it on your 401(k) website.)

You know how I love reducing choice to get people to take action? Well, the companies that offer 401(k)s take this to an extreme: They offer a few investment funds for you to choose from—usually the options are called something like aggressive investments (which will be a fund of mostly stocks), balanced investments (this fund will contain stocks and bonds), and conservative investments (a more conservative mix of mostly bonds).

If you're not sure what the different choices mean, ask your HR representative for a sheet describing the differences in funds. Note: Stay away from "money market funds," which is just another way of saying your money is sitting, uninvested, in cash. You want to get your money working for you.

As a young person, I encourage you to pick the most aggressive fund they offer that you're comfortable with. As you know, the more aggressive you are when younger, the more money you'll likely have later. This is especially important for a 401(k), which is an ultra-long-term investment account.

Depending on what company your employer uses to administer your 401(k), your fund options may be a little pricey in terms of expense ratios (I consider anything over 0.75 percent expensive), but on balance, you're getting huge tax advantages and employer-match benefits. So it's worth it to invest in these funds, even if they aren't perfect.

Investing
Using Your Roth IRA

After your 401(k) match, the next best place to invest is your Roth IRA. (I'm sure I don't need to remind you that in addition to accruing earnings tax-free, one of the primary benefits of Roth IRAs is the flexibility of choosing any funds you want.)

When you send money to your Roth IRA account, it just sits there. You'll need to invest the money to start making good returns. The easiest investment is a target date fund. You can just buy it, set up automatic monthly contributions, and forget about it.

Choosing a Target Date Fund for Your Roth Ira

Let's assume you're looking for a target date fund through Vanguard, which I recommend (though there are many other solid companies that offer target date funds).

You'll notice that Vanguard offers funds with names like "Target Retirement 2040," "Target Retirement 2045," and "Target Retirement 2050." The main difference among these funds is how they're allocated: The larger the number (which represents the year you'll retire), the more equities (stocks) the fund has.

To find the right fund, choose the year you're likely to retire. If like most people you're thinking about age sixty-five, look up the fund that's closest to that year for you (e.g., 2050). You can also search for "Choosing Vanguard target date fund."

Like most target date funds, these funds have very low fees. Best of all, they automatically reallocate over time, so you don't have to worry about rebalancing (or buying and selling to maintain your target asset allocation). In short, they do all the hard work for you. All you have to do is contribute as much as possible.

A few notes you may want to keep in mind as you research these funds: Some companies call them "target date" funds, while others call them "target retirement" or "lifecycle" funds. They're all the same thing. Some companies require you to invest a minimum amount—usually $1,000 to $3,000—but that fee can often be waived if you agree to automatic investing, which you should. Finally, you can choose any target date fund, depending on your age and risk tolerance. So if you're twenty-five and pretty risk averse, you can pick a fund designed for someone older, which will give you a more conservative asset allocation.

Buying into Your Target Date Fund

Now that you've identified a target date fund to invest in, actually buying it is an easy process.

Log in to your Roth IRA (which you opened in Chapter 3). Your login information should be handy if you followed my tip on page 118.

You'll need to have at least enough cash in it to cover the minimum investment of the fund, which is usually between $1,000 and $3,000.

The Rule of 72

The Rule of 72 is a fast trick you can do to figure out how long it will take to double your money. Here's how it works: Divide the number 72 by the return rate you're getting, and you'll have the number of years you must invest in order to double your money. (For the math geeks among us, here's the equation: 72 ÷ return rate = number of years.) For example, if you're getting a 10 percent return rate from an index fund, it would take you a little more than seven years (72 divided by 10) to double your money. In other words, if you invested $5,000 today, let it sit there, and earned a 10 percent return, you'd have $10,000 in about seven years. And it doubles from there, too. Of course, you could accumulate even more using the power of compounding by adding more every month. As a rule of thumb, you should assume 8 percent returns.

Some companies waive the minimums if you set up an automatic $50 or $100 investment every month (which you should). But some, like Vanguard, won't waive the fees no matter what. If you really want a fund that requires a minimum investment but you don't have the money, you'll need to save up the necessary amount before you can buy into the fund. So, once you have enough money in your account, type in the ticker symbol for your target date fund (it will look something like VFINX). If you don't know it, you can search for it right from your account.

Then, click "buy." Voilà!

With each fund you buy, you'll be able to set up automatic contributions so you don't have to contribute manually each month.

Since reading IWT, I have probably saved and earned at least $70,000-plus over the past four years. This was accomplished by reading the 401(k) and Roth IRA (Vanguard) sections and investing in target date funds. **—JENNA CHRISTENSEN, 26**

This Small Investing Mistake Cost Her $9,000

An IWT reader wrote me about a conversation she had with her friend. The friend mentioned she'd been contributing to her IRA for almost ten years.

And then . . . she sent me this email describing their conversation.

IWT READER: "Ten years! Wow, that's great!"

FRIEND: "Yeah, but it's barely increased at all." My IWT reader had a sinking feeling.

IWT READER: "You know you have to buy the funds, right? It's not enough to transfer money into an IRA. You have to choose the allocation."

FRIEND: "What?"

RAMIT, MY FRIEND HAS BEEN PUTTING MONEY INTO A ROTH FOR TEN YEARS AND NEVER SELECTED FUNDS. IT'S A GLORIFIED SAVINGS ACCOUNT. SHE'S MISSED TEN YEARS OF INVESTMENT GROWTH WITH COMPOUND INTEREST. I DON'T KNOW IF I'M MORE ANGRY OR SAD.

Do you see what happened here? Her friend opened a Roth IRA (as you did in Chapter 3) and even transferred money over, but never took the final step: *making sure that money got invested.*

Very few experts are ever crystal clear in telling you that you need to actually INVEST your money when you have a Roth IRA.

The worst part? The $3,000 her friend "invested" could have been worth more than $12,000. That's $9,000 in effortless money—and because it's a Roth IRA, those earnings would have been tax-free.

You know I had to ask how her friend felt when she learned the truth.

"I feel kind of cheated," her friend said. "I could have been earning more money for all of these years, yet no one ever told me about this important step."

This is why I started writing about money. This woman went out of her way to get educated. She went as far as opening a Roth IRA and even contributed thousands of dollars. But because she didn't understand the tiny technical features of this retirement account, she lost out on $9,000 of tax-free earnings.

Should she take some responsibility for not knowing exactly how a Roth IRA worked? Of course.

But it shouldn't be this hard. You shouldn't have to be a financial expert to have your money do the right thing, just like I shouldn't have to understand how a carburetor works to drive my car.

A ROTH IRA IS JUST AN ACCOUNT. Once your money is in there, you have to start investing in different funds to see your money grow.

Do me a favor: Share this information with someone you know who's just getting started investing. We could literally help them earn thousands over the years.

So You Want to Do It on Your Own

So you aren't satisfied with one target date fund, and you want to pick your own index funds to construct your portfolio in your Roth IRA.

Are you sure?

If you're looking for one investment that gets you 85 percent of the way there—which you won't have to monitor, rebalance, or even pay attention to—then just use a target date fund from the above section.

(Can you tell that I'm a big target date fan?)

Remember, most people who try to manage their own portfolios fail at even matching the market. They fail because they sell at the first sign of trouble, or because they buy and sell too often, thereby diminishing their returns with taxes and trading fees. The result is tens of thousands of dollars lost over a lifetime. Plus, if you buy individual index funds, you'll have to rebalance every year to make sure your asset allocation is still what you want it to be (more on this in a minute). Target date funds do this for you, so if you just want an easy way to invest, use one.

But if you want more control over your investments and you just know you're disciplined enough to withstand market dips and to take the time to rebalance your asset allocation at least once a year, then choosing your own portfolio of index funds is the right choice for you.

All right, let's do this. If you've read this far, I guess my warnings didn't dissuade you from building your own portfolio. If I can't scare you, I might as well help you.

As we discussed earlier, the key to constructing a portfolio is not picking killer stocks! It's figuring out a balanced asset allocation that will let you ride out storms and slowly grow, over time, to gargantuan proportions. To illustrate how to allocate and diversify your portfolio, we're going to use David Swensen's recommendation as a model. Swensen is pretty much the Beyoncé of money management. He runs Yale's fabled endowment, and for more than thirty years he has generated an astonishing 13.5 percent annualized return, whereas most managers can't even beat 8 percent. That means he has almost doubled Yale's money every five years from 1985 to today. Best of all, Swensen is a genuinely good guy. He could be making hundreds of millions each year running his own fund on Wall Street, but he chooses to stay at Yale because he loves academia. "When I see colleagues of mine leave universities to do essentially the same thing they were doing but to get paid more, I am disappointed because there is a sense of mission," he's said. I love this guy.

Anyway, Swensen suggests allocating your money in the following way:

30 percent—Domestic equities: US stock funds, including small-, mid-, and large-cap stocks

15 percent—Developed-world international equities: funds from developed foreign countries, including the United Kingdom, Germany, and France

5 percent—Emerging-market equities: funds from developing foreign countries, such as China, India, and Brazil. These are riskier than developed-world equities, so don't go off buying these to fill 95 percent of your portfolio.

20 percent—Real estate investment trusts: also known as REITs. REITs invest in mortgages and residential and commercial real estate, both domestically and internationally.

15 percent—Government bonds: fixed-interest US securities, which provide predictable income and balance risk in your portfolio. As an asset class, bonds generally return less than stocks.

15 percent—Treasury inflation-protected securities: also known as TIPS, these treasury notes protect against inflation. Eventually you'll want to own these, but they'd be the last ones I'd get after investing in all the better-returning options first.

THE SWENSEN MODEL OF ASSET ALLOCATION

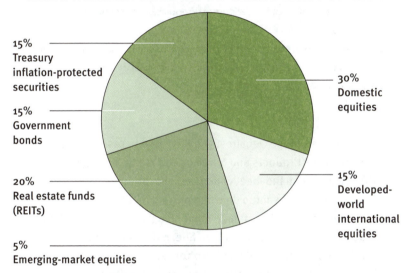

15%
Treasury
inflation-protected
securities

15%
Government
bonds

20%
Real estate funds
(REITs)

5%
Emerging-market equities

30%
Domestic
equities

15%
Developed-
world
international
equities

A significant amount of math went into Swensen's allocation, but the most important takeaway is that no single choice represents an overwhelming part of the portfolio. As we know, lower risk generally equals lower reward. But the coolest thing about asset allocation is that you can actually reduce your risk while maintaining an equivalent return.

Swensen's theories are great, but how do we make them real and pick funds that match his suggestions? By picking a portfolio of low-cost funds, that's how.

Choosing your own index funds means you'll need to dig around and identify the best index funds for you. I always start researching at the most popular companies: Vanguard, Schwab, and T. Rowe Price; check out their websites.

Keep It Manageable

Q: *HOW MANY FUNDS SHOULD I INVEST IN?*

A: If you're wondering how many funds you should own, I'd encourage you to keep it simple. Ideally you should have just one (a target date fund). But if you're picking your own index funds, as a general guideline, you can create a great asset allocation using anywhere from three to seven funds. That would cover domestic equities, international equities, real estate investment trusts, and perhaps a small allocation to treasury bonds. Remember, the goal isn't to be exhaustive and to own every single aspect of the market. It's to create an effective asset allocation and move on with your life.

When you visit these websites, you'll be able to research funds (you may have to click "Products and Services" on many of the sites) to make sure they're low-cost and meet your asset allocation goals.

The first thing you want to do when picking index funds is to minimize fees. Look for the management fees ("expense ratios") to be low, around 0.2 percent, and you'll be fine. Most of the index funds at Vanguard, T. Rowe Price, and Fidelity offer excellent value. Remember: Expense ratios are one of the few things you can control, and higher fees cost you dearly—and they just put money in Wall Street's pocket. See the chart on page 237 for a comparison of how these fees can affect you.

Second, you want to make sure the fund fits into your asset allocation. After all, the reason you're choosing your own index funds is to have more control over your investments. Use David Swensen's model as a baseline and tweak as necessary if you want to exclude certain funds or prioritize which are important to you. For example, if you have limited money and you're in your twenties, you'd probably want to buy the stock funds first so you could get their compounding power, whereas you could wait until you're older and have more money to buy the bond funds to mitigate your risk. In other words, when you look for various funds, make sure you're being strategic about your domestic equities, international equities, bonds, and all the rest. You cannot just pick random funds and expect to have a balanced asset allocation. To analyze your own current portfolio, log in to your investment account and use their investment tools. For example, I log in to Vanguard and I can see what percentage of my portfolio is in equities vs. bonds or international vs. domestic. You can do the same for any fund you're considering. (Every major investment company offers this. If yours doesn't, use the online site Personal Capital.) This is a great way to drill into your asset allocation and make sure your funds are well diversified.

Third, note that you should absolutely look at how well the fund has returned over the last ten or fifteen years, but remember that, as they say, past performance is no guarantee of future results.

To make this a little easier, when you click "Products and Services" on most sites, you'll be able to find a fund screener that will let you add search filters like "international index funds with an expense ratio of less than 0.75%" to find funds that fit your criteria. Remember, this isn't simple. Creating your own portfolio takes significant research.

As an example of what you might end up with, here's a sample portfolio made of all Vanguard funds:

Stocks ("Equities")

30 percent—Total Market Index/equities (VTSMX)

20 percent—Total International Stock Index/equities (VGTSX)

20 percent—REIT index/equities (VGSIX)

Bonds

5 percent—Short-Term Treasury Index Fund (VSBSX)

5 percent—Intermediate-Term Treasury Index Fund (VSIGX)

5 percent—Long-Term Treasury Index Fund (VLGSX)

15 percent— Short-Term Inflation-Protected Securities Index Fund (VTAPX)

These are just a few of the literally thousands of index funds that exist. You can be flexible with the funds. If you want to be more or less aggressive, you can change the allocation to match your risk tolerance. For example, if you look at those funds and say, "Man, I'll never get

Dollar-Cost Averaging: Investing Slowly Over Time

When I want to sound smart and intimidate people, I calmly look at them, chew on a muffin for a few seconds, and then throw it against a wall and scream, "DO YOU DOLLAR-COST AVERAGE???" People are often so impressed that they slowly inch away, then whisper to people around them. I can only guess that they're discussing how suave and knowledgeable I am.

Anyway, "dollar-cost averaging" is a phrase that refers to investing regular amounts over time, rather than investing all your money in a fund at once. Why would you do this? Imagine if you invest $10,000 tomorrow and the stock drops 20 percent. At $8,000, it will need to increase 25 percent (not 20 percent) to get back to $10,000. By investing at regular intervals over time, you hedge against any drops in the price—and if your fund does drop, you'll pick up shares at a discount price. In other words, by investing over time, you don't try to time the market. You use time to your advantage. This is the essence of automatic investing, which lets you consistently invest in a fund so you don't have to guess when the market is up or down. In Chapter 5, we covered your automatic infrastructure. To set up automatic investing, configure your accounts to automatically pull a set amount of money from your checking account each month. See page 180 for details. Remember: If you set it up, most funds waive transaction fees.

But here's a question: If you have a big pile of money to invest, what's the better option: Dollar-cost averaging it or investing the entire lump sum all at once? The answer might surprise you. Vanguard research found that lump-sum investing actually beats dollar-cost averaging two-thirds of the time. Because the market tends to go up and stocks and bonds tend to outperform cash, investing all at once produces higher returns in most situations. But—and there are several buts—this isn't true if the market is going down. (Of course, nobody can predict where the market will go, especially in the short term.) And investing isn't just about math, but about the very real effects of your emotions on your investing behavior.

In short, most of us already dollar-cost average since we take part of our monthly paycheck and invest it. But if you have a lump sum of money, most of the time you'll get better returns by investing it all at once.

around to owning seven funds," then be realistic with yourself. Maybe you want to buy the stock funds but just one bond fund for now. Maybe you don't need to think about treasury inflation-protected securities yet. Pick the number of funds that will let you get started, realizing that you can adjust it later on to get a balanced asset allocation.

Spend time identifying the funds that will help you build a full, balanced asset allocation over time. You don't need to get all seven funds I just listed—even one is better than nothing. But you should have a list of funds that you'll eventually buy to round out your allocation.

Buying into Individual Index Funds

Once you've got a list of index funds you want to own in your portfolio—usually three to seven funds—start buying them one by one. If you can afford to buy into all of the funds at once, go for it—but most people can't do this, since the minimum for each fund is between $1,000 and $3,000.

Just like with a target date fund, you want to set a savings goal to accumulate enough to pay for the minimum of the first fund. Then you'll buy that fund, continue investing a small amount in it, and set a new savings goal to get the next fund. Investing isn't a race—you don't need a perfect asset allocation tomorrow. Here's how to handle buying multiple index funds over time.

Let's say you check your Conscious Spending Plan from Chapter 4, and it allows you to invest $500 per month after contributing to your 401(k). Assuming all of your funds have a $1,000 minimum, you'd set a savings goal of $1,000 for Index Fund 1 and save for two months. Once you accumulated enough to cover the minimum, transfer that $1,000 from savings to your investment account and buy the fund. Now, set up a contribution of $100 per month to the fund you just bought. Then take the remaining $400 per month set aside for investing ($500 total minus the $100 you're investing in Index Fund 1) and start another savings goal toward Index Fund 2. Once you've saved enough, buy Index Fund 2. Repeat this process as necessary. Sure, it may take a few years to get to the point where you own all the index funds you need, but remember, you're taking a forty- or fifty-year outlook on investing—it's not about the short term. This is the cost of constructing your own perfect portfolio.

Note: Once you own all the funds you need, you can split the money across funds according to your asset allocation—but don't just split it evenly. Remember, your asset allocation determines how much money you invest in different areas. If you have $250 to invest per month and you buy seven index funds, the average person who knows nothing (i.e., most people) will split the money seven ways and send $35 to each. That's wrong. Depending on your asset allocation, you'll send more or less money to various funds, using this calculation: (Your monthly total amount of investing money) (Percentage of asset allocation for a particular investment) = Amount you'll invest there. For example, if you're investing $1,000 per month and your Swensen allocation recommends 30 percent for domestic equities, you'll calculate ($1,000) (0.3) = $300 and put that toward your domestic-equity fund. Repeat for all other funds in your portfolio.

Finally, if you opt for investing in your own index funds, you'll have to rebalance about once a year, which will keep your funds in line with your target asset allocation. I'll cover that in the next chapter.

What About Other Kinds of Investments?

There are many different investments besides stocks, bonds, and index and target date funds. You can invest in precious metals, real estate, private startups, cryptocurrency, or even art; just don't expect very good returns. And despite all my dire warnings, you can also buy a couple of individual stocks in companies you really like.

Real Estate

For most Americans, their home is their biggest "investment," and yet, as investments go, your primary residence is not a very good one for individual investors. Why? Because the returns are generally poor, especially when you factor in costs like maintenance and property taxes—which renters don't pay for, but homeowners do. I'll cover real estate more in Chapter 9, but in general, most people confuse their house with an investment that they buy and sell for profit. Think about it. Who sells their house for profit and keeps the money? If your parents ever sold their house, did they move into a smaller house and enjoy the rest of that money? No! They rolled it over to the down payment for their next, more expensive house.

You want to keep each part of your portfolio balanced so no one area overshadows the rest. If you're spending $2,000 per month on your mortgage and don't have enough left over to diversify into other areas, that's not a balanced portfolio. If you do buy real estate, regardless of whether it's to live in or to invest in, be sure to keep funding the rest of your investment areas—whether that's a target date fund or your own portfolio of index funds.

Art

Art advisers report annual returns for the index of fine art sales to be around 10 percent. However, as research done by Stanford analysts in 2013 found, "The returns of fine art have been significantly overestimated, and the risk, underestimated." They found that the real annual return of art over the past four decades is closer to 6.5 percent versus the 10 percent that is claimed. The main reason for the overestimation is due to selection bias, in which the repeat sale of popular pieces isn't taken into account. Also, by choosing particular art pieces as investments, you're doing essentially the same thing as trying to predict winning stocks, and after reading Chapter 6, you know how difficult that is to do.

In aggregate, art investments may be quite profitable, but the trick is choosing which individual pieces will appreciate—and as you can imagine, that isn't easy. To show you how hard it is to select art as an investment, the *Wall Street Journal* wrote about John Maynard Keynes's massive art collection: In 2018 dollars, he spent $840,000 to amass an art collection that is now worth $99 million. That return works out to 10.9 percent per year—an excellent return, except for one thing: Two pieces of art account for half the value of the collection. Think about that: One of the world's best art collectors carefully bought 135 pieces, and just two generated half the value of the entire collection. Could you predict which two would be worth that much? For most people, the answer is no.

High-Risk, High-Potential-for-Reward Investments

Life isn't just about target date funds and index funds. Lots of people understand that, logically, they should create a well-diversified portfolio of low-cost funds. But they also want to have fun investing. If you feel this way, sure, use a small part of your portfolio for "high risk" investing—but treat it as fun money, not as money you need. I set

My Counterintuitive $297,754 Lesson

When you were fifteen, a lot of your dads were teaching you how to drive, showing you how to use a razor, or throwing you a quinceañera. My dad told me to open a Roth IRA.

A fifteen-year-old is too young to open a Roth IRA, so my dad and I opened a "custodial" account together at E-Trade. I had a few thousand bucks from a few high school jobs I worked—pizza maker, soccer referee, and sales guy for an internet company—so I started looking for what to invest in.

For lil' gangster Ramit, this was about as exciting as it got! So I started doing my research, which consisted of:

- Looking up which stocks went really high and really low (because I thought "Higher risk = higher reward, and I'm young, so I can stand high risk so I get high reward!!" God, I hate myself.)

- Restricting it to tech ("Because I understand technology!")

- Reading magazines like the *Industry Standard*, which breathlessly hyped different companies as they swelled to hundreds of pages of ads during the dot-com boom

- Back then, I thought investing meant picking individual stocks, so I ended up buying three stocks

I bought stock in a company called JDS Uniphase (JDSU), an optical communications company. The stock effectively went to zero.

I bought stock in a company called Excite, an early search engine, which was renamed Excite@Home after being acquired. It went bankrupt.

And then I bought roughly $11,000 in a little company called Amazon .com.

My investment of a few thousand bucks turned into $297,754. I should be proud of myself, right?

WRONG. It might seem like I won, but you can learn a lot of counterintuitive lessons from this example.

What are the lessons here?

THE SUPERFICIAL LESSON: *"You're so smart for picking Amazon!"*

THE REAL LESSON: That is exactly the wrong lesson to take away. If that's your reaction, please read carefully: It's very important to know WHY you win and why you lose. I won with this Amazon investment, but it wasn't because I was a good investor. It was, purely and simply, luck— a freakish once-in-a-generation winner.

THE SUPERFICIAL LESSON: *If you pick the next Amazon, you'll be rich.*

THE REAL LESSON: Investing isn't about picking individual stocks. Research shows that even veteran portfolio managers will, on average, fail to beat the market. I could have picked another one hundred stocks, and statistically, I would not have even beaten the market. It was pure luck. I've actually made much more money on long-term, low-cost investing.

THE SUPERFICIAL LESSON: *Getting the right stock matters a lot.*

THE REAL LESSON: Getting started early mattered a lot. I was extremely lucky to have a dad who pushed me to start investing early. If you had the same, awesome. But let's say you didn't grow up with parents who knew a lot about money. Or, until recently, you thought the only way to invest was to "pick stocks." I hear you—we all start from different places in life. Hey, my dad didn't teach me about the importance of engaging my core when deadlifting. We all start with the cards we're dealt. But you've read this book. Now you can start investing aggressively.

aside about 10 percent of my portfolio for fun money, which includes particular stocks I like, know, and use (companies like Amazon that focus on customer service, which I believe drives shareholder value); sector funds that let me focus on particular industries (I own an index fund that focuses on health care); and even angel investing, which is personal investing for private ultra-early-stage companies. (I occasionally see these angel opportunities because I've worked in Silicon Valley and have friends who start companies and look for early friends-and-family money.) All of these are very-high-risk investments, and they're funded by just-for-fun money that I can afford to lose. Still, there is the potential for great returns. If you have the rest of your portfolio set up and still have money left over, be smart about it, but invest a little in whatever you want.

"What About Crypto?"

I thought you only found mindless, roving hordes in zombie movies—until I met crypto "investors." I use that term loosely, since the majority of cryptocurrency fanboys have no other investments. They are "investors" in the same way that I am a mermaid because I can swim.

The next time you hear someone ranting and raving about why crypto is the future, ask them this simple, devastating question:

"Besides crypto, what does the rest of your portfolio look like?"

Their answer will instantly reveal that they are speculators, not investors, because they almost never have a diversified portfolio.

Here are the three answers you will get:

- "LOL. I don't invest in fiat currency."

- "Traditional investments are so boring."

- "You don't understand blockchain."

These answers are contrarian, that's for sure. The only catch with being a contrarian is you have to actually be right.

When you get one contrarian, they just sound a little crazy. Put two of them in the same room, though, and you're suddenly witnessing a convention of people with all the hallmarks of brain-dead speculators. These people are almost always young, libertarian, and disaffected. You're not seeing a lot of people with successful careers spending four hours a day posting "HODL" (crypto investors' take on the word "hold" from "buy and hold") on social media. See for yourself at bitcoin.reddit.com. It gets a little quiet when crypto investments drop 80 percent though.

I have no problem with alternative investments when they are part of an overall portfolio. I have a real problem with mob mentalities around money-making ideas that then get rationalized and twisted from "currency" to "investments" to scathing (and shortsighted) criticisms of worldwide currency.

To make this easy, I've created *Ramit's Guide to Understanding Crypto as an Investment.*

THEY SAY: *Cryptocurrency is a form of currency that you can use to pay for various goods.*

REALITY: Very few merchants accept cryptocurrency. Also, one thing people seem to like is their currency being stable, meaning one dollar is worth one dollar. What happens when your cryptocurrency swings over 25 percent in one week? That's right, people tend to not spend it, because your TV might be 25 percent cheaper next week.

THEY SAY: *Cryptocurrency allows people to use cryptography and decentralization to remain anonymous.*

REALITY: This is true, and there are some valid reasons for people to purchase anonymously. However, for now crypto largely gets used to buy drugs.

THEY SAY: *It is better than fiat currency.*

REALITY: If you spend more than three minutes talking about crypto with a fanatic—excuse me, fan—they will surely bring up the argument of fiat money. This quickly progresses to referencing Nixon's 1971 decoupling from the gold standard, followed by "Money isn't real." I just stare at them, blinking.

THEY SAY: *It's not about Bitcoin, it's about blockchain.*

REALITY: Bitcoin is one example of a cryptocurrency using "blockchain" technology, which uses cryptography and a decentralized architecture. The technology is legitimately impressive. It is also used by fans to distract from the constant failings of the actual usage, like Bitcoin and the thousands of applications. In one study, 80 percent of ICOs (initial coin offerings) were, and I quote, "identified as scams." Fans ignore these and instead point to the blockchain as the panacea for all of societal ills: Hungry? Blockchain will solve that. Need to walk your dog? What about using blockchain? Hey, I need to change my underwear. Got blockchain?

THEY SAY: *Well, crypto is an amazing investment.*

REALITY: Investment returns in Bitcoin increased hugely in 2017. From January to June, it had increased by 240 percent compared to 9 percent for the S&P 500. Hard to argue against that. But irregular returns are a larger problem than most people realize. In just three months, Bitcoin soared over 340 percent, then dropped like a rock. Just like in any other type of high-risk gambling, you get addicted to the highs, but when it goes down, you begin hiding your losses and not talking about them. True to form, that's exactly what we saw. The number of people who searched for Bitcoin soared at the same time its price did—and, of course, once the price dropped, people stopped talking about Bitcoin as an investment.

In crypto, you see the same signs of gambling and cultlike behavior:

- Questioning anything is verboten and harshly punished

- Engaging in increasingly risky behavior (e.g., borrowing money to "invest" in crypto)

- Whether prices increase or decrease, explaining it through the lens of why crypto will eventually replace all currency

- Making increasingly irrational claims, such as "disrupting fiat currency"

- Moving goalposts ("It's a currency . . . No, it's an investment . . . No, we're here to change the world.")

If you want to invest in cryptocurrency, be my guest. As I said, once you have a solid portfolio in place, I encourage you to invest 5 to 10 percent in something fun! Just make sure you have a fully functioning portfolio first, meaning you've completed the Ladder of Investing, you have six months of emergency funds, and you limit your exposure by periodically rebalancing. Of course, if you had a question about crypto in the first place, you're not reading this anymore. You're already on a Bitcoin forum chanting "HODL" and "FIAT." Why am I even writing this?

ACTION STEPS

WEEK SIX

1 **Figure out your investing style (thirty minutes).** Decide whether you want the simple investment options of a target date fund or the increased control (and complexity) of index funds. I recommend a target date fund as the 85 Percent Solution.

2 **Research your investments (three hours to one week).** If you've decided on a target date fund, research the funds from Vanguard, T. Rowe Price, and Schwab (see page 114 for contact info). This should take a few hours. If you're constructing your own portfolio, it will take more time (and more money to meet the minimums of each fund). Use the Swensen model as a basic template and prioritize which funds you'll buy today and which you'll get later. Once you decide on an asset allocation, research funds using a fund screener like the one at Vanguard (search "Vanguard fund screener").

3 **Buy your fund(s) (one hour to one week).** Buying a target date fund is easy: First, transfer money to your investment account. (For 401(k)s, you should already be directing money from each paycheck into your 401(k) account. For Roth IRAs, this money should be waiting in your savings account from Chapter 5. If you don't have cash lying around to invest, set a savings goal and wait until you have enough to invest in your first fund.) Once the money is ready and has been transferred to your investment account, log in to your account, enter the ticker symbol, and you're finished. If you're buying individual index funds, you'll usually need to buy one at a time and set up savings accounts for the others.

Yes! You're now an investor! And not only that, but you've reached the end of the six-week program. You've optimized your credit cards and bank accounts and started investing—and, even better, you've tied your system together so it works automatically with hardly any effort on your part. There's just a little more: In the next chapter, we'll focus on how to maintain and grow your investments. Then, in the final chapter, I'll address all those random questions you have about money and life in general. But the truth is, by making it all the way through this chapter, you've already done the hard work.

CHAPTER 8

HOW TO MAINTAIN AND GROW YOUR SYSTEM

You've done the hard work. What's next?
Here's how to maintain (and grow) your
financial infrastructure to achieve your Rich Life.

You may have noticed that this chapter is one of the shortest in the book. That's because you've already put the 85 Percent Solution into place and dealt with the most important parts of your finances: your credit cards, bank accounts, spending, and investments. You've consciously decided what your Rich Life is, and you've built a financial system that is essentially on autopilot, letting you spend your time pursuing the things you love. You're doing great. Especially considering that most people are still struggling with paying their monthly bills. So congratulations. But—of course there's a "but"—if you're seriously nerdy and want to know more about enhancing your finances, this is the chapter for you. We'll cover a few topics that will help you maintain your system. We'll also cover optimizing your investments even further. Remember, though: This is extra credit, so don't feel the need to follow the advice in this chapter unless you really want to.

Get Honest About Why You Want More

I was raised to be the best—to study harder, work longer, and perform better than everyone else. In many ways, those lessons have paid off. But I also see the dark side of blindly following the idea of being the best without reflecting on why you're working so hard. So before you read on, ask yourself what the point of all of this work is. Is it to earn an extra $10,000? Or to actually live a Rich Life?

Sometimes financial advice just blindly encourages people to do "more, more, more" without stopping to ask, "Is this enough?" The concept of winning becomes the goal instead of knowing why you're playing in the first place. When do you get to stop and enjoy all the hard work you've done?

I've seen too many people decide to take control of their finances (good), then change their lives to save money (good), then continue saving and become increasingly aggressive (not so good), and finally end up "living in the spreadsheet," where they spend each day counting how much their money has grown (very bad). They've become obsessed with the game without realizing why they're playing.

You do not want to live in the spreadsheet. Life is more than tweaking your asset allocation and running Monte Carlo simulations on your investments.

At this level, you've already won the introductory game. Now it's time to ask *why* you want to keep going. If the answer is, "I want to take a lavish vacation every year and splurge on first-class tickets," great! If your answer is, "I'm saving aggressively for the next three years so we can afford to move into our dream neighborhood," awesome. I can show you how to achieve both of those goals even faster.

To do that, let's go through an exercise I call "Taking It From the Clouds to the Street."

When I ask you, "Why do you want more?" the common answers are "freedom" or "security." Those are fine, but I want to challenge you to go deeper. The problem is that high-level, vague visions never motivate us as much as we'd hope. True motivation is often real, concrete—on the street. It's something that affects our day-to-day.

If you had to get extremely specific about why you want to earn your next $10,000 and you had to bring your answer from the clouds to the street, what would you say?

What's your street-level motivation? You could create some lofty life purpose—or you could take a ten-minute walk and figure out what gets you excited at this exact moment. The answers are often a lot simpler than you think.

Your motivation could be taking a taxi to happy hour at five p.m. instead of sweating on the train, or paying for a friend to join you on a glamping trip. One of my early street-level motivations was being able to order appetizers when I ate out!

For this book, my street-level motivation is to answer the same questions I get asked every day about money . . . and to tell a few jokes. It's as simple as that.

So: Why do you want to earn the next $1,000 or $10,000 or $25,000? Don't give me an answer that's in the clouds. Get brutally honest and bring your answer down to the street.

Two of my favorite things are concerts and coaching high school lacrosse. Thanks to my job and salary I am able to buy VIP tickets to concerts and have scheduling flexibility to hold a full-time job in addition to coaching high school lacrosse.

—DANIEL SNOW, 38

When I go grocery shopping, I don't look at the prices of things. I get whatever I need and want. Before, I needed to figure out how to make $50 work for the week. Now, if a recipe calls for a pound of Gruyère, I'll get it. I might be surprised at the register, but it's all good. I don't need to take anything back. **—ELZ JONES, 44**

If you've gotten clear about why you want more, let me show you a few things you can do to achieve it.

How to Accumulate More and Grow Faster: Feed Your System

I n the previous chapter, you chose your investments and set things up so they run automatically. The automatic system is great, but it's fueled by only one thing: the money you feed it. That means that your system is only as strong as the amount you put in it.

The earlier chapters in this book were about implementing the 85 Percent Solution—getting started was the hardest and most important step. It didn't matter if you were contributing only $100 per month. But now it's about the raw volume you put into your system—more in, more out.

This is where your purpose comes in handy. For example, if you want to FIRE (become Financially Independent and Retire Early) in fifteen years, you know to double down and save/invest aggressively. Alternatively, if you want to live large in Manhattan, you could give yourself a generous spending plan for cocktail bars and Seamless delivery (a decision I know well).

Of course, the very best is to say "yes and yes"—yes, I want to save aggressively, and yes, I want to live an incredibly Rich Life. With enough planning (and, depending on your goals, a high enough income), you can often do both.

Remember: Because the rewards of investing as early as possible are so tremendous, one of your key drivers will be feeding as much as possible into your system.

I automated my savings so that I was saving a substantial amount while paying off credit card debt. This allowed me to pay for a wedding and also buy a house at the bottom of the market in San Diego. My home increased in value from $250,000 to $700,000, and the absurdly low mortgage payment allows us to live relatively stress free in a popular, beautiful area. **—ALISSA MCQUESTION, 34**

To put it another way, if you found a magical money machine that took $1 in and spit $5 out, what would you do? You'd put as much as you could in it! The only catch is, it takes time: Every dollar you invest today will be worth many more tomorrow.

How Rich Will I Be In . . .

How much will your monthly investment be worth, assuming an 8 percent return?

IF YOU INVEST . . .	$100/ month	$500/ month	$1,000/ month
After 5 years . . .	$7,347	$36,738	$73,476
After 10 years . . .	$18,294	$91,473	$182,946
After 25 years . . .	$95,102	$475,513	$951,026

Note: For simplicity, this calculation ignores taxes.

Don't just take it from me, though. Go to bankrate.com and open up one of their investment calculators. Enter in your monthly investment contribution, assuming an 8 percent return. You'll likely see that your current contributions will grow more slowly than you thought. But by adding a small amount per month—even $100 or $200 more—the numbers will change dramatically.

In Chapter 4, I outlined a Conscious Spending Plan that suggested general percentages of income to allocate for savings and investing. Your first goal was to aim for those percentages. Now it's time to move beyond those amounts so you can save and invest as much as possible. I know, I know. "Invest more? I can't squeeze out another cent!"

This is not about me wanting to deprive you. Actually, quite the opposite: Because compounding works so effectively, the more you save now, the more you'll have later (by a huge amount). You saw this in the Bankrate calculator. Now go in and play around with your Conscious Spending Plan to see how you can eke out a little more to put toward your investments every month. Optimizing your plan might involve doing some serious bargaining when you make major purchases like a car or house (see Chapter 9). Or you might need to cut your expenses as ruthlessly as possible, which I cover on my website (search for "ramit savings"). You may even think about negotiating a higher salary or getting a higher-paying job (see page 307). No matter how you go about it, be sure that you're shoveling the maximum amount possible into your system every month. Remember, it's never easier to do this than now—and the more you feed into your system now, the sooner you'll reach your goals.

I went from manually paying my bills every month to automatically paying my bills, automating savings, and planning the whole year's worth of expenses. Now I have even automated monthly donations to charity as well. I almost never worry about money now, and after growing up with the constant struggle of money being short, this really makes me feel a lot better.

—MICHAEL STEELE, 40

Rebalancing Your Investments

If you've chosen to manage your own asset allocation, you're going to have to rebalance from time to time—which is one more reason I highly recommend target date funds (see page 238), which handle rebalancing for you. (If you've chosen a target date fund—good news—you can skip this section.) But if you haven't, here's what you need to know about rebalancing. When you have a diversified portfolio, some of your investments, such as international stocks, will outperform others. To keep your asset allocation on track, you'll want to rebalance once a year so your international stocks don't become a larger part of your portfolio than you intended. Think of your investment portfolio like your backyard: If you want your zucchini to be only 15 percent of your backyard and they grow like crazy and end up taking over 30 percent, you'll want to rebalance by either cutting the zucchini back or by getting a bigger yard so that the zucchini is back to covering only 15 percent. I know, I know—first personal finance, next organic gardening. A true Renaissance man.

Let's say you create an asset allocation based on the Swensen model:

TARGET ASSET ALLOCATION

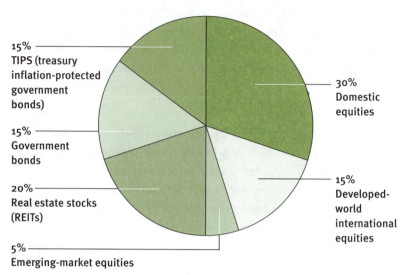

15%
TIPS (treasury
inflation-protected
government
bonds)

15%
Government
bonds

20%
Real estate stocks
(REITs)

5%
Emerging-market equities

30%
Domestic
equities

15%
Developed-
world
international
equities

Now let's assume that domestic equities gain 50 percent one year. (For easy calculations, let's hold all other investments constant.) All of a sudden, domestic equities represent a larger part of your portfolio and all the other numbers are out of whack.

ALLOCATION AFTER DOMESTIC EQUITIES JUMP 50%

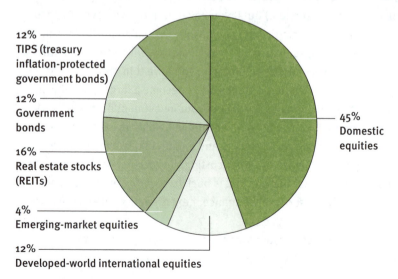

12%
TIPS (treasury
inflation-protected
government bonds)

12%
Government
bonds

16%
Real estate stocks
(REITs)

4%
Emerging-market equities

12%
Developed-world international equities

45%
Domestic
equities

Although it's great that one of your investment areas is performing well, you want to keep your allocation in check so one sector isn't disproportionately larger or smaller than the others. Rebalancing your portfolio will make sure your assets remain properly allocated and protect you from being vulnerable to a specific sector's ups and downs.

The best way to rebalance is to plow more money into the other areas until your asset allocation is back on track. How? Assuming your domestic equities now represent 45 percent of your asset allocation—but should actually be only 30 percent—stop sending money there temporarily and redistribute that 30 percent of your investment contribution evenly over the rest of your investment categories. You can do this by "pausing" your automatic investment to particular funds from within your investment account. Log in to your account, find the fund that's out of whack with your initial asset allocation, and stop your automatic contributions. (Don't worry, you can resume automatic payments at any time.) In other words, stop investing in the outperforming area and grow the other areas of your portfolio until your allocation is back in line with your goals.

Check out the chart on the next page to see how it works. In this case, you can see that after eight months you're more or less back on target, so you can go back to your original allocations.

Note: There is another way to rebalance, but I don't like doing it. You can rebalance by selling the outperforming equities and plowing the money into other areas to bring the allocation back under control. I hate selling, because it involves trading fees, paperwork, and "thinking," so I don't recommend this.

Don't forget to set a calendar reminder to resume your automatic payments for the asset class you paused once your portfolio is rebalanced.

If, on the other hand, one of your funds has *lost* money, that will also knock your asset allocation out of whack. In this case, you can pause the other funds and add money to the loser until it returns to where it should be in your portfolio. To keep the math simple, I recommend the free financial dashboard at personalcapital.com to help guide your rebalancing.

And remember, if you've invested in a target date fund (see page 238), this will be automatically taken care of for you—yet another reason I like them.

Rebalancing Your Portfolio

$10,000 PORTFOLIO AFTER GAIN OF 50% IN DOMESTIC EQUITIES

Value	$12,727		New portfolio value
	Allocation	Value	
Domestic	45%	$5,727	←
International	12%	$1,500	←
Emerging Markets	4%	$500	←
REITs	16%	$2,000	←
Bonds	12%	$1,500	←
TIPS	12%	$1,500	←

	Month 2		Month 3		Month 4	
Value	$13,727		$14,727		$15,727	
	Allocation	Value	Allocation	Value	Allocation	Value
Domestic	42%	$5,727	39%	$5,727	36%	$5,727
International	12%	$1,710	13%	$1,920	14%	$2,130
Emerging Markets	4%	$610	5%	$720	5%	$830
REITs	16%	$2,260	17%	$2,520	18%	$2,780
Bonds	12%	$1,710	13%	$1,920	14%	$2,130
TIPS	12%	$1,710	13%	$1,920	14%	$2,130

Note: In some cases, the numbers in the above columns don't add up to 100%

Because your domestic equities now represent 45 percent of your portfolio, rather than the targeted 30 percent, you have to take action. Pause your automatic contribution to domestic equities and reallocate that 30 percent by distributing it evenly to the other five asset classes (each would get an additional 6 percent). $1,000 monthly contributions will now be allocated as follows:

———— 0%: Put this investment on pause and evenly distribute the 30% across the other asset classes (i.e., 6% for each).

———— 21%: The target is 15%, so add 6% and you'll get 21%. Monthly contribution: $210

———— 11%: The target here is 5%, so you again add 6%. Monthly contribution: $110

———— 26%: Target is 20%. Monthly contribution: $260

———— 21%: Target is 15%. Monthly contribution: $210

———— 21%: Target is 15%. Monthly contribution: $210

Month 5		Month 6		Month 7		Month 8	
$16,727		$17,727		$18,727		$19,727	
Allocation	Value	Allocation	Value	Allocation	Value	Allocation	Value
34%	$5,727	32%	$5,727	31%	$5,727	29%	$5,727
14%	$2,340	14%	$2,550	15%	$2,760	15%	$2,970
6%	$940	6%	$1,050	6%	$1,160	6%	$1,270
18%	$3,040	19%	$3,300	19%	$3,560	19%	$3,820
14%	$2,340	14%	$2,550	15%	$2,760	15%	$2,970
14%	$2,340	14%	$2,550	15%	$2,760	15%	$2,970

because of the variables of rounding.

Stop Worrying About Taxes

Taxes are tribal. They're one of the most politically heated topics of all. And when it comes to taxes, I've learned that people really, really don't like being told that what they've believed for twenty-five-plus years is wrong.

So when I share six thoughts about taxes, some of you are probably going to get mad. That's okay with me.

I want you to be educated about taxes. And then I want you to notice how many people unthinkingly repeat tropes and clichés about them.

Tax Truth #1: People think getting a tax refund is bad. In reality, it's great.

The Myth: Getting a tax refund is bad because you've given Uncle Sam an interest-free loan.

Reality: You would have spent that money. We know this because data shows that small tax refunds that are gradually added to your paycheck get spent. Big tax refunds get saved or used to pay off debt.

Surprising Fact: This is why politicians have a hard choice to make when it comes to tax cuts. Give people small tax refunds over the year and they'll spend it, stimulating the economy . . . but they won't realize they're getting more money and give the politicians credit. Or, give them a big tax refund and your administration will get credit—but people will save it or pay off debt, not stimulate the economy.

Tax Truth #2: The US is not "the highest-taxed nation in the world."

The Myth: America is the highest-taxed nation in the world.

Reality: Not even close.

Surprise: Notice how many basic facts like this are simply lied about. If we can't even agree on basic facts, how can we expect to agree on tax policy? Also, if you're a tax nut opening up your email to send me thirty pages of crackpot theories and YouTube videos, don't bother. I'm right.

Tax Truth #3: People actually think that it's better to NOT make more money for tax reasons. They are wrong.

The Myth: Making more money will move you up in tax brackets, causing you to get taxed more and actually earn less.

Reality: Please, for the love of God, spend three minutes learning about something called "marginal tax brackets." If you start earning more and move up tax brackets, the "marginal" amount—or the money in the higher tax bracket—is taxed at a higher rate, *not the entire amount you earn.*

As "Kristi," a commenter on my website, wrote:

I've known people who refused raises for years because they think the new tax bracket will lower their income. If you try to explain the reality to them, they become furious. They are so convinced, they would rather complain about it than learn how it works. At this point, if they learned they were wrong all this time they would feel so foolish that they would rather go on believing incorrect things than learn they were wrong. I know someone who believes that he has to pay his $3,000 deductible up front every single time he goes to see a doctor. He becomes irate and refuses to listen if you try to explain how deductibles work. He'd rather just complain about his health and not go to a doctor because each trip would cost $3,000 so he can't afford it. He tells everyone about Obamacare ruining his life. I think he just enjoys complaining.

Surprise: The people who believe this will go their entire lives without spending five minutes learning how tax rates actually work. At a certain point, their incorrect opinions become so entrenched that it's impossible for them to admit they were wrong and accept the truth. Good times.

Tax Truth #4: People get really angry about how their taxes are spent but actually have no goddamn idea where the money goes.

The Myth: We spend a ton of money on foreign aid.

Reality: Out of every $100 in federal taxes you pay, around 1 percent goes toward foreign aid, which is dramatically lower than most people think.

Surprise: People are clueless about what their taxes are spent on. Also, they love to say, "I don't mind paying taxes as long as it doesn't go toward XYZ." Thank you, but that's not how taxes work in a democracy.

Tax Truth #5: People think rich people just use loopholes to never pay taxes.

The Myth: There are a lot of loopholes for the rich.

Reality: I know about these loopholes. There are a few legit ones—like tax efficiency in your investment accounts, maxing out your tax-advantaged accounts, and a few more—but not nearly as many as you think. In general, those loopholes are few and far between and largely available to the super-rich who earn millions via capital gains (not ordinary salaries or even the high salaries of lawyers and bankers).

Surprise: There are certain loopholes for the super-rich that you probably haven't heard about. If you earn multiple six figures, go to my website for my course on advanced personal finance.

Tax Truth #6: Your politics cloud your rational judgment on taxes.

The Myth: People think their beliefs about taxes are rational and fair. Yes, even you!

Reality: Your personal psychology, along with your sources of information, play a huge role in your beliefs about taxes. As *Psychology Today* noted, "People have a number of general beliefs about what kinds of exchanges should be taxable, and they want tax law to fit with those beliefs. When tax law conflicts with those beliefs, then people think the tax is unfair." Here's one idea: Next time you hear someone ranting and raving about taxes, ask them this: "It sounds like you don't like taxes. What do you think your taxes get you?" This does two things: (1) It shifts the conversation away from the scarcity-based pandemic of people who see taxes as taking something away from them to seeing them as the price you pay as part of a democracy . . . and (2) You will quickly determine whether this person is worth having a rational discussion with (e.g., if they say, "We should privatize roads" or "All taxation is theft," just stand up and silently walk away).

Whenever taxes come up, you're going to hear a lot of nonsense. Take note of it. Analyze it critically. And make your own decisions.

Here's my take.

I'm happy to pay my taxes. I take advantage of every legal tax advantage I have, like using tax-advantaged accounts, but I know that my taxes contribute to an overall system of stability. I also know that I can always earn more, so I don't use taxes as the primary factor in my decisions. Finally, if you ever get the urge to complain about taxes, go take a ride on a road anywhere else in the world. Notice the difference in infrastructure? So give me a break, pay your taxes, and be a contributing member of society.

Taxes are a great example of where the 85 Percent Solution applies. (Quick refresher on the 85 Percent Solution: Make a few key decisions, get "good enough" to be mostly right, then move on with your life.) The solution here is to take full advantage of your tax-deferred accounts (more on this below). If you're doing this, you're saving thousands of dollars in taxes every year.

Once you get deeper into personal finance, you're going to stumble across lots of outlandish claims of ways you can shield your money from taxes. I have expensive advisers, and I've looked into all these options. Nearly all of them are BS.

Yes, if you earn hundreds of thousands of dollars every year, you may have a few additional options. But the real "rich people" tax benefits begin when you're earning millions of dollars from your existing investments. So focus on growing your money and hitting the 85 Percent Solution with taxes.

The One Thing You Need to Know About Taxes and Investments

Invest as much as possible into tax-deferred accounts like your 401(k) and IRA. Because retirement accounts are tax advantaged, you'll enjoy significant rewards. Your 401(k) money won't be taxed until you withdraw it many years down the line, and your Roth IRA earnings won't be taxed at all. More important, you won't have to worry about the minutiae, including picking tax-efficient funds or knowing when to sell to beat end-of-year distributions. By moving toward investing in tax-advantaged retirement accounts, you'll sidestep the vast majority of tax concerns.

Investing in tax-advantaged retirement accounts is the 85 Percent Solution for taxes. Set it up, then move on.

The Annual Financial Checklist

It's important to maintain your automated financial system. Every year, I spend a few hours re-reviewing my system and making any changes necessary. For example, have I added subscriptions that I don't need anymore? Should I adjust my Conscious Spending Plan to account for new short-term goals? Set aside some time every year—I recommend December so you can start the next year off right—to go through each of the steps below.

EVALUATE YOUR CONSCIOUS SPENDING PLAN (THREE HOURS) Use these as general guidelines, but take them seriously: If your money is following these suggested percentages, that's a Big Win toward a Rich Life.

- ☐ Fixed costs (50–60%)
- ☐ Investments (10%)
- ☐ Savings (5–10%)
- ☐ Guilt-Free Spending (20–35%)
- ☐ Reassess current subscriptions (cut if necessary).
- ☐ Renegotiate cable and internet bills.
- ☐ Revisit spending goals: Are they accurate? Are you actively saving for them?
- ☐ If your fixed costs are too high, it may be time to look at a cheaper rent (or AirBnB'ing a room out, or earning more).
- ☐ If you aren't investing at least 10 percent, it's worth finding the money from somewhere else—usually guilt-free spending—and reallocating it to investments.

NEGOTIATE ANY FEES (TWO HOURS) Many companies will offer you introductory rates or lower your monthly fees if you ask. Use my word-for-word scripts at iwillteachyoutoberich.com/negotiate.

- ☐ Cell phone bill
- ☐ Car insurance
- ☐ Cable and internet
- ☐ Bank fees

INVESTMENTS (TWO HOURS)

☐ Confirm you're contributing the max to your 401(k), that your money is being invested (not just sent over and sitting there—for a cautionary tale, see page 244), and that it's being invested in the right fund(s).

☐ Confirm you're contributing the max to your Roth IRA, that your money is being invested (not just sent over and sitting there), and that it's being invested in the right fund(s).

☐ Be sure you're taking advantage of all the tax-advantaged accounts you can (Chapter 4)

DEBT (TWO HOURS)

☐ Revisit your debt payoff plan: Are you on track? Can you pay any of your debt off sooner?

☐ Check your credit report and credit score.

☐ Renegotiate your credit cards' APRs.

CREDIT CARDS (ONE HOUR)

☐ Make a plan to use your credit card points! (Some might expire, some might not—but you earned them. Now have fun with them!)

☐ Call to ask what other perks your credit card offers that you haven't taken advantage of.

☐ Confirm you're not paying any unnecessary fees. If you are, try to negotiate them down.

EARN MORE (ONGOING)

☐ Negotiate a raise (see page 155).

☐ Make money on the side (visit iwillteachyoutoberich.com for ideas, examples, and courses).

(We cover these at iwillteachyoutoberich.com.)

OTHER

☐ Review your insurance needs, including renters insurance and life insurance.

☐ If you have dependents, create a will.

Why You Should Think Twice About Selling

I've never sold a single one of my investments. Why would I? I'm investing for the long term. But I still get questions about selling investments. In general, anytime you sell your investments, you'll be eligible to pay taxes when April 15 rolls around. The government has created incentives for long-term investing: If you sell an investment that you've held for less than a year, you'll be subject to ordinary income tax, which is usually 25 to 35 percent. Most people who buy a stock and make $10,000 in nine months and stupidly decide to sell it really pocket only $7,500.

If, however, you hold your investment for more than a year, you'll pay only a capital-gains tax, which is much lower than your usual tax rate. For example, take the same person who sold their stock in nine months and paid 25 percent in ordinary income taxes. If they'd held that stock over a year, *then* sold it, they would have only paid 15 percent in capital-gains taxes. Instead of only netting $7,500, they would have ended up with $8,500. (Now imagine that happening with $100,000, or $500,000, or millions of dollars. If you save and invest enough by following the IWT system, that's extremely likely.) This is a small example of big tax savings from holding your investments for the long term.

Here's the trick: If you've invested within a tax-advantaged retirement account, you don't have to pay taxes in the year that you sell your investment. In a 401(k), which is tax deferred, you'll pay taxes much later, when you withdraw your money. In a Roth IRA, by contrast, you've already paid taxes on the money you contribute, so when you withdraw, you won't pay taxes at all.

Since you presumably made a good investment, why not hold it for the long term? In Chapter 6, we covered how people can't time the market. In Chapter 3, I showed you how buy-and-hold investing produces dramatically higher returns than frequent trading. And once you've factored in taxes, the odds are stacked against you if you sell. This is yet another argument for not buying individual stocks and instead using target date funds or index funds to create a tax-efficient, simple portfolio. Remember, all of this assumes that you made a good investment.

Bottom line: Invest in retirement accounts and hold your investments for the long term.

Knowing When to Sell Your Investments

When you're young, there are only three reasons to sell an investment: You need the money for an emergency, you made a terrible investment and it's consistently underperforming the market, or you've achieved your specific goal for investing.

You Need the Money for an Emergency

If you suddenly need money for an emergency, here's your hierarchy of where to get it.

1. Use your savings account, which you established in Chapter 2.

2. Earn additional money. Drive for Uber, sell old clothes, pick up tutoring. You might not be able to earn a huge amount in a short time, but selling some of your own goods is an important psychological step— it will let you prove how serious you are both to yourself and to your family (which will be useful if you're asking them for help).

3. Ask your family if you can borrow the money from them. Note: This doesn't work if your family is crazy.

4. Use the money in your retirement accounts. You can always withdraw the principal you contributed to your Roth IRA penalty-free, although you'll be severely retarding your money's ability to compound over time. With a 401(k), you can take money out for "hardship withdrawals," which typically include medical expenses, buying a home, tuition, preventing foreclosure, and funeral expenses, but you'll probably still pay early withdrawal fees. If it comes to this, consult your HR representative. But I urge you to avoid cashing out your retirement accounts because of the penalties and taxes involved.

5. Use your credit card *only* as a last resort. I can't emphasize this enough: The chances are very good that your credit card will gouge you as you're repaying it, so don't do this unless you're truly desperate.

Financial Options for Super-Achievers: Make the Ten-Year Plan That Few Others Do

I love getting emails from people who have optimized their personal finances and want to know, "What's next?" My answer: Just ask people five to ten years older than you what they *wish* they had started earlier, then do that. You'll get three answers right off the bat:

1. CREATE AN EMERGENCY FUND. An emergency fund is simply another savings goal that is a way to protect against job loss, disability, or simple bad luck. Especially if you have a mortgage or you need to provide for your family, an emergency fund is a critical piece of being financially secure. To create one, just set up an extra savings goal and then funnel money to it in the same way you would your other goals. Eventually, your emergency fund should contain six to twelve months of spending money (which includes everything: your mortgage, payments on other loans, food, transportation, taxes, gifts, and anything else you would conceivably spend on).

2. INSURANCE. As you get older and more crotchety, you'll want more and more types of insurance to protect yourself from loss. This includes homeowner insurance (fire, flood, and earthquake) and life insurance. If you own a home, you do need insurance, but young, single people don't need life insurance. First of all, statistically, we hardly ever die, and the insurance payout is useful only for people who depend on your livelihood, like your spouse and kids. Beyond that, insurance is really out of the scope of this book, but if you're truly interested, I encourage you talk to your parents and their friends and search for "life insurance" online to research the various options. You likely don't need to buy a bunch of insurance options right now, but you can certainly set up a savings goal so that when you do need them, you'll have money to use. One last thing: Insurance is almost never a good investment, despite what financial salespeople (or clueless parents) will tell you. So use it as protection from downside risk—like for fires or accidental death when you have a family—but don't think of it as a growth investment.

3. CHILDREN'S EDUCATION. Whether or not you have children yet, your first goal should be to excel financially for yourself. I'm always confused when I see people online who are in debt yet want to save for their children's education. What the hell? First, get out of debt and save for your own retirement. Then you can worry about your kids. That said, just as Roth IRAs are great retirement accounts, 529s—educational savings plans with significant tax advantages—are great for children's education. If you've got kids (or know that one day you will) and some spare cash, pour it into a 529.

If you're younger, these are just a few of the things you may be forced to think about in the next ten years. The best way to prepare yourself is to talk to successful people who are somewhat older than you and have their act together. Their advice can be invaluable—and can give you an edge on planning for the next decade.

You Made a Terrible Investment That's Consistently Underperforming

This point is largely moot if you invested in an index fund or series of index funds, because they reflect the entire index's performance. To oversimplify it, if your "total market index fund" is going down, that means the entire market is down. If you believe the market will recover, that means investments are on sale for cheaper prices than before, meaning not only should you *not* sell, but you should keep investing and pick up shares at a cheaper price.

But let's talk about this conceptually to understand when to sell an investment for poor performance. If you discovered that the share price of a stock you own is down by 35 percent, what would you do?

"Ramit," you might say frantically, "this stock sucks! I need to sell it before I lose all my money!"

Not so fast. You have to look at the context before you decide what to do. For instance, if the example is a consumer goods stock, how is the rest of the consumer goods industry doing?

By looking at the stock *and* the surrounding industry, you see that the entire industry is in decline. It's not your particular investment. They're *all* doing poorly. Now, this raises questions about the industry, but it also gives you a context to explain your stock's plunging returns. And just because they're plunging doesn't mean that you should sell immediately. All industries experience declines at one time or another. Find out what's happening with the industry. Is it still viable? Are there competitors replacing it? (For example, if you own shares in a company that's producing CD players, chances are that business is not coming back.) If you think the industry or investment is simply going through a cyclical downturn, then hang on to the investment and continue regular purchases of shares. If, however, you think the industry won't recover, you may want to sell the investment.

Now, if your stock's share price has plummeted, but the share prices of other companies in the industry are high, then consider selling.

Once you decide it's time to sell an investment, the process is easy. You simply log in to your investment account, browse to the investment you want to sell, and then click "Sell." If you're selling outside of a retirement account, there are many tax considerations, such as tax-loss harvesting (which lets you offset capital gains with losses), but since most of us will start by investing all of our money in tax-efficient retirement accounts, I'm not going to get into these issues here. I want to emphasize that I almost never have to sell investments, because I rarely make specific stock investments. If you pick a target date fund or build a portfolio of index funds instead, you rarely have to think about selling. My advice: Save your sanity and focus on more important things.

You Achieved Your Specific Goal

Buying and holding is a great strategy for ultra-long-term investments, but lots of people invest in the medium to short term to make money for specific goals. For example, "I'm going to invest for a dream vacation to Thailand . . . I don't need to take the trip anytime soon, so I'll just put $100/month into my investment account." Remember, if your goal is less than five years away, you should set up a savings goal in your savings account. But if you've invested money for a longer-term goal that you've achieved, sell and don't think twice. That's a great investing success, and you should use the money for whatever your original goal was.

You're Almost There

We've got one last chapter to read. From the thousands of emails and blog comments I've received over the years, I've learned that there are a few common issues that lots of people have questions about. In the next chapter, I'll cover the juicy specifics of money and relationships, buying a car and your first house, and managing the daily questions that come up in your financial life. Last chapter!

Let's do it.

CHAPTER 9

A RICH LIFE

The finances of relationships, weddings, buying a car,
your first house, and more

I'll never forget the conversation I had with my then-girlfriend (now wife), Cass. It was right before Thanksgiving and we'd decided it was time to talk about kids, marriage, money—the big things.

I told you I love systems, so true to form I created an agenda with my talking points. Here it is:

Number of kids		Wedding
When?		Where to live
Names of kids		Lifestyle—who works?

First up was getting engaged. We'd been dating for years and Cass was ready to get married. In fact, she said, "I'd really like to be engaged by Q1 of next year." This was the moment I fully realized I'd found the love of my life: when I heard her speaking about our relationship in financial quarters.

We talked about how many kids we wanted to have, who would work, where we wanted to live, and the kind of lifestyle we wanted to lead.

Toward the end of the conversation, I took a deep breath and said something I'd been thinking about for a long time. "There's one other thing I want to talk about. It's important to me that we sign a prenup."

More on that in a moment.

In this book, I've written about money, which I believe is a small but important part of a Rich Life.

What about the rest?

What about challenging conversations about love and money, like the one I had with Cass? Or the decision to buy a house? Or negotiating your salary? Once you've automated your finances, what's next?

Living a Rich Life happens outside the spreadsheet. It's tempting to tinker with online calculators and asset allocations for years and years, but at a certain point—especially for my readers who have followed my lessons and automated their money—there's a point where you got it right. You won the game. Now it just takes time, patience, and feeding the system.

The next layer of a Rich Life isn't about recalculating your returns from compound interest. It's about designing the lifestyle you want. Kids? Taking a two-month vacation every year? Flying your parents out to meet you? Increasing your savings rate so you can retire in your forties?

I'm writing this from a safari lodge in Kenya—part of a six-week honeymoon that Cass and I are taking. One of our dreams was to invite our parents for the first part of the trip in Italy—to treat them and create new memories together. It was truly an unforgettable Rich Life experience.

For me, a Rich Life is about freedom—it's about not having to think about money all the time and being able to travel and work on the things that interest me. It's about being able to use money to do whatever I want—and not having to worry about taking a taxi or ordering what I want at a restaurant or how I'll ever be able to afford a house.

That's just me. Being rich probably means something different to you. Now it's time to focus on designing your Rich Life.

Student Loans— Pay Them Down or Invest?

The Federal Reserve reports that the average college graduate has around $35,000 of student loans—and those of you carrying such debt may find it an impediment to achieving your Rich Life. But the surprisingly good news is that student loans were probably an excellent financial decision.

Statistics clearly show that college graduates far outearn those with only a high school diploma. (That said, you should take responsibility for researching college majors and their average salaries.) Please don't listen to the pundits who have jumped on the bandwagon of saying student loans are "evil" and you should skip college. God, if I hear this nonsense one more time, I'm going to jump up and beat someone with an onion. (That way it's unclear why they're crying.)

We already talked about getting out of student debt in Chapter 1, but there's one additional question I constantly get asked: "Should I invest or pay off my student loans?"

> *I used to have anxiety wondering how I would ever be able to pay off my student loans, have savings, and have a retirement plan. Now my student loans are almost entirely paid off, I have savings accounts (plural), have two retirement accounts, and have no stress around those things. I have all of it automated, and I know how much money comes in, where it goes, and how much goes out.*
>
> **—DEANNA BEATON, 30**

Investing vs. Paying Off Student Loans

It can be difficult to hear the drumbeat of "Invest early!" when you're scrambling to pay $500 or $1,000 toward your student loans each month. But when it comes to paying down your loans or investing, you really have three choices:

- Pay the minimum monthly payment on your student loans and invest the rest.

- Pay as much as possible toward your student loans and then, once they are paid off, start investing.

- Do a hybrid 50/50 approach, where you pay half toward your student loans (always paying at least the minimum) and send the other half into your investment accounts.

Technically, your decision comes down to interest rates. If your student loan has a super-low interest rate of, say, 2 percent, you'd want to pursue option one: Pay your student loans off as slowly as possible, because you can make an average of 8 percent by investing in low-cost funds.

However, notice I said "technically." That's because money management isn't always rational. Some people aren't comfortable with debt and want to get rid of it as quickly as possible. If having debt keeps you awake at night, follow option two and pay it off as soon as possible—but understand that you could be losing lots of growth potential just so you can be more comfortable.

I recommend you take a close look at option three, and here's why: The interest rate on most student loans these days is similar to what you'd get in the stock market, so frankly your decision will be a toss-up. All things being equal, the money you stand to make by investing is about the same amount that you'll pay out in interest on your student loan, so basically it's a wash. It won't really matter whether you pay off your student loans or invest, because you'll get roughly the same return. Except for two things: compound interest and tax-advantaged retirement accounts. When you invest in your twenties and early thirties, you get huge benefits from compound interest. If you wait until you're older to invest, you'll never be able to catch up on those earnings. Plus, if you're investing in tax-advantaged accounts like 401(k)s and Roth IRAs (see Chapter 3), you're getting gains from tax benefits. That's why I would consider a hybrid split, paying off your debt with part of your money and investing with the rest. The exact split depends on your risk tolerance. You could choose a fifty-fifty split to keep things simple, but if you're more aggressive, you'll probably want to invest more.

LOVE AND MONEY

After you know the basics of personal finance, it's easy to live in the spreadsheet. What's harder is knowing how to navigate money with the people around you: your friends, your parents, your partner.

There are infinite situations where love and money play out: eating out with the friend who never tips, realizing your parents are in debt, or combining money with your new partner. I believe mastering love and money is one of the most complex—and rewarding—parts of a Rich Life.

That's why I want to spend some time talking about how to handle money with the people around you. Sure, there are some easy formulas you can use for situations like splitting rent when one partner earns more than the other.

But that's just the spending. I believe the real challenges—and opportunities—lie in the softer discussions. For example, should you tell your friends how much you earn? What about your parents? What's the role of money in getting married? Should you get a prenup?

I don't have all the answers, but I'll tell you exactly what I've chosen to do—and why.

Ignore the Noise of Money Advice

Now that you've mastered the basics of personal finance, you're going to notice how "noisy" the world of money is. There are your uncle's "hot stock tips," random money-management apps, and your friend's scoffing that you haven't used a certain obscure tax-avoidance strategy (LOL when you get financially judged by someone who can't save enough to buy a bag of jelly beans).

Everyone's got advice. Everyone has a different way they handle money. Some know more than others, but everyone has an opinion on what *you* should do. Suddenly you'll be hyperaware of how other people handle their money.

You'll also notice that as soon as they hear that you've taken control of your money, they'll begin to act weirdly—making excuses for why they can't do it, putting your efforts down.

■ "Ugh, it's impossible to get ahead . . ."

- "Retire? LOL! I'm going to have to work forever . . ."

- "Must be nice to have savings like you . . ."

I've had over fifteen years to think of comebacks. Here's my fantasy.

RAMIT'S FANTASY SITUATION: Someone who absolutely sucks at personal finance and is deeply in debt starts telling me how I "need" to drop everything I'm doing and invest in real estate, Bitcoin, and other assorted idiotic suggestions.

COMEBACK: I look up from my Thai papaya salad, lower my fork, use a cloth napkin to wipe my lips, examine them from head to toe, and say, "Why would I take advice from you?" The music stops, everyone in the restaurant claps, and the chef comes out to shake my hand and give me free dessert.

After years of hearing these comments, I've learned what's really going on. When you first begin taking control of your money, people will notice. (Candidly, you're probably talking about it more than before. You know the saying "How do you know if someone is vegan? Don't worry, they'll tell you." Same with taking control of your finances. My suggestion: Be mindful of how you discuss money and who you discuss it with.) By mastering your money, you're disrupting the normal relationship pattern you've had with others, which makes them uncomfortable and causes them to react in odd ways. Don't take it personally. Smile and say, "Thank you." As the people around you get more comfortable with the new you, the comments will gradually fade away.

But at that point, you'll be hearing other noise: the chaos of advice on the internet. As my readers get more comfortable implementing the IWT system, they start to seek out more information on investing and personal finance. Maybe you end up on reddit or investing forums. Suddenly, you'll be hit with tons of "advanced" tactics that anonymous commenters will urge you to use.

- "Tax-loss harvesting is the most important thing on earth!"

- "Wait, you don't have captive insurance?"

- "LOL, I can't believe you still believe in index investing. That's cute. It's so obvious that Apple is going to the moon." (Or is it Tesla? Or Bitcoin? Or ICOs?)

If anything, I've learned to have compassion. Remember that just a few weeks ago, you didn't know much about money. It may have taken you a long time to get mentally ready to even buy a finance book and go through it—and now you understand concepts, like automation and IRAs, that would have seemed foreign just a few weeks ago. The best thing you can do is be a great example to others and, if they want your advice, share this book with them.

Ignore the noise. Remember, investing shouldn't be dramatic or even fun—it should be methodical, calm, and as fun as watching grass grow. (What you can *do* with your investments—and your Rich Life—*that's* fun!)

Log in to your investment account no more than once a month—that's it. If you've set up your asset allocation and are consistently funding it, stick to your guns. You're investing for the long term, and when you look back, day-to-day changes will seem like minor blips—which they are.

I understand that you'll want to seek out more information. Do it. Just keep it in perspective and realize that everyone has an angle but there are no tricks or hacks to long-term personal finance. After you read the hundredth breathless post about how index investing is only for beginners (it's not), you'll realize you know more than most of the advice out there. That's the magic moment: Instead of "living in the spreadsheet," tweaking random numbers, and searching out endless reddit threads about personal finance, you can spend less than ninety minutes a month on your finances—and instead live your Rich Life outside the spreadsheet doing things that matter.

How to Help Parents Who Are in Debt

This is one of the most difficult situations you may face in your financial life: realizing that your aging parents are in financial trouble.

As likely as not, they won't come out and admit it (and in my experience with thousands of readers, your parents will never ask for help—it's too embarrassing). They might drop little clues here and there, saying things like "Money is tight right now."

Discussing their situation may be among the most challenging conversations you'll ever have—and one of the most necessary. Your parents have spent decades raising you and have formed patterns that are very difficult to change. *You* are more likely to bring up money than they are. And you have the perfect excuse—this book. Like this: "Mom, I've been reading this book on personal finance. I learned a lot of things I never knew. How did you learn about money?" Watch the floodgates open.

If your parents are in debt, it can be very tough on your relationship with them. Your biggest challenge is not going to be coming up with a technical personal finance solution for their problem. Instead, it's going to be asking lots of questions, listening carefully, and deciding if they actually want help, and if they're ready to receive it.

If they do, great! You can help them. But if they don't, one of the most difficult things you'll ever do is respect their decision, even as their situation might become increasingly dire.

In my experience, if you approach the topic of money with your loved ones in a careful, compassionate way, they'll open up to you.

Every situation is different, but here are some questions you can ask. (Remember: Tread gently. Nobody likes talking about money— especially if it means having to admit to their kids that they need help.)

- Where did they learn about money? What did their parents teach them?

- If they could wave a magic wand and be in any financial situation, what would it be? (Let them dream here. If they say "win the lottery," encourage them. What would that mean? What would they do? Then get more realistic: "Okay, let's assume you can't win the lottery. What would your ideal situation look like five years from now?" Most parents have pragmatic dreams.)

- How much do they make per month? How much do they spend?

- What percentage of their income are they saving? (Almost nobody knows this. Be reassuring, not judgmental.)

- Do they pay fees for their bank accounts and credit cards?

- What's their average monthly credit card balance? Out of curiosity (use that phrase), why isn't it zero? How could they get it there?

- Do they have any investments? If so, how did they choose them?

- Do they own a mutual fund or funds? How much are they paying in fees?

- Are they maximizing their 401(k)s, at least contributing as much as their company matches?

- What about other retirement vehicles, like a Roth IRA? Do they have one?

- Do they read iwillteachyoutoberich.com? NO? WHY NOT, DAD?!?! (Note: I highly recommend that you scream this really loudly at them.)

Your parents might not have answers to all these questions, but listen closely to what they do tell you. I'd encourage you to take the 85 Percent Solution approach and figure out one or two major actions they could take to improve their financial situation. Maybe it means setting up an automatic savings account, or focusing on paying off one credit card so they can feel a small sense of accomplishment. Think back to when you didn't know anything about money and it was incredibly overwhelming. Now you can use what you've learned to help your parents make small changes that will have big results.

Should You Tell Your Parents and Friends How Much Money You Have?

Years ago, I started to feel that I should talk to my parents about money. My business had grown. I'd become more financially secure than I'd ever imagined. And when my parents asked how business was going, I'd answer in generalities—"Things are good!"— when in reality, I knew that sharing a single revenue number would be more specific than anything else I could say.

I called my friend Chris for advice.

"Should I tell my parents?"

Chris is an author who was raised in a household similar to mine. He instantly understood what I meant.

"Why do you want to tell them?" he asked. I told him it would answer a lot of questions I felt were beneath the surface. Am I doing fine, financially speaking? Did my parents do the right thing by moving to this country? Are they proud of me?

But I was nervous because I thought sharing specific details about my success might change my relationship with my parents. "It might get weird," I said, using a loaded word that anyone with ethnic parents will understand. Chris, more than almost anyone else, knew what it was like to grow up as an Asian kid with frugal parents, then earn more than you ever imagined.

Ultimately, I realized that I wanted my parents to know I was doing fine—that they'd prepared me for life, that I'd learned their lessons, and that they didn't need to worry.

Chris pointed out that I'd been thinking a single number would communicate all of this, but in reality, I could assure my parents in lots of different ways. I could simply tell them my business was doing well. I could thank them for teaching me the discipline to grow a business. And I could do the thing that's most meaningful to parents: spend time with them.

Chris was right. He taught me that my intention was right, but I didn't have to get into exact dollar figures to communicate that I was secure. In reality, my parents don't care about the number in my bank account—they just want to know that I'm happy (and of course that I'm married and having kids—these are Indian parents I'm talking about).

The next time I spoke to my parents and they asked how things were going, I took extra time to thank them for everything they'd taught me and told them that, thanks to them, I was fortunate enough to have a dream business that let me live an incredible life.

My lessons:

■ As you become more financially successful, your relationships with others might change. Be aware of it. (For example, I'm hyperconscious about different people's ability to spend on a dinner or vacation. If I'm meeting a group of friends for dinner, I'll always pick a restaurant that we can all easily afford. My nightmare is choosing a place that makes them feel financially pressured.)

■ You might be tempted to share specific numbers. If it's with your spouse or a very close friend or family member, okay. But beyond those people, ask yourself why: Is it to communicate that you're doing well? Or is it to subtly show off? Are there other ways of communicating this? Remember, sharing numbers without context is a bad move. Your intention might be good, but to someone who earns $60,000, telling them you're on track to have a $1 million portfolio (or much more) doesn't communicate safety and security. It communicates arrogance.

Talking Money with Your Significant Other

My fantasy is to host a TV show where couples have their first conversations about money together. No, I'm not going to mediate it. I'll just be sitting in the background stirring the pot with crazy money questions ("What's a money secret you haven't told your partner yet?"), eating chips and salsa, grinning as I watch the nervous hands, the sweaty foreheads, and the stammering words. Damn, I live for this shit. HBO, give me a call.

Sure, you and your boyfriend or girlfriend might have had an occasional chat about money. But when you're getting serious—maybe you just moved in together, or you just got married and you're merging your finances together—it's important to spend some time talking about your money and your financial goals. Talking about money with your partner might sound awkward, but I promise you it doesn't have to be painful. As corny as it sounds, it can actually bring you closer together—if you know what to ask and you stay calm.

The specific tactics aren't as important as your attitude going in.

The key is to be nonjudgmental and to ask lots of questions. Here are some sample questions:

- "I've been thinking about my personal finances a lot and I'd love to get on the same page with you. Can we talk about it?"

- "How do you think about money? Like some people like to spend more on rent and other people like to save a certain percentage. I think I overspend on eating out. Speaking broadly, what are your general thoughts about money?" (Notice that I started off broad, then offered examples, then offered a confession about an area I'm not great in. Start by being vulnerable with your own finances.)

- "If you could wave a magic wand, what would you be doing with your money? For me, I know I should be investing in my 401(k),

but to tell you the truth, I haven't filled out the paperwork yet."
(Another admission—only if true, of course.)

- "How should we use our money together? Have you thought about whether you'd want to change anything?" (This is where you can discuss how you share expenses, if you're saving toward joint goals, or what fun things you want to use your money for.)

Notice that we're not getting into the tactics of different investment options or making each other feel bad about things we "should have done." The goal of this conversation should be to agree that money is important to both of you and that you want to work together to help each other with finances. That's it—end on a high note!

The Big Meeting

This is the big day when you both lay bare all your finances and work through them together. But remember, it's not really such a dramatic step, since you've been slowly working toward this for weeks.

It should take about four or five hours to prepare for this meeting. You'll each want to bring the following:

- A list of your accounts and the amount in each

- A list of debts and what the interest rates are

- Monthly expenses (see page 141 for details on how to determine this)

- Your total income

- Any money that is owed to you

- Your short-term and long-term financial goals

My wife and I did this with our finances. We started with the big picture—how much we earned and how much we'd saved—and over the course of many months, we went deeper into our accounts and our attitudes toward money. (It probably won't take you that long to explore your accounts, but to fully understand each other's money attitudes can take years.)

When you sit down, put the paper aside and start by talking about goals. From a financial perspective, what do you want? What kind of lifestyle do you expect? What about vacations in the next year? Does either of you need to support your parents?

Then look at your monthly spending. This will be a sensitive conversation, because nobody wants to be judged. But remember, keep an open mind. Show yours first. Ask, "What do you think I could be doing better?" And then it's your partner's turn.

Spend some time talking about your attitudes toward money. How do you treat money? Do you spend more than you make? Why? How did your parents talk about money? How did they manage it? (One of my friends has horrible money management skills, which is confusing because she's so disciplined and smart. After years of knowing her, one day she told me that her dad had declared bankruptcy twice, which helped me understand the way she approached her finances.)

The most important goal of this conversation is to normalize talking about money, which is why we want to keep it as light as possible. The second goal is for you both to get to a "baseline" of money management, making sure you're each saving and investing and paying off debt (if applicable). Essentially, you want to work through this book with your partner. You can get to all the complicated stuff, like joining accounts together, later!

Now, in the spirit of keeping this upbeat: I want you to set up a few short- and long-term savings goals, such as a year-end trip. At this point, it's probably better not to run through all the numbers for a really large purchase, because that can get overwhelming. Just establish a savings goal or two and set up an automatic monthly transfer for each of you. Longer term, you and your partner should work together to get on the same page with your money attitudes. When you set a goal together ("We're going to save enough to put a $30,000 down payment on a house"), you'll both be able to commit to working toward it.

When One Person Earns More Than the Other

Once you and your significant other start sharing expenses, questions will invariably come up about how to handle money on a daily basis—especially if one of you has a higher income than the other. When it comes to splitting bills, there are a few options.

The first, and most intuitive, choice is to split all the bills fifty-fifty. But is that really fair to the person who earns less? They're spending disproportionately more, which can lead to resentment and, often, bad money situations.

As an alternative, how about this idea from Suze Orman? She encourages dividing expenses based proportionately on income.

For example, if your monthly rent is $3,000 and you earn more than your partner, here's how you might split it up:

DIVIDING EXPENSES BASED ON INCOME		
	You	Your partner
Monthly income	$5,000	$4,000
Rental payment	$1,680	$1,320
	(5,000/9,000 = 56%)	(4,000/9,000 = 44%)

There are lots of other options. You can each contribute a proportional amount into a joint household account and pay bills out of that. Or one person can cover certain expenses, like groceries, while the other handles rent.

The key takeaway here is to discuss it, come to an agreement that feels fair (remember, fifty-fifty is not the only definition of "fair"), and then check in every six to twelve months to make sure your agreement is still working for both of you.

What to Do if Your Partner Spends Money Irresponsibly

This is the most common complaint I hear from married readers. "Ramit," they write, "my husband spends way too much money on video games. How are we supposed to save money? When I tell him this, he tunes me out and the next day, he's buying something else."

The solution is to elevate the conversation beyond you and your partner. If you keep trying to tell your partner not to spend money on something, he or she will resent it and ignore you. People absolutely hate to be judged for their spending, so if you continue making it personal ("You can't spend that much on shoes each month!"), you'll get nowhere.

Instead, keep it simple—the food analogy is to stop discussing how much dessert they eat and instead to agree on filling your plates with mostly vegetables and protein first. Turn to page 146 in Chapter 4 and look at how much it costs to save for common purchases like vacations, Christmas gifts, or a new car. Then have a conversation about what your savings goals are and how much you need to save to reach them—and come to a savings plan that you both agree on.

If you do this, the next time you have an argument about spending, you can steer it away from you and your partner and instead refocus on the plan. Nobody can get defensive when you're pointing to a piece of paper (rather than pointing at the other person). It's not about you deciding to splurge on a fancy dinner or them paying extra for a direct flight. It's about your plan. Note that you and your partner will almost certainly have different approaches to reaching your savings and investing goals. For example, you might want to prioritize spending on organic food, while your partner might prioritize travel. As long as you both reach the goal, be flexible on *how* you arrive there. By focusing on the plan, not the person, you're more likely to be able to sidestep the perception of being judgmental and work on bringing spending in line with your goals. This is the way handling money is supposed to work.

The $35,000 Question: Why We're All Hypocrites About Our Wedding (and How to Save for Yours)

After the first edition of this book was published, I went on book tour across the country. I met readers in cities like New York, San Francisco, and Salt Lake City. I'll never forget a young woman I met at my Portland meetup.

She came up after my talk and said, "I just wanted to thank you for your advice on weddings." I was thrilled. She told me she'd set up a sub-savings account for her wedding and was automatically saving for her wedding every month.

I got excited. I love seeing real people who've applied my material. I asked if I could take a quick video where she shared her story.

Suddenly, she got visibly uncomfortable.

I could tell she was not into it, but I couldn't figure out why. So I asked her. She looked down and said, "Because I'm not even engaged yet."

Think about that: She thought it was "weird" to save for her wedding because she wasn't engaged yet—that she would get judged by people.

I LOVED IT!

You know what I think is weird? NOT saving for predictable expenses you *know* will be coming. It's too far off or too big to think about—so we avoid planning for the very items that will make a massive impact on our finances. These are the Big Wins.

Buckle up, because I'm about to break down my perspective on weddings—one that lots of people think is "weird." But I don't care if people think my techniques are weird. I care about designing our Rich Lives, together.

Of Course *Your* Wedding Will Be Simple

When my sister called me to tell me that she'd gotten engaged, I was out with my friends. I ordered champagne for everyone. When my other sister told me she was getting married a few months later, I ordered another round. Then I found out they were each having both an East Coast wedding and a West Coast wedding—for a total of four Indian weddings in a few months! Damn, this shit just got real.

That's what got me started thinking about weddings. The average American wedding costs almost $35,000, which, the *Wall Street Journal* notes, is "well over half the median annual income in US households." Hold on: Just wait a second before you start rolling your eyes. It's easy to say, "These people should just realize that a wedding is about having a special day, not about putting yourself in crippling debt."

But guess what? When it's your wedding, you're going to want everything to be perfect. Yes, you. So did I. It'll be your special day, so why not spend the money to get the extra-long-stemmed roses or the filet mignon? My point isn't to judge people for having expensive weddings. Quite the opposite: The very same people who spend $35,000 on their weddings are the ones who, a few years earlier, said the same thing you're saying right now: "I just want a simple wedding. It's ridiculous to go into debt for just one day." And yet, little by little, they spend more than they planned—more than they can afford—on their special day. Look, there's nothing wrong with wanting your day to be perfect. Let's just acknowledge it and figure out how to achieve our goals.

So What Should You Do?

Knowing the astonishingly high costs of weddings, what can you do?
I see three choices:

Cut costs and have a simpler wedding. Great idea, but frankly, most people are not disciplined enough to do this. I don't say this pejoratively, but statistically: Most people will have a wedding that costs tens of thousands of dollars.

Do nothing and figure it out later. This is the most common tactic. I spoke to a recently married person who spent the previous eight months planning her wedding, which ended up becoming a very expensive day. Now, months later, she and her husband don't know how to deal with the resulting debt. If you do this, you made a huge mistake. But you are in good company, because almost everybody else does it too.

Acknowledge reality and plan for the wedding. Ask ten people which of these choices they'll make, and every single one of them will pick this one. Then ask them how much money they're saving every month for their wedding (whether they're engaged or not). I guarantee the sputtering and silence will be worth it. Then again, I live for uncomfortable conversations.

If you think about it, we actually have all the information we need. The average age at marriage is about twenty-nine for men and twenty-seven for women. (I'm assuming a heterosexual marriage because we have more long-term data.) We know that the average cost of a wedding is about $35,000. So, if you really are committed to not going into debt for your wedding, here's the astonishing amount you should be saving, whether you're engaged or not:

HOW MUCH SHOULD YOU BE SAVING FOR YOUR FUTURE WEDDING?

BASED ON THE AVERAGES IF YOU'RE A WOMAN:

Your age	Months until wedding	Monthly amount needed to save
22	60	$583.33
23	48	$729.17
24	36	$972.22
25	24	$1,458.33
26	12	$2,916.67
27	1	$35,000

BASED ON THE AVERAGES IF YOU'RE A MAN:

Your age	Months until wedding	Monthly amount needed to save
22	84	$416.67
23	72	$486.11
24	60	$583.33
25	48	$729.17
26	36	$972.22
27	24	$1,458.33
28	12	$2,916.67
29	1	$35,000

This can be intimidating, but I think of it differently. This is an eye-opener. Remember that these numbers are averages. You may decide to get married earlier, later, or not at all. I got married at 36! The key point here is that when you plan ahead, time is on your side.

Most of us haven't even conceived of saving this amount for our weddings. Instead, we say things like:

- *"Wow, that's a lot. There's no way I can save that. Maybe my parents will help . . ."*

- *"My wedding won't be like that. I'm just going to keep it small and simple . . ."*

- *"I'll think about it when I get engaged."*

- *"It would be weird to start saving for a wedding. I'm not even engaged yet . . ."*

- *"I guess I have to marry someone rich."* (I've heard people say this, and they were only half joking.)

More commonly, though, we don't think about this at all: one of the biggest expenditures of our lifetimes, which will almost certainly arrive in the next few years, and we don't even sit down for ten minutes to think about it. Something's broken here.

Surprising Wedding Math

I set up a simulation to see which levers were the most powerful in reducing wedding costs. To be honest, I thought reducing the number of guests would produce the biggest result.

I was wrong.

Interestingly, changing the number of guests doesn't change the cost as much as you'd imagine. In the example on the next page, reducing the head count by 50 percent reduces the cost by only 25 percent.

Beyond the obvious—negotiating for better prices on the venue and food—the best suggestion I've heard about cutting wedding costs is to tackle the fixed costs. One of my friends, for example, actually flew in a photographer from the Philippines for his wedding. It sounds extravagant, but even with the flight, he saved $4,000. In another example, my sister had her invitations designed and printed in India for a fraction of what it would have cost in the United States.

SAMPLE WEDDING COSTS

Variable costs	150 guests	75 guests
Open bar/person	$20	$20
Lunch/person	$30	$30
Reception/person	$120	$120
Subtotal	$25,500	$12,750
Fixed costs		
DJ	$1,000	$1,000
Photographer	$4,000	$4,000
Rentals: tables, chairs, linens	$1,500	$1,250
Flowers	$750	$600
Hotel for guests	$750	$750
Invitations	$1,000	$750
Rehearsal dinner	$1,500	$1,500
Honeymoon	$5,000	$5,000
Dress	$800	$800
Limo	$750	$750
Rings	$5,000	$5,000
Bridesmaids' gifts	$4,000	$4,000
Misc.	$2,000	$2,000
Subtotal	$28,050	$27,400
Grand total	**$53,550**	**$40,150**

Should You Sign a Prenup?

One of my friends recently hosted a "prenup night," where he invited several high-net-worth individuals to discuss their thoughts on prenuptial agreements. Among the people he invited—men, women, single people, married people, and a lawyer to answer common questions—one wrote back declining the invitation.

"Dude, this is the last thing I'd ever come to," he said. He was married and had signed a prenup years earlier. When my friend asked why, he replied, "Imagine taking the person you love, then introducing lawyers to communicate with each other for months . . . all to create a contract of what happens if you get divorced. It was the worst time of my life."

I didn't have as bad an experience, but the financial conversations with Cass during the months when we developed our prenup were the hardest I've ever had. In fact, before getting into a serious relationship, I never thought I would have a prenup: I didn't know anyone who had one, I didn't think it applied to me, and I didn't like the idea of "planning to fail."

But I changed my mind. My wife and I signed a prenup. After months of researching it, hours of discussion, and tens of thousands of dollars of legal fees, this is what I learned.

The first thing I wondered is: Who needs a prenup? In pop culture, it's celebrities, industrial tycoons, and wealthy heirs—three groups I'm not a member of.

As I researched further, I found that most people don't need a prenup unless one of you has a disproportionate amount of assets or liabilities relative to the other—or there are complications like one of you owning a business or having an inheritance. Ninety-nine percent of people don't need one. I learned that, in movies and on TV, prenups are portrayed as the tool that one person (the wealthier one) uses to screw the other. In reality, a prenup is an agreement on assets that were accumulated *before* the marriage, not just what's jointly accumulated *during* the marriage— plus an agreement on what to do if the marriage ends.

I own a business, of course, so technically I should have one, but the decision went deeper than numbers; it went to *identity*. Am I the kind of person who should get a prenup? I remember calling my dad and asking him if Indian people ever got prenups. I was 100 percent sure he would be against it, since we'd never talked about prenups—ever—and my dad is very relaxed about money. Imagine my shock when he said, "No . . .

I don't think so. But I can see why people do it." In retrospect, I think I was looking for my dad to validate my doubts by saying, "No way! We don't do that." When he didn't, my mind was blown.

As I talked to more friends and told them that Cass and I were getting serious, a surprising number of them—especially the entrepreneurs—said, "You're getting a prenup, right?"

I started to pay attention.

The next thing I realized was that the best information about prenups isn't available publicly. For example, I tried searching for sample agreements and found virtually nothing. Much of the information online is written by anonymous redditors or, at worst, factually wrong. I later discovered that because prenups are, by definition, customized, high-stakes legal agreements for wealthy individuals, there is no incentive to publicize how they actually work. Take what you read online with a grain of salt.

I realized that in most other parts of life, we plan ahead: our investments, buying a house, where we want to live, getting a raise at work. But somehow, magically, when it comes to our relationships, we're told that planning ahead is "unromantic." As one divorced friend admitted, "I never thought I'd have to use this agreement. But I'm glad I signed it."

Finally, after researching it for months, and because I was bringing a business and a much higher net worth to the marriage, I made the decision that I wanted to sign one.

Marriage is about finding a partner you love and want to spend the rest of your life with. It's also a legal contract with significant financial ramifications. I plan for other financial contingencies, so after getting educated and consulting lots of experts, I realized that—of course— I should plan for the largest financial decision I'd ever make. As one friend said, "We signed our prenup at our best to prepare for the worst."

How do you talk about this? Most of the information online is about how to bring up the issue with your significant other (and it's almost always from the perspective of "how a guy should bring this up without making his female partner angry"). Some common advice recommends blaming your lawyers ("They made me do it!"). I hated this approach.

Here's what I did.

Cass and I jointly decided to have a conversation about our future: kids, marriage, money, the works. In that conversation, I brought it up: "There's something I want to talk about, and it's important to me. It's important to me that we talk about a prenup and sign one before we get married."

Cass sat back, clearly not expecting this. "Wow," she said. "I'm just absorbing this."

We talked more and I told her *why* I wanted us to sign a prenup.

I reassured her that I planned for our marriage to be forever. "I love you and I'm excited to get married and be with you for the rest of my life."

I told her why we were even talking about this. "Because of a few decisions and a lot of luck with my business, I'm coming to this relationship with more money than most people. I don't think we'll ever need to use a prenup, but it's important to me that I protect the assets I've accumulated before we get married."

I emphasized marriage was about creating a team. "When we get married, we're a team. I want you to know I'll look out for you, and I know you'll look out for me."

I emphasized our lifestyle. "You and I grew up almost the same. Both our moms are teachers. You see what I spend my money on—it's not sports cars or bottle service. It's basically living a comfortable life (with a few nice things). I love sharing this lifestyle with you and with our families."

But I was firm about wanting to sign a prenup. "I'm proud of what I've accomplished with my business and finances. It's important to me that I protect those assets in the worst case that we separate."

Notice that:

- I started by emphasizing that I love her and want to spend my life with her.

- I took responsibility for bringing this up. It wasn't my lawyers or accountants or anybody else forcing me to. This was something I wanted and it was important to me.

- I spent the majority of the time talking about *why* I wanted a prenup (not how it's structured or the numbers).

Cass told me she was open to it and she wanted to research more. And thus began a multi-month conversation about our prenup. We talked about what money meant to us, we circled back to why I wanted one, and when we dug in to the actual numbers, we talked about what those numbers meant.

At one point, Cass said, "You know, I've been really open with my finances. I feel a little uncomfortable because I don't really know anything about your finances."

DUH. I'd never actually walked her through my numbers. In fact, only my bookkeeper and accountant knew everything. That was a big mistake on my part. I shared my numbers with her that same day.

We talked about how we would travel: What if I want to stay at a nicer hotel and she wants to save money?

We talked about our businesses: Mine has been around for many years, while hers is just starting up. What if she didn't hit her numbers one month? Or for three months in a row? What if my income decreased?

We talked about risk and security. How does money make you feel? Do you need a certain amount in your bank account to feel safe? Are you risk-averse? I'm willing to bet your partner thinks about risk and security differently than you do. Find out.

In retrospect, I really should have started our conversation six months before I proposed. I would have shared my finances with Cass earlier and spent a lot of time talking about what money means to each of us. For me, money represents hard work and luck. It also represents the opportunity to design our Rich Life—together.

I'd been thinking about money for fifteen years, especially as my assets began to grow. Cass had not. I was more casual about certain expenses, knowing that my financial team would figure out how to categorize and reconcile them down to the last penny. Cass was not.

I would have taken the time to gradually discuss different money issues regularly—not just telling her some of my financial decisions, but also asking about hers. For example, "I'm calling my bookkeeper to prepay my taxes. Here's why I like to do that" and "How do you decide what to spend money on and what's not worth it? Here's how I think about it."

That way, money wouldn't be a surprise that was "sprung" on her. It would have been normal to talk about it regularly.

As the months went on, things got really tough. I felt resentful; she felt misunderstood. We both felt stuck—and this is when Cass brought up the idea of getting help. The minute she suggested it, I agreed: We ended up seeing a counselor who helped us navigate the tricky emotional issues of money. Imagine getting new conversational tools to talk about your hopes for money, your fear of money, your pride in money, and ultimately what your marriage will be about. This was immensely useful. We should have done it earlier. I've heard there are counselors who specialize in financial counseling, but we were in a rush and we found our counselor on Yelp.

In retrospect, I would have talked through how to manage our lawyers. Your lawyer naturally wants to protect you from every contingency, while your partner's lawyer wants to protect them. But ultimately, you need to manage them, not let the lawyers lead the process.

Prenups dictate the terms of what happens in the case of divorce. What happens to your premarital assets (money you've earned before you marry)? What if you've bought a house—who moves out? How fast? What if you get divorced in one year? Twenty years? What if you have kids?

These are complex topics. There are prenups, postnups, amendments, and so much more. There are no easy formulas, which is why you need the help of lawyers.

Ultimately, we signed an agreement that we're both satisfied with.

Going through this process, I was shocked at how nobody talks about this publicly—it's completely taboo. Yet when I started discussing it privately with friends and advisers, I discovered that a surprising number of people actually had one! I want to shine a light on this topic and encourage you to discuss it openly with your partner.

The prenup process taught me more about how we both think about money than anything I'd ever done. We both hope we never have to use it.

WORK AND MONEY

Fundamentally, there are two ways to get more money. You can earn more or you can spend less. Cutting costs is great, but I personally find increasing earnings to be a lot more fun. Because most of our income comes from work, it's an excellent place to optimize and earn more. In fact, negotiating your salary at a new job is the fastest legal way to make money. Your starting salary is even more important than you think, because it sets the bar for future raises and, in all likelihood, your starting salary at future jobs. A $1,000 or $2,000 salary increase, in other words, can equal many times that over your career. Now let me show you how to get thousands by negotiating for a better salary.

Negotiating Your Salary, *I Will Teach You to Be Rich* Style

In Chapter 4, I wrote about asking for a raise at your current job. But the single best time to negotiate salary is when you're starting a new job. You have the most leverage then, and—with some basic preparation—you can earn $5,000 or $10,000 in a simple ten-minute conversation. Thousands of my students have used my YouTube videos, courses, and the scripts below to increase their salaries.

When I coach people on negotiation, I pretend to be the hiring manager and ask the toughest questions they might get. When we're finished—four to five hours later—they're exhausted and cranky. But the people I've coached end up negotiating, on average, $6,000 more in salary. On my website, we offer a course that includes videos of actual negotiations and word-for-word scripts—but for now, let me give you some of our best material right here.

Negotiating is 90 percent about mindset and 10 percent about tactics. Most people don't believe they should negotiate. They're afraid of being "rude" or of having the employer rescind their offer. That almost never happens, especially because the company may have already spent up to $5,000 recruiting you. If you negotiate, you explicitly communicate that you value yourself more highly than the average employee. Are you average? If not, why would you settle for an average salary?

Because of your book, and subsequent teachings, my salary has gone from $25,000 a year to $80,000 a year. It doesn't matter if it's a yard sale, buying a car, or getting a higher salary, I hit negotiations hard and prepared. I get something extra, whether it's time or money, every time I negotiate. Your book set me on that path. **—JASON FLAMM, 35**

The basics of negotiating are very simple:

1. Remember that nobody cares about you. Most new employees come to the table talking about how much *they* want to make. To be totally honest, as a hiring manager, I don't really care what you want to make. Personally, I'd like to be fed octopus ceviche on command. So what? When you're negotiating, remember this: When it comes to you, your manager cares about two things—how you're going to make him or her look better, and how you're going to help the company do well.

Negotiating tactic: Always frame your negotiation requests in a way that shows how the company will benefit. Don't focus on the amount you'll cost the company. Instead, illustrate how much value you can provide the company. If your work will help them drive an initiative that will make $1 million for the company, point that out. Tie your work to the company's strategic goals—and show the boss how you'll make her look good. Highlight the ways you'll make your boss's life easier by being the go-to person she can hand anything to. And remember that your company will make much more off your work than they pay you, so highlight the ways you'll help your company hit its goals. Your key phrase here is "Let's find a way to arrive at a fair number that works for both of us."

2. Have another job offer—and use it. This is the single most effective thing you can do to increase your salary. When you have another job offer, your potential employers will have a newfound respect for your skills. People like others who are in demand.

Negotiating tactic: Interview with multiple companies at once. Be sure to let each company know when you get another job offer, but don't reveal the amount of the exact offer—you're under no obligation to. In the best case, the companies will get into a bidding war and you'll profit while watching two multinational firms rumble over you. I can think of no better way to spend a casual weekday.

3. Come prepared (99 percent of people don't). Don't just pick a salary out of thin air. First, visit salary.com and payscale.com to get a median amount for the position. Then, if you can, talk to people currently at

Five Things You Should *Never* Do in a Negotiation

1. DON'T TELL THEM YOUR CURRENT SALARY. Why do they need to know? I'll tell you: So they can offer you just a little bit more than what you're currently making. If you're asked, say, "I'm sure we can find a number that's fair for both of us." If they press you, push back: "I'm not comfortable revealing my salary, so let's move on. What else can I answer for you?" (Note: Typically first-line recruiters will ask for these. If they won't budge, ask to speak to the hiring manager. No recruiter wants to be responsible for losing a great candidate, so this will usually get you through the gatekeeper. If the gatekeeper insists on knowing, I recommend you play ball, realizing you can negotiate later.) And in New York, asking for your current salary is actually against the law.

2. DON'T MAKE THE FIRST OFFER. That's their job. If they ask you to suggest a number, smile and say, "Now come on, that's your job. What's a fair number that we can both work from?"

3. IF YOU'VE GOT ANOTHER OFFER FROM A COMPANY THAT'S GENERALLY REGARDED TO BE MEDIOCRE, DON'T REVEAL THE COMPANY'S NAME. When asked for the name, just say something general but true, like "It's another tech company that focuses on online consumer applications." If you say the name of the mediocre company, the negotiator is going to know that he's got you. He'll tear down the other company (which I would do too), and it will all be true. He won't focus on negotiating, he'll just tell you how much better it will be at his company. So withhold this information.

4. DON'T ASK "YES" OR "NO" QUESTIONS. Instead of "You offered me fifty thousand dollars. Can you do fifty-five thousand?" say, "Fifty thousand dollars is a great number to work from. We're in the same ballpark, but how can we get to fifty-five thousand?"

5. NEVER LIE. Don't say you have another offer when you don't. Don't inflate your current salary. Don't promise things you can't deliver. You should always be truthful in negotiations.

the company (if you know someone who has recently left, even better—they'll be more willing to give you the real information) and ask what the salary range really is for the job. Finally—and this is important—bring a plan of how you'll hit your goals to the negotiating session.

Negotiating tactic: Most of the negotiation happens outside the room. Call your contacts. Figure out the salary amount you'd love, what you can realistically get, and what you'll settle for. And don't just ask for money. Literally bring a strategic plan of what you want to do in the position and hand it to your hiring manager. Do you realize how few people come to a negotiation with a plan for their role? This alone could win you $2,000 to $5,000. And, of course, it allows you to negotiate on the value you're going to bring to the company, not just the amount they'll pay you.

4. Have a toolbox of negotiating tricks up your sleeve. Just as in a job interview, you'll want to have a list of things in your head that you can use to strengthen your negotiation. Think about your strong points and figure out ways you might be able to bring them to the hiring manager's attention. For example, I often ask, "What qualities make someone do an extraordinary job in this position?" If they say, "The person should be very focused on metrics," I say, "That's great that you said that—we're really on the same page. In fact, when I was at my last company, I launched a product that used an analytical package to . . ."

Negotiating tactic: Have a repertoire of your accomplishments and aptitudes at your fingertips that you can include in your responses to commonly asked questions. These should include the following:

- Stories about successes you've had at previous jobs that illustrate your key strengths

- Questions to ask the negotiator if the conversation gets off track ("What do you like most about this job? . . . Oh, really? That's interesting, because when I was at my last job, I found . . .")

5. Negotiate for more than money. Don't forget to discuss whether or not the company offers a bonus, stock options, flexible commuting, or further education. You can also negotiate vacation and even job title. Note: Startups don't look very fondly on people negotiating vacations, because it sets a bad tone. But they love negotiating stock options, because top performers always want more, as it aligns them with the company's goals.

Negotiating tactic: Your line is "Let's talk about total comp," which refers to your total compensation—not just salary, but everything. Treat them each as levers: If you pull one up, you can afford to let another fall. Use the levers strategically—for example, by conceding something you don't really care about—so you can both come to a happy agreement.

6. Be cooperative, not adversarial. If you've gotten to the point of negotiating a salary, the company wants you and you want them. Now you just need to figure out how to make it work. It's not about you demanding more or them screwing you for less. Negotiation is about finding a cooperative solution to creating a fair package that will work for both of you. So check your attitude: You should be confident, not cocky, and eager to find a deal that benefits you both.

Negotiating tactic: The phrase to use here is "We're pretty close . . . Now let's see how we can make this work."

7. Smile. I'm not joking. This is one of the most effective techniques in negotiation. It's a disarming technique to break up the tension and demonstrates that you're a real person. When I was interviewing for college scholarships, I kept getting passed over until I started smiling— and then I started winning a bunch of them.

Negotiating tactic: Smile. Really, do it.

8. Practice negotiating with multiple friends. This sounds hokey, but it works better than you can imagine. If you practice out loud, you'll be amazed at how fast you improve. Yet nobody ever does it because it feels "weird." I guess it also feels "weird" to have an extra $10,000 in your pocket, jackass. For example, one of my friends thought it was too strange to practice negotiating, so when he faced a professional hiring manager, he didn't have a prayer. Later, he came to me like a clinically depressed Eeyore, whining about how he didn't negotiate. What could I say? This lack of practice can cost, on average, $5,000 to $10,000.

How My Friend Got a 28 Percent Raise by Doing Her Homework

I helped my friend Rachel, who's twenty-five, negotiate a job offer, and at my request, she wrote up the process. Here's what she said:

First the big picture: I got a 28 percent raise in base salary, which comes out to more than $1,000/hour based on how much time I spent getting the job. Plus stock options, which at least allow me the luxury of dreaming about being a gazillionaire.

I've applied to, and been ignored for, many, many job openings—more than I care to share. Despite this, I decided to jump back into the job market a few months ago after doing marketing for a large hotel in San Francisco. I found a marketing manager position on a website and through it I sent in a résumé, which snagged a phone interview, which was followed by an in-person interview, which was followed by an offer letter.

Sounds like a cakewalk, right? Actually, the VP of marketing told me that I had the least experience of anyone she was interviewing—then she hired me anyway. I can't pinpoint exactly why I was successful in getting this job in contrast to all of my past attempts, but I can think of a few things that probably made the difference. My strategies weren't rocket science, but they involved time and effort, two things that definitely make a difference in separating you from the pack.

1. I BROKE DOWN THEIR JOB POSTING line by line and wrote down my skills and projects I'd worked on that directly related to their description.

2. I RESEARCHED THEIR WEBSITE EXTENSIVELY, read articles about the company, and looked up the management teams' backgrounds so that I could speak knowledgeably about the company and why I was a good fit.

3. I PREPARED A SPIEL ABOUT MY SOMEWHAT ECLECTIC RÉSUMÉ, which can look unfocused if not set in the proper context.

4. I CALLED AN EXPERT ON STARTUPS, finance, bargaining, and a half dozen other things to get some outside counsel. Ramit gave me some key advice, including "Tell them you want to get your hands dirty" and "Suggest three things you would do to improve/enhance their marketing efforts." Yes, he does talk just like he writes on his blog.

5. I ACTUALLY TOOK RAMIT'S ADVICE, which is where a lot of my work came in. I dreamed up three proposals for generating greater interest at trade shows, better responses to direct marketing efforts, and increased name recognition in the general population.

Wow! So the interview must have gone really well, right? Not quite . . . and Rachel's description of what she did is a classic case of turning a missed opportunity into a chance to win.

I never actually found a good opportunity to mention my ideas (this despite a four-hour interview). I emailed the proposals to my potential boss instead. I then individually emailed every person I spoke to that day to thank them for their time. Might have been overkill, but then again, my email flurry may have been the tipping point for my hiring.

My references later told me that the VP had been impressed with my energy and intelligence and had decided she would rather train someone with potential than hire a more experienced, and perhaps less flexible, individual. Three weeks of research and planning paid off with an entirely new career—a pretty stellar return on the investment of my time.

Just notice how this is the exact embodiment of everything this book stands for. Rachel carefully researched her options, took action, reached out to more experienced people for advice, and came in with a presentation that was better than everyone else's (so much so that she actually didn't have to negotiate much). And when she didn't get a chance to show off all of her presentation, she sent it by email—even though some people would think that was "weird."

Getting rich isn't about one silver bullet or secret strategy. It happens through regular, boring, disciplined action. Most people see only the results of all this action—a winnable moment or an article in the press. But it's the behind-the-scenes work that really makes you rich.

Negotiating tactic: Call over your toughest, most grizzled friend and have them grill you. Don't laugh during the role play—treat it like it's a real negotiation. Better yet, videotape it—you'll be surprised how much you learn from this. If it sounds ridiculous, think about the benefits of not only the additional money, but the respect you'll get from your boss for a polished, professional negotiation.

9. If it doesn't work, save face. Sometimes the hiring manager simply won't budge. In that case, you need to be prepared to either walk away or take the job with a salary that's lower than you wanted. If you do take the job, always give yourself an option to renegotiate down the line—and get it in writing.

Negotiating tactic: Your line here is "I understand you can't offer me what I'm looking for right now. But let's assume I do an excellent job over the next six months. Assuming my performance is just extraordinary, I'd like to talk about renegotiating then. I think that's fair, right?" (Get the hiring manager to agree.) "Great. Let's put that in writing and we'll be good to go."

When I first read the IWT book (around 2012), I was making $10.25 per hour, working full-time at a hotel front desk. After reading your section on negotiation, I negotiated my first raise. Not a crazy raise, but I wouldn't have gotten it if I hadn't read your book. Money Made: $520. I've used your advice to negotiate two raises since then, once to go from $35,000 to $42,000, and once to go from $40,000 (I moved jobs and started in a new field) to $50,000. Money Made: $7,000 + $1,000 (YTD). So in raises alone, I figure I've made about $8,500 due to buying your book.
—ELIZABETH SULLIVAN-BURTON, 30

If you want to learn more about negotiation, I've put together a package of in-depth negotiation videos and tips. Check out iwillteachyoutoberich.com/bonus/ for details.

HOW TO SAVE THOUSANDS ON BIG-TICKET ITEMS

When it comes to saving money, big purchases are your chance to shine—and to dominate your clueless friends who are so proud of not ordering Cokes when they eat out, yet waste thousands when they buy large items like furniture, a car, or a house. When you buy something major, you can save massive amounts of money—$2,000 on a car or $40,000 on a house—that will make your other attempts to save money pale in comparison. Big-ticket items like these, however, are where people most commonly make mistakes. They don't comparison shop, they overpay because a salesperson cons them into spending too much, and worst of all, they then think they got a good deal. Don't be one of these people!

A Fresh Look at Buying a Car

It's strange how many people make an effort to save on things like clothes and eating out, but when it comes to large purchases like cars, make poor decisions and erase any savings they've accumulated along the way.

Let me first tell you that the single most important decision associated with buying a car is not the brand or the mileage. Surprisingly, from a financial perspective, the most important factor is how long you keep the car before you sell it. You could get the best deal in the world, but if you sell the car after four years, you've lost money. Instead, understand how much you can afford, pick a reliable car, maintain it well, and drive it for as long as humanly possible. Yes, that means you need to drive it for more than ten years, because it's only once you finish the payments that the real savings start. And by taking good care of your car, you can save even more enormous piles of money over the long term—and you'll have a great car.

There are four steps to buying a car: Budgeting, Picking a Car, Negotiating Like an Indian, and Maintaining Your Car.

First, ask yourself how buying a car fits into your spending and saving priorities (see Chapter 4). If you're satisfied with a used Toyota Corolla and would rather put your extra money toward investing for growth, great. On the other hand, if you really love BMWs and can afford to buy one, then you should do it. This is conscious spending, applied.

Once you've thought about where your car fits into your priorities, you need to look at your Conscious Spending Plan and decide what you're willing to allocate toward your car each month. This is the number you keep in your back pocket as the number you can afford to spend up to. Ideally you'll spend less. (Note: Ignore the random offers for "$199/ month." Those are scammy introductory rates that are simply not real.)

So, knowing that there will be other expenses involved in the total expense of having a car, you want to decide how much you want to spend on the car itself. For example, if you can afford a total monthly payment of $500 toward your car, you can probably afford a car that costs $200 to $250 per month. (For example, when I lived in San Francisco, my monthly car payment of $350.75 actually added up to around $1,000 when I factored in insurance, gas, maintenance, and $200/month in parking.) With a budget of around $200 per month for your car itself, that means you can afford a car that costs around $12,000 over five years. Pretty sobering compared with what most people think they can afford, right? This shows you how easy it is to overspend on a car.

Don't Buy a Horrible Car

Please, pick a good car. There are some cars that are just objectively bad decisions that nobody should ever buy. For example, has anyone with an IQ over 42 ever consciously chosen to buy a Ford Focus? Sadly, many people I know are seduced by the shiny new cars at the dealership. But it's important to remember that you're not just buying the car for today— you're buying it for the next ten-plus years. I have friends who've bought expensive cars. Some of them love cars and they love driving every single day. For others, the "newness" wore off and now it's just a tool for their daily commute—an expensive tool they regret.

First, any car you evaluate must fit within your budget. This will eliminate most cars automatically. Do not even look at cars you can't afford.

Second, the car must be a good car. "But, Ramit," you might say, "who can say what a good car is? One man's trash is another man's treasure." Listen, there is one person who will say what a good car is: me. Here's what makes a good car:

- **Reliability.** When I bought my car, above all, I wanted one that would not break down. I have enough stuff going on in my life, and I want to avoid car-repair issues that cost time and money as much as possible. Because this was a high priority, I was willing to pay slightly more for it.

- **A car you love.** I've written time and time again about consciously spending on the things you love. For me, since I'd be driving the car for a long time, I wanted to pick one that I really enjoyed driving. And like a dutiful Indian son, I love not having to worry about it breaking down.

- **Resale value.** One of my friends bought a $20,000 Acura, drove it for about seven years, and then sold it for 50 percent of the price. That means she got a fantastic deal on driving a new car for seven years. To check out how your potential cars will fare, visit the Kelley Blue Book site at kbb.com and calculate resale prices in five, seven, and ten years. You'll be surprised how quickly most cars depreciate and how others (Toyotas and Hondas especially) retain their value.

- **Insurance.** The insurance rates for a new and used car can be pretty different. Even if they're only slightly different (say, $50/month), that can add up over many years.

- **Fuel efficiency.** It makes a lot of sense to factor this in, especially if you drive a lot. This could be an important factor in determining the value of a car over the long term.

- **The down payment.** This is important. If you don't have much cash to put down, a used car is more attractive because the down payment (i.e., the money you have to pay up front when you buy the car) is typically lower. And if you put $0 down, the interest charges on a new car will be much more. In my case, I had cash available to put down.

Dos and Don'ts for Buying a Car

DO

- **CALCULATE TOTAL COST OF OWNERSHIP (TCO).** This means you figure out how much you'll be spending over the life of the car—these expenses can have a big effect on your finances. Besides the cost of the car and the interest on your loan, the TCO should include maintenance, gas, insurance, and resale value. By understanding even a rough ballpark of how much these "invisible" costs will run you, you'll be able to save more accurately—and avoid surprises when you get a $600 car repair fee.

- **BUY A CAR THAT WILL LAST YOU AT LEAST TEN YEARS,** not one that looks cool. Looks fade, and you're still going to be stuck with the payments. Optimize for the long term.

DON'T

- **LEASE.** Leasing nearly always benefits the dealer, not you. The two exceptions are people who want the newest car and are willing to pay a lot for it, and the occasional business owner who leases a car for tax benefits. For most IWT readers, leasing is a bad decision. Buy a car and hold it for the long term. Years ago, *Consumer Reports* found that buying an average sedan, the Honda Accord, would cost "$4,597 less over five years than leasing the exact same model." I ran the same calculation with a new model Toyota Camry and found the same thing: Buying would save $6,000 over six years versus leasing—and even more over time.

- **SELL YOUR CAR IN FEWER THAN SEVEN YEARS.** The real savings come once you've paid off your car loan and driven it for as long as possible. Most people sell their cars far too early. It's much cheaper to maintain your car well and drive it into the ground.

- **ASSUME YOU HAVE TO BUY A USED CAR.** Run the numbers. Over the long term, a new car may end up saving you money if you pick the right new car, pay the right price, and drive it for a long time. See page 320 for my story on buying a new car.

■ **STRETCH YOUR BUDGET FOR A CAR.** Set a realistic budget for your car and don't go over it. Be honest with yourself. Other expenses will come up—maybe car related, maybe not—and you don't want to end up struggling because you can't afford your monthly car payment.

■ **Interest rate.** The interest rate on your car loan will depend on your credit, which is why having a good credit score matters (see page 29). If you have multiple sources of good credit, your interest rate will be lower. This becomes more important over a longer-term loan. Each car dealership will negotiate differently. Don't be afraid to walk out if the dealer tries to change the finance terms on you at the last minute. This is a common trick.

Conquering Car Salespeople by Outnegotiating Them

I've seen more than my share of negotiations—including watching my dad negotiate with car dealers for multiple days. I think we actually ate breakfast at a dealership once.

You must negotiate mercilessly with dealers. I have never seen as many people make bad purchasing decisions as when they're in a car dealer's office. If you're not a hardball negotiator, take someone with you who is. If possible, buy a car at the end of the year, when dealers are salivating to beat their quotas and are far more willing to negotiate. Their saliva is your salvation!

I also highly recommend using Fighting Chance (fightingchance .com), an information service for car buyers, to arm yourself before you negotiate. For the price, the service is completely worth it. You can order a customized report of the exact car you're looking for, which will tell you exactly how much car dealers are paying for your car—including details about little-known "dealer withholding." For instance, I spent a month on the site researching and planning and then bought my car for $2,000 under invoice. The service also provided specific tips for how to negotiate from the comfort of your sofa. You don't even have to set foot in a dealership until the very end.

Here's how I did it: When I decided to buy—at the end of December, when salespeople are desperate to meet their quotas—I reached out to seventeen car dealers and told them exactly which car I wanted. I said I was prepared to buy the car within two weeks and, because I knew exactly how much profit they would make off the car, I would go with the lowest price offered to me. The same day, as I sat back with a cup of Earl Grey tea and three tacos with habanero salsa, responses started rolling in from the dealers. After I had all the offers, I called the dealers, told them the lowest price I'd received, and gave each of them a chance to beat it. This resulted in a bidding war that led to a downward spiral of near-orgasmic deals.

In the end, I chose a dealer in Palo Alto who sold me the car for $2,000 under invoice—a nearly unheard-of price. I didn't have to waste my time going to multiple dealerships, and I didn't have to bother with slimy car salespeople. I went into only one dealer's office: the winning one.

Boring but Profitable: Maintaining Your Car

I know that keeping your car well maintained doesn't sound sexy, but it will make you rich when you eventually sell your car. So take your car's maintenance as seriously as your retirement savings: As soon as you buy your car, enter the major maintenance checkpoints into your calendar so you remember them. Here's a hint: The average car is driven about fifteen thousand miles per year. You can use that number as a starting point to calculate a maintenance schedule based on the car manufacturer's instructions.

Of course, you also need to have regular oil changes, watch your tire pressure, and keep your car clean. I keep a record of each service I have, along with any notes. When I sell my car, I'll show the documentation to the buyer to prove how meticulous I've been (and charge the buyer accordingly). People often forget this and slap their foreheads when they go to sell their car, only to be negotiated down (by someone like me) for not keeping detailed maintenance records. Don't let yourself get outmaneuvered by a lack of paperwork.

The Biggest Big-Ticket Item of All: Buying a House

I f I asked people, "Hey, would you like to make a hundred thousand dollars in one year?" who wouldn't say yes? And if I sweetened the offer by saying you'd have to spend only ten hours per week that year to do it, I guarantee every single person I asked would go for it. So why don't people spend that amount of time researching the biggest purchase of their lives? By doing the research that 99 percent of other people don't, you can save tens of thousands of dollars on your house over the life of your loan.

Buying a house is the most complicated and significant purchase you'll make, so it pays to understand everything about it beforehand. I mean everything. This isn't a pair of pants at Banana Republic. When you buy a house worth hundreds of thousands of dollars, you should be an expert on common mistakes most home buyers make. You should know all the common real estate terms, as well as how to push and pull to get the best deal. And you should understand that houses are primarily for living in, not for making huge cash gains.

Look, if you buy a house without opening up a spreadsheet and entering some numbers, you are a fool. Remember, if you can save $75,000 or $125,000 over the entire course of a thirty-year loan just by educating yourself a little, it's certainly worth your time. I'm going to help you figure out if buying a house is right for you, and then I'm going to give you an overview of the things you'll need to do over the next few months—at least three months, probably twelve—to prepare to buy. I can't cover all the tips here, but I'll get you started with the basics.

Who Should Buy a House?

From our earliest days, we're taught that the American dream is to own a house, have 2.5 kids, and retire into the sunset. In fact, I have friends who, when they graduated from college, wanted their first major purchase to be a house. What the hell? No spending plan, no 401(k), but they wanted to buy a house? When I ask my younger friends why they want to buy a house, they stare at me blankly. "They're a good investment," they reply like brainless automatons who are at risk of being smacked by me.

Actually, houses really aren't very good investments in general. But I'll cover that in a minute. Back to who should buy:

First and foremost, you should buy a house only if it makes financial sense. In the olden days, this meant that your house would cost no more than 2.5 times your annual income, you'd be able to put at least 20 percent of the purchase price down, and the total monthly payments (including the mortgage, maintenance, insurance, and taxes) would be about 30 percent of your gross income. If you make $50,000 per year before taxes, that means your house would cost $125,000, you'd put $25,000 down, and the total monthly payments would be $1,250 per month. Yeah, right. Maybe if you live in the Ozarks.

Things are a little different now, but that doesn't explain the stupidity of people who purchase houses for ten times their salaries with zero money down. Sure, you can stretch those traditional guidelines a little, but if you buy something you simply can't afford, it will come around and bite you in the ass.

Let me be crystal clear: Can you afford at least a 20 percent down payment for the house? If not, set a savings goal and don't even think about buying until you reach it. Even if you've got a down payment, you still need to be sure you make enough money to cover the monthly payments. You might be tempted to think, "Oh, I'm paying $1,000/ month for my apartment, so I can definitely afford $1,000 for a house!" Wrong. First off, chances are you'll want to buy a nicer house than you're currently renting, which means the monthly payment will likely be higher. Second, when you buy a house, you'll owe property taxes, insurance, and maintenance fees that will add hundreds per month. If the garage door breaks or the toilet needs repairing, that's coming out of your pocket, not a landlord's—and home repairs are ridiculously expensive. So even if your mortgage payment is the same $1,000/month as your rental, your real cost will be about 40 to 50 percent higher—in this case, more like $1,500/month when you factor everything in.

Bottom line: If you don't have enough money to make a down payment and cover your total monthly costs, you need to set up a savings goal and defer buying until you've proven that you can hit your goal consistently, month after month.

Next thing to think about: Are the houses you're looking at within your price range? It's funny how so many people I know want to live only in the grandest possible house. Sure, your parents may live in one of those now, but it probably took them thirty or forty years to be able to afford it. Unless you're already loaded, you need to readjust your expectations and begin with a starter house. They're called that for a reason—they're simple houses that require you to make trade-offs but allow you to get started. Your first house probably won't have as many bedrooms as you want. It won't be in the most amazing location. But it will let you get started making consistent monthly payments and building equity.

Finally, will you be able to stay in the house for at least ten years? Buying a house means you're staying put for a long time. Some people say five years, but the longer you stay in your house, the more you save. There are a few reasons for this: When you go through a traditional real estate agent, there are large transaction fees—usually 6 percent of the selling price. Divide that by just a few years, and it hits you a lot harder than if you had held the house for ten or twenty years. There are also the costs associated with moving. And depending on how you structure your sale, you may pay a significant amount in taxes. The bottom line here: Buy only if you're planning to live in the same place for ten years or more.

I have to emphasize that buying a house is not just a natural step that everyone has to take at some point. Too many people assume this and then get in over their heads. Buying a house changes your lifestyle forever. No matter what, you have to make your monthly payment every month—or you'll lose your house and watch your credit tank. This affects the kinds of jobs you can take and your level of risk tolerance. It means you'll need to save for a six-month emergency plan in case you lose your job and can't pay your mortgage. In short, you really need to be sure you're ready for the responsibility of being a homeowner.

Of course, there are certainly benefits to buying a house, and, like I said, most American households will purchase one in their lifetime. If you can afford it and you're sure you'll be staying in the same area for a long time, buying a house can be a great way to make a significant purchase, build equity, and create a stable place to raise a family.

The Truth: Real Estate Is a Poor Investment for Most Individual Investors

Americans' biggest "investments" are their houses, but real estate is also the place where Americans lose the most money. Real estate agents (and most homeowners) are not going to like me after this section, but in truth, real estate is the most overrated investment in America. It's a purchase first—a very expensive one—and an investment second.

If you're thinking of your primary residence as an investment, real estate provides mediocre returns at best. First, there's the problem of risk. If your house is your biggest investment, how diversified is your portfolio? If you pay $2,000 per month to a mortgage, are you investing $6,000 elsewhere to balance your risk? Of course not. Second, the facts show that real estate offers a very poor return for individual investors. Yale economist Robert Shiller found that from 1915 through 2015, home prices have increased, on average, only 0.6 percent per year.

I know this sounds crazy, but it's true. We fool ourselves into thinking we're making money when we're simply not. For example, if someone buys a house for $250,000 and sells it for $400,000 twenty years later, they think, "Great! I made $150,000!" But actually, they've forgotten to factor in important costs like property taxes, maintenance, and the opportunity cost of not having that money in the stock market. The truth is that, over time, investing in the stock market has trumped real estate quite handily—which is why renting can be a great decision. I rent by choice!

I'm not saying buying a house is always a bad decision. (In fact, I created a sub-savings account called "Down Payment for Future House," knowing that I will eventually buy.) It's just that you should think of it as a purchase, rather than as an investment. And, just as with any other purchase, you should buy a house and keep it for as long as possible. Do your homework and then negotiate. And know your alternatives (like renting).

Buying vs. Renting: The Surprising Numbers

I want to show you why renting is actually a smart decision for many people, especially if you live in an expensive area like New York or San Francisco. But first, let's get rid of the idea that renters are "throwing away money" because they're not building equity. Any time you hear clichés like that—from any area of personal finance—beware. It's just not true, and I'll show you the numbers to prove it.

The total price of buying and owning a house is far greater than the house's sticker price. Take a look at some sample numbers.

THE COST OF BUYING A HOME OVER 30 YEARS	
Purchase price (typical single-family home)	$220,000
Down payment (10%)	$22,000
Closing costs	$11,000
Private mortgage insurance (76 payments of 0.5% PMI at $82.50)	$6,270
Interest @ 4.5%	$ 163,165.29
Taxes & insurance ($3,400/year)	$102,000
Maintenance ($2,200/year)	$66,000
Major repairs & improvements	$200,000
Total costs	$778,408.73

Note: Mortgage rates change over time. Calculate your own numbers at mortgagecalculator.org.

In the example above, your $220,000 house actually costs you over $775,000. And I'm not even including moving costs, the cost of new furniture, renovations, and the real estate fees when you sell the house—all of which will add up to tens of thousands of dollars.

You can agree or disagree with my exact numbers; regardless, run them yourself. I want you to understand all the phantom costs involved.

When you rent, you're not paying all those other assorted fees, which effectively frees up tons of cash that you would have been spending on a mortgage. The key is investing that extra money. If you do nothing with it (or, worse, spend it all), you might as well buy a house and use it as a forced savings account. But if you've read this far, chances are good that you'll take whatever extra money you have each month and invest it.

Of course, like buying, renting isn't best for everyone. It all depends on your individual situation. The easiest way to see if you should rent or buy is to use the *New York Times*'s excellent online calculator "Is It Better to Rent or Buy?" It will factor in maintenance, renovations, capital gains, the costs of buying and selling, inflation, and more.

Becoming a Homeowner: Tips for Buying Your New House

Like any area of personal finance, there are no secrets to buying a house. But it does involve thinking differently from most other people, who make the biggest purchase of their lives without fully understanding the true costs. Although I may be aggressive with my asset allocation, I'm conservative when it comes to real estate. That means I urge you to stick by tried-and-true rules, like 20 percent down, a 30-year fixed-rate mortgage, and a total monthly payment that represents no more than 30 percent of your gross income. If you can't do that, wait until you've saved more. It's okay to stretch a little, but don't stretch beyond what you can actually pay. If you make a poor financial decision up front, you'll end up struggling—and it can compound and become a bigger problem throughout the life of your loan. Don't let this happen, because it will undo all the hard work you put into the other areas of your financial life.

If you make a good financial decision when buying, you'll be in an excellent position. You'll know exactly how much you're spending each month on your house, you'll be in control of your expenses, and you'll have money to pay your mortgage, invest, take vacations, buy a TV, or whatever else you want to do.

Here are some of the things you'll need to do to make a sound decision.

1. *Check your credit score.* The higher your score, the better the interest rate on your mortgage will be. If your credit score is low, it might be a better decision to delay buying until you can improve your score. (See page 38 for details on increasing your score.) Good credit translates into not only a lower total cost, but lower monthly payments. The table below from myfico.com shows how interest rates affect your mortgage payments on a thirty-year fixed $220,000 loan.

THE EFFECT OF CREDIT SCORES ON A MORTGAGE PAYMENT			
FICO score	**APR***	**Monthly payment**	**Total interest paid**
760–850	4.18%	$1,073	$166,378
700–759	4.402%	$1,102	$176,696
680–699	4.579%	$1,125	$185,021
660–679	4.793%	$1,153	$195,200
640–659	5.223%	$1,211	$216,022
620–639	5.769%	$1,287	$243,146

These numbers change over time. For the latest figures, search for "my FICO loan savings calculator."

2. *Save as much money as possible for a down payment.* Traditionally, you have to put 20 percent down. If you can't save enough to put 20 percent down, you'll have to get something called Private Mortgage Insurance (PMI), which serves as insurance against your defaulting on your monthly payments. PMI typically costs between 0.5 percent to 1 percent of the mortgage, plus an annual charge. The more you put down, the less PMI you'll have to pay. If you haven't been able to save at least 10 percent to put down, stop thinking about buying a house. If you can't even save 10 percent, how will you afford an expensive mortgage payment, plus maintenance and taxes and insurance and furniture and renovations and . . . you get the idea. Set a savings goal (page 142) for a down payment, and don't start looking to buy until you reach it.

Myths About Owning a Home

"PRICES IN REAL ESTATE ALWAYS GO UP" (OR "THE VALUE OF A HOUSE DOUBLES EVERY TEN YEARS"). Not true. Net house prices haven't increased when you factor in inflation, taxes, and other homeowner fees. They appear to be higher because the sticker price is higher, but you have to dig beneath the surface.

"YOU CAN USE LEVERAGE TO INCREASE YOUR MONEY." Homeowners will often point to leverage as the key benefit of real estate. In other words, you can put $20,000 down for a $100,000 house, and if the house climbs to $120,000, you've effectively doubled your money. Unfortunately, leverage can also work against you if the price goes down. If your house declines by 10 percent, you don't just lose 10 percent of your equity—it's more like 20 percent once you factor in the 6 percent Realtor's fees, the closing costs, new furniture, and other expenses.

"I CAN DEDUCT MY MORTGAGE INTEREST FROM MY TAXES AND SAVE A BUNCH OF MONEY." Be very careful here. Tax savings are great, but people forget that they're saving money they ordinarily would never have spent. That's because the amount you pay out owning a house is much higher than you would for any rental when you include maintenance, renovations, and higher insurance costs, to name a few. Furthermore, 2018 laws reduced the benefit of these tax deductions.

3. Calculate the total amount of buying a new house. Have you ever gone to buy a car or cell phone, only to learn that it's way more expensive than advertised? I know I have, and most of the time I just bought it anyway because I was already psychologically set on it. But because the numbers are so big when purchasing a house, even small surprises will end up costing you a ton of money. For example, if you stumble across an unexpected cost for $100 per month, would you really cancel the paperwork for a new home? Of course not. But that minor charge would add up to $36,000 over the lifetime of a thirty-year loan—plus the opportunity cost of investing it. Remember that the closing costs—including all administrative fees and expenses—are usually between 2 and 5 percent of the house price. So on a $200,000 house, that's $10,000. Keep in mind that ideally the total price shouldn't be much more than three times your gross annual income. (It's okay to stretch here a little if you don't have any debt.) And don't forget to factor in insurance, taxes, maintenance, and renovations. If all this sounds a little overwhelming, it's telling you that you need to research all this stuff before buying a house. In this particular case, you should ask your parents and other homeowners for their surprise costs or just search "surprise costs of owning a house."

4. Get the most conservative, boring loan possible. I like a thirty-year fixed-rate loan. Yes, you'll pay more in interest compared with a fifteen-year loan. But a thirty-year loan is more flexible, because you can take the full thirty years to repay it or pay extra toward your loan and pay it off faster if you want. But you probably shouldn't: *Consumer Reports* simulated what to do with an extra $100 per month, comparing the benefits of prepaying your mortgage versus investing in an index fund that returned 8 percent. Over a twenty-year period, the fund won 100 percent of the time. As they said, ". . . the longer you own your home, the less likely it is that mortgage prepayment will be the better choice."

5. Don't forget to check for perks. The government wants to make it easy for first-time home buyers to purchase a house. Many state and local governments offer benefits for first-time home buyers. Check out hud.gov/topics/buying_a_home to see the programs in your state. Ask—it's worth it. Finally, don't forget to check with any associations you belong to, including local credit unions, alumni associations, and teachers' associations. You may get access to special lower mortgage rates. Hell, even check your Costco membership (they offer special rates for members too).

6. Use online services to comparison shop. You may have heard about zillow.com, which is a rich source of data about home prices all over the United States. Also check out redfin.com and trulia.com, which give you more information about buying a house, including tax records and

neighborhood reviews. For your homeowner's insurance, check insure
.com to comparison shop. And don't forget to call your auto insurance
company and ask them for a discounted rate if you give them your
homeowner's insurance business.

How to Tackle
Future Large Purchases

We've covered weddings, cars, and houses, but there are plenty
of other major expenses that people don't plan ahead for—just
think about having kids! The problem is that, as we've seen,
if you don't plan ahead, it ends up costing you much more in the end.
The good news is that there is a way to anticipate and handle almost any
major expense you'll encounter in life.

*1. Acknowledge that you're probably not being realistic about how much
things will cost—then force yourself to be.* If you've read this whole
book (and taken even half of my advice), you're probably better at
your finances than 95 percent of other people, but you're still human.
Sorry, but your wedding will be more expensive than you planned. Your
house will have costs you didn't account for. Having a head-in-the-sand
approach, however, is the worst thing you can do. Bite the bullet, sit
down, and make a realistic plan for how much your big purchases will
cost you in the next ten years. Do it on a napkin—it doesn't have to be
perfect! Just spend twenty minutes and see what you come up with.

2. Set up an automatic savings plan. Because almost nobody will take
my recommendation to make a budget to forecast major purchases,
I suggest just taking a shortcut and setting up an automatic savings
plan (see page 213). Assume you'll spend $35,000 on your wedding,
$20,000 on a car, $20,000 for the first two years of your first-born kid,
and however much you'll need for a typical down payment for a house in
your city. Then figure out how much you need to save. If you're twenty-
five, and you're going to buy a car and get married in three years, that's
$45,000/36 months = $1,250 per month. I know, I know. That's more
than $1,000 per month. You might not be able to afford it. Better to
know now than later. Now ask yourself this: Can you afford $300? If so,
that's $300 more than you were doing yesterday.

3. You can't have the best of everything, so use the P word. Priorities are essential. Like I said, it's human nature to want the best for our wedding day or first house, and we need to be realistic about acknowledging that. But we also need to acknowledge that we simply can't have the best of everything. Do you want the filet mignon or an open bar at your wedding? Do you want a house with a backyard or a neighborhood with better local schools? If you have the costs down on paper, you'll know exactly which trade-offs you can make to keep within your budget. If you haven't written anything down, there will appear to be no trade-offs necessary. And that's how people get into staggering amounts of debt.

For the things you decide aren't that important, beg, borrow, and steal to save money: If you're getting married and you decide location is important, spend on it—but choose the cheapest options for chairs and cutlery and flowers. If you're buying a car, skip the sunroof so you can get the model you want. And whatever you do, negotiate the hell out of big-ticket purchases. This is where, if you plan ahead, time can take the place of money.

Giving Back: Elevating Your Goals Beyond the Day to Day

Most people spend their entire lives handling the day-to-day issues of money and never get ahead. Oh man, why did I buy that $300 jacket? Damn, I thought I canceled that subscription. If you've followed the steps in this book, you've moved past these basic questions. Your accounts work together automatically. You know how much you can afford to spend going out and how much you want to save each month. If something goes wrong, your system lets you easily see if you need to cut costs, make more money, or adjust your lifestyle. It's all there.

That means it's time to think about elevating your goals beyond the day to day. Whereas most people may be so consumed with the minutiae of money that they've never thought about getting rich ("I just want to pay off this debt"), you can set larger goals of doing the things you love using money to support you.

I believe that part of getting rich is giving back to the community that helped you flourish. There are lots of traditional ways to do this, like volunteering at a soup kitchen or becoming a Big Brother or Big Sister. You don't need to be rich to give back. Even $100 helps. Sites like Pencils of Promise or kiva.org let you give directly to poor developing communities. (I was very proud that the *I Will Teach You to Be Rich* community raised over $300,000 for Pencils of Promise, which resulted in building thirteen schools for impoverished children around the world.) Or you can donate to your high school, local library, environmental action groups—whatever means the most to you. And if you're short on cash, donate your time, which is often more valuable than money.

If you think about it, philanthropy mirrors the very same *I Will Teach You to Be Rich* principles you read in this book: The simplest step can get you started. Pick an organization to support or a place to volunteeer your time. You don't have to be rich to be a philanthropist, just as you don't have to be rich to invest.

The point is that now you've got a personal finance system that few others have. This allows you to elevate your goals beyond making it through the daily grind. When you think back to last year, what was the one big thing you accomplished for others? What will it be this year?

If I could hope for one thing from this book, it would be that you become a master of conscious spending—and then apply those skills to helping those around you. Maybe it will be by mentoring a needy kid, or establishing a scholarship, or even just helping your friends manage their money for free. Whatever it is, you're now in the top tier of investing knowledge. You've moved beyond managing your money for short-term goals and you're thinking strategically about your money and how it can help you to be rich—and how to share that with others.

If this were a movie, it would be raining, violin music would be swelling in the background, and a young soldier would slowly raise his hand to salute an elderly general who has a single tear rolling down his cheek.

A Rich Life for You— and Others

I f I've been successful, the end of this book is the beginning of a rich future for you. We know that being rich isn't just about money. We know that most people around us have strong opinions about money yet are clueless with their own. And we know that conscious spending can be fun (especially when it's automated). But now that you know how money really works, there's one other thing: Not enough people know about being rich. It's not some mythical thing that happens only to Ivy League grads and lottery winners. Anyone can be rich—it's just a question of what rich means to you. You've learned it: You know that money is a small, but important, part of a Rich Life. You know life is meant to be lived outside the spreadsheet. And you know how to use money to design your Rich Life.

Would you do me a favor and pass the word along to your friends to help them focus on their goals, too? A Rich Life is about more than money. It starts by managing your own. And it continues by helping others become rich.

I'd like to share some bonus resources with you to help you earn more money. Get them at iwillteachyoutoberich.com/bonus.

And one last thing: Send me an email (ramit.sethi@iwillteachyouto berich.com, subject: my Rich Life) to let me know one thing you learned from this book. I'd love to hear from you.

Acknowledgments

Nobody writes a book alone. In my case, this book came to life with the help of researchers who found elusive data, teammates who ran operations while I hunkered down to write, readers who openly shared their money stories, family support, and an entire team of editors and designers who helped bring the book to life.

Finally, I get to acknowledge all the people who helped turn this book into its final form.

Thank you to Chris Neal, my book researcher who found information on every topic I could possibly think of—always with a smile. Eric Meermann and Paul Jacobs, both CFPs from Palisades Hudson Financial Group, did final fact checks. And a special thanks to Jeff Kuo, the researcher for the first version of this book.

Thank you to my friends at Workman Publishing: Anna Cooperberg, Orlando Adiao, Moira Kerrigan, Rebecca Carlisle, and Lathea Mondesir. And of course my long-time editor, Margot Herrera, who's mastered the art of the gentle phone call asking when my next manuscript will be ready.

To my family—Prab and Neelam Sethi, Roy and Tricia, Nagina, Ibrahim, Rachi, Haj, Maneesh, Nikki, Carlos, and all of the kids—thank you for being incredible role models to me.

Immense gratitude to my mentors and teachers, who taught me about consistency, ethics, and just plain hard work.

And to my friends, who have an endless supply of insane money stories.

To my agent, Lisa DiMona. Here we go again!

To my wife, Cass, who is infinitely patient and supported me every step of the way.

And finally, to my new readers. I hope this book helps you design your Rich Life.

Index

down payments
  for car, 317
  for house, 146, 252,
    322, 325, 327
  Roth IRAs and, 112
  savings accounts
    and, 76, 86, 142,
    330

E

early withdrawal
  penalties, 108
earnings
  controlling, 20
  extra, 163–164
  increasing, 155–161,
    219, 306–307
  unequal, 294–295
education expenses, 279
80/20 analysis, 147, 149
85 Percent Solution, 16,
  67, 259, 273
Einstein, Albert, 95
emergencies/emergency
  funds, 277, 278
emerging-market
  equities, 246–247
employer matches, 104,
  105–106, 120, 240
envelope system,
  153–155
excuses, 14–15
expense ratios, 234, 248
expenses
  dividing by income,
    295
  unexpected, 162–163
expertise, myth of,
  188–189

F

FatFire, 217, 218
features
  bank, 83
  brokerage, 115

fee-based financial
  advisors, 199–200
feeding system, 263–265
fees
  avoiding monthly,
    87, 89
  for index funds, 207
  for mutual funds,
    206–207, 234
  for passive
    versus active
    management,
    207–209
  wealth managers
    and, 204
FICO score. *See* credit
  score
Fidelity, 114, 195
fiduciaries, 199, 201
Fighting Chance, 319
financial advisors
  being taken for a ride
    by, 198–199
  commission-based,
    197
  fee-based, 199–200
  introductory email
    to, 201
  invisible money
    scripts on, 210
  questions to ask, 201
  robo-advisors and,
    117
  as unnecessary, 197,
    199–200
financial checklist,
  annual, 274–275
financial experts
  hiding poor
    performance,
    193–196
  ignoring, 190–193
  as unnecessary,
    189–190
  worth reading, 203
financial independence
  (FI), 216–220
financial literacy tests,
  189

FIRE, 217, 218, 219
first-time home buyers,
  perks for, 329
529 accounts, 279
fixed costs, 140–142
food, money compared
  to, 7
401(k)
  advantages of,
    109–110
  allocation in, 240–
    241
  common concerns
    about, 108–109
  conscious spending
    plan and, 142
  employer matches
    for, 104
  mastering, 105–110
  maximum
    contributions to,
    120
  mutual funds and,
    233
  paying off debt
    versus, 285
  setting up, 110, 125
  stats on, 96
  taking money from,
    66
  taxes and, 273
freelance work, 161,
  181–182, 185
fuel efficiency, 317
fund managers, 191–193

G

gifts, 143, 145, 163–164
giving back, 184,
  331–332
goals, realistic, 151
government bonds, 229,
  247. *See also* bonds
growth stocks, 229
guilt, 144–145
guilt-free spending
  money, 140, 147

H

health insurance, 120–122
Health Savings Account (HSA), 105, 120–124
Hepburn Capital, 192
high-deductible health plans, 120–122
high-risk, high-potential-for-reward investments, 253, 255–256
holding out, 82
home equity lines of credit (HELOC), 38, 66
homeowner insurance, 278
Hood, Randolph, 221
house, buying, 146, 321–329
Housel, Morgan, 203
Hulberg, Mark, 192, 236
Hulbert Financial Digest, 192
Hutchins, Chris, 37

I

illusory superiority, 234
income. *See* earnings
index funds, 207, 209, 222, 223, 235–238, 245–246, 251–252
inflation, 95
information glut, 9
installment loans, 38
insurance
  car, 317
  car rental, 45
  health, 120–122
  homeowner, 278, 330
  life, 199, 278
  Private Mortgage Insurance (PMI), 327
  trip-cancellation, 45
insure.com, 330

interest rates
  annual percentage rate (APR), 26, 41, 64
  for car loans, 319
  changes in, 4–5
  credit rating and, 24
  credit score and, 30–32
  for mortgage, 327
  for savings accounts, 76–77
international stocks, 229, 230
investing
  automatic, 107–108, 213–216
  building blocks of, 222–225
  fear of, 215
  invisible money scripts on, 99
  number of funds for, 248
  overview of, 94–96, 220–222
  paying off student loans versus, 284–285
  reasons people avoid, 96–102
  regrets regarding, 97
  returns on, 103
  steps for, 104–105
investing style, 212, 259
investment account, feeding, 119
investment brokerages
  choosing, 115–116
  discount versus full-service, 114
  recommended, 114
investment plan, 21, 22
investment portfolio, 212–213, 221–222

investments
  choosing and buying, 240
  choosing your own, 245–252
  rebalancing, 265–269
  selling, 276–280
  underperforming, 279–280
invisible money scripts, 3, 51–54, 75, 99, 174, 210
IRA accounts, 108–109
irregular expenses, 162–163

J

Jaffe, Chuck, 225
Jenkins, Richard, 143
jobs, higher-paying, 160–161. *See also* earnings
judging, 139

K

Kelley Blue Book, 317
key messages, 16–18
Keynes, John Maynard, 253
Klontz, Brad, 51

L

large purchases
  car, 315–320
  future, 330–331
  house, 321–329
large-cap stocks, 229, 230
LastPass, 118
late payments, 39–40, 42
lawyers, 306
LeanFire, 217, 218
leasing a car, 318
Lieber, Ron, 203

retail store credit cards,
34–35
retiring early (RE), 217,
218
returns
asset allocation and,
226–227
average, 14–15
calculations of, 264
on investing, 103
on stocks and bonds,
95, 223, 227
Rich Lives
defining, 18–19
rules for, 20–21
risk tolerance, 227–228
risk-parity, 119
Robin, Vicki, 216–217
robo-advisors, 116–119
rollovers, 109
Roth 401(k), 109
Roth IRAs, 105, 111–114,
125, 241–245, 273,
285
Rule of 72, 243
running out of money, 97

S

salary, negotiating,
307–314
"Save $1,000 in 30 Days
Challenge," 12
savings, 140, 142–143
savings accounts, 76–79,
85–86, 92. *See also*
bank accounts
scare tactics, credit cards
and, 25–26
Schwab, 71, 80, 84–85,
114
Schwartz, Barry, 9
sector funds, 255
selection bias, 253
self-employment tax, 185
selling, 276–280
SEP-IRA, 182
service credit, 38
Shiller, Robert, 324
short-term bonds, 229

significant other
irresponsible
spending by,
295–296
talking money
with, 282–283,
292–294
unequal earnings
and, 294–295
Simon, W. Scott, 236
60 Percent Solution, 143
six-week plan, overview
of, 21–22
*Skating Where the Puck
Was* (Bernstein),
230–231
small-cap stocks, 229,
230
*Smartest Investment
Book You'll Ever
Read, The* (Solin),
193, 211
snowball method, 63
Society for Human
Resource
Management (SHRM),
155
Solin, Daniel, 193, 203,
211
Solo 401(k), 182
spending, categories
of, 140, 165, 171.
See also conscious
spending
spending, irresponsible,
295–296
spending after saving,
184
spending frameworks, 20
spending money, guilt-
free, 140, 147
starter houses, 323
starting early, 10
stock market
average annual
returns for, 95
dips in, 215–216
returns on, 223
timing the, 191, 192

stock-picking,
engineering perfect
record for, 196
stocks, 223–224, 226–
227, 228, 229–230
street-level motivation,
262
student loans, 27–29, 54,
56, 284–285
subscriptions, 136–137
survivorship bias,
194–196
sustainable change,
152–153
Swensen, David, 195,
246–248, 259
Swensen model, 247,
259, 265–266
systems, 167–169

T

Taking It From the Clouds
to the Street, 262
target date funds, 220,
222, 223, 238–240,
242–243, 259, 268
tax-advantaged
accounts, 285
tax-deferred accounts,
273, 276
taxes
401(k) accounts and,
105, 108
freelancers and, 185
mortgages and, 328
Roth IRAs and,
111–112
stop worrying about,
270–273
wealth managers
and, 202
teaser rates, 82
30-Second Test, 71
TIAA, 71
timing the market, 191,
192
tools for tracking
finances, 148–149

WHAT'S NEXT?

LISTEN TO MY PODCAST, *Money for Couples*, and watch my Netflix show, *How to Get Rich.*

GET MONEY COACHING with a supportive community and live Q&A that I host every month. Learn more at iwt.com/moneycoaching.

EARN MORE MONEY by using my digital programs at iwt.com/products. An extra $1,000/month can make a big difference in your Rich Life.

NEW FROM RAMIT:
HOW TO BUILD A RICH LIFE TOGETHER!

What if talking about money with your partner actually felt good?
Now from bestselling author Ramit Sethi comes the definitive book on dealing with money in your relationship. Built around a 10-step program, it goes beyond the usual "make a budget" advice and gives couples a clear plan to transform their financial lives in a way that's exciting and fun, including how to:

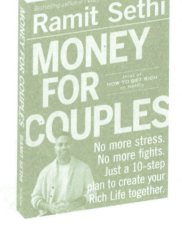

- Stop fighting over money
- Save, invest, pay down debt, and plan for major purchases
- Handle money disagreements, including specific words to use (and avoid)
- Navigate one partner being the Saver and the other the Spender

Money for Couples will show you how to use your money to live a more adventurous, spontaneous, and generous life—together.

Available wherever books are sold.